Numbers on the maps denote music venues, pubs, bars, shops, attractions and restaurants of interest in the Dublin area. A full listing follows the city centre map. For a listing by genre, see the appendix on page 233.

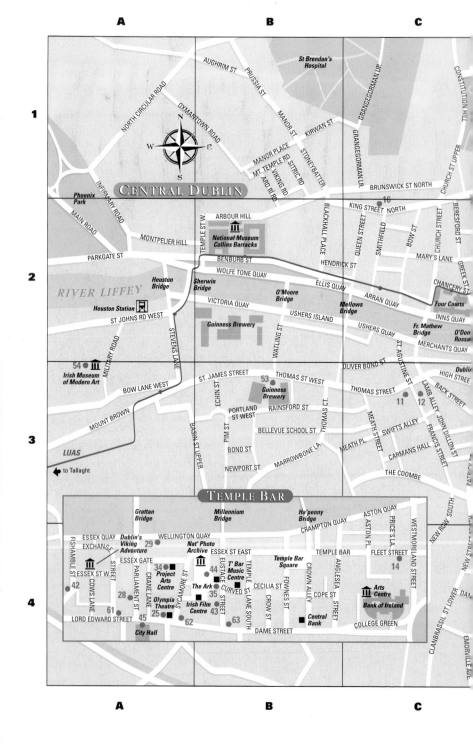

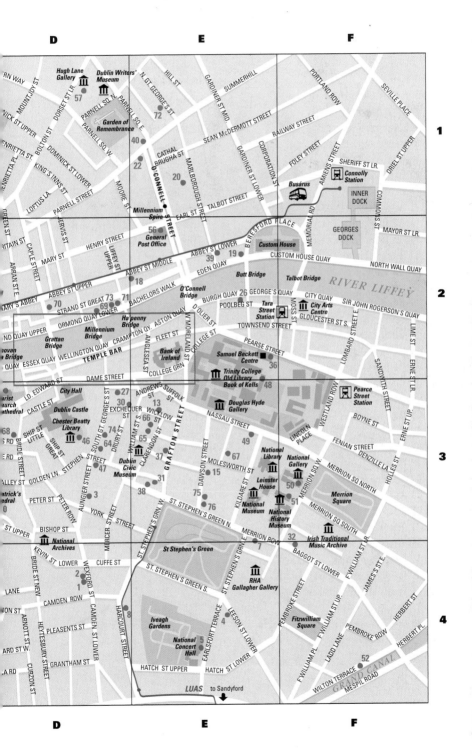

Waking Up In
Dublin

Printed and bound by L.E.G.O. SpA, Vicenza, Italy

Published by Sanctuary Publishing Limited, Sanctuary House, 45–53
Sinclair Road, London W14 0NS, United Kingdom

Distributed in the US by Publishers Group West
www.sanctuarypublishing.com

ISBN: 1-86074-591-1

Waking Up In
Dublin

Neil Hegarty

Sanctuary
www.sanctuarypublishing.com

Contents

Acknowledgements

My thanks to all those who appear in this book; and also to the following, for their assistance and advice:

Agnes Aylward, Maarten Bongenaar, Paul Byrne, Orla Cunningham, Paul Delaney, Eugene Downes, Regina Fallon, Maeve Gebruen, Treasa Harkin, Patricia Higgins, Sinead Higgins, Cormac Jackson, Martina Kelly, Philip Kelly, Darragh Kettle, Willeen Keough, Ossie Kilkenny, Anna Mary Luttrell, Ciaran McGahon, John McManus, Grainne Millar, John Murphy, Beth O'Halloran, Paul O'Neill, Jeroen van Rens, Dave Ross, Tom Sherlock, Catherine Toal, Michael Wall and Aoife Woodlock.

Particular thanks to John Lovett, to Albert DePetrillo at Sanctuary, to Marie Gethins and to my family.

N.H.
Dublin, April 2004.

Introduction

The Sensual World

IT IS a fine, still morning in mid-June. It is very, very early – just after four o'clock – but I am wide awake. I pull the blinds and see the sun already rising, the thin cirrus clouds stretched, rose-washed and clean in the sky. I open the window and hear not a sound: no cars, no sirens, not even any screeching prostitutes who like to congregate in my part of town. The early light is tinged with violet, and the air is deliciously

Still Wheeling that Wheelbarrow: Molly Malone, Grafton Street

fresh. I hang out of the window for a moment and close my eyes. But I'm not up at the crack of dawn to look at the view: after a moment I shake myself, go downstairs, get into the car and begin the drive down to the Dublin docks.

The Irish have a difficult relationship with boats and with harbours. For generations, the docks and quays of Ireland witnessed heartbreaking scenes as a country that could not provide its young people with homes, jobs or livelihoods, packaged them up and sent them off on the boat to Britain and Australia, North America and New Zealand. Times have changed and today people more often emigrate only if they want to – not because they have to. But somewhere in the collective psyche of this country, the quaysides and harbours all over the country are associated with throngs of ghosts – the women and men torn from their homes and all their associations and forced by need to go abroad.

These ghosts are much on my mind as I collect my yawning friends, comment on their black-rimmed eyes, and drive on through the early morning streets of the city centre. I avert my gaze from the detritus that remains from a typical Dublin night out: the broken bottles, litter and worse – much worse. I turn onto the city quays, past the elegant, domed Custom House and through what seems like miles of desolate docklands that surround Dublin port, past the containers, trailers and depots and down, eventually, into the shadow of the vast ferry. The docks are potent in my imagination too, but the heartbreaking past – the emigrations and exile – these don't apply to me, not this morning anyway. I shake my head a little and dislodge these imaginings. I have a project underway.

I am going to shop.

I am going, in fact, to IKEA.

In the absence of latter-day emigrants, the Irish Sea ferry companies have caught onto a new market. IKEA has failed – so far, at any rate – to tap into the Irish passion for spending money on their beautiful homes and so eager Irish shoppers are forced to take to the ferries and travel to Greater Manchester for the day to do their Scandinavian-themed shopping. This is the first time I have ever joined the crowds and it's all something of a novelty, since it's also the first time I have ever been Britain-bound on an Irish Sea ferry. Soon enough, we are settled in the saloon of the ship, drinking bad coffee and noticing with a grimace, the smell of bad breakfasts frying away, frying to death somewhere out of sight. Ireland drops from view.

It is late when the ferry returns and we are all exhausted. Of course, the IKEA trip has been a success – it ought to have been, since it was planned with military, forensic efficiency. The catalogue was consulted, the measurements made, the boot measured too, and the calculations coldly made. The car is now full of all manner of ENETRI wall units, BONDE bookcase combinations and KAJAK storage cases, and our stomachs are full of Swedish meatballs and gravlax. It has been a long day nevertheless and a long drive through Wales and England. We slump in our seat and I look out of the saloon window, watching the sun set and the Irish coast slowly approach. This is the first time I have ever come to Dublin from the sea. People have always told me that it is quite a spectacle and I know I ought to be out on deck, experiencing it for myself. So I sigh, heave myself up, make my excuses (nobody pays any attention) and take myself out on deck again to gaze at the views. I stumble out, close the heavy door behind me and roll my way to the deck rail, exchanging the smell of long-dead sausage rolls and bacon for salt and sea air. When I get there and right myself, I understand what people mean.

The city of Dublin is beautifully set on the curving shore of its bay, with the Wicklow Mountains to the south and the flatlands of Meath to the north. On this warm summer evening, even after a long, long day, I can appreciate this beauty for myself, especially as the city is topped with an extravagant sunset and the city lights are beginning to twinkle along the edge of the water. The lighthouses are already shining to the north and south, smoothly across the smooth sea. The first stars are out overhead and the sea seems perfectly calm. I hold onto the ship's rail and find myself thinking about the emigrants once more. On a beautiful evening such as this, with such a vista open before me, the heartbreak of it all comes sharply and mercilessly into focus.

THE EMIGRANTS took their music with them when they left. They had a good deal of it to take, for the history of Ireland and of Dublin has always been bound up with the idea of music as a means of expression. There's nothing new in that; music has always had a central place in the history and culture of every community. It reflects, broadcasts and carries forward a community's history and culture. It expresses the dreams, the imaginings and emotions, the anger, longing, love and hate of societies the world over, and Ireland is no exception.

The path of Irish history, of course, follows that of many other lands: the country was settled and invaded countless times, colonised and planted and slowly and reluctantly decolonised. This is the usual story of cultures and societies around the world, but what makes Ireland exceptional and unique is the prominence its history and culture has enjoyed and continues to enjoy on the world stage. The Irish diaspora has carried the idea of this country around the earth, so that today, Ireland punches extravagantly above its weight on the world stage. Fewer than six million people live on this island and a quarter of these live in and around Dublin. This is not a large population, then, and not a large city – not by any means – but still, Dublin and Ireland are extraordinarily, enormously, and prodigiously influential.

Music has played its part in this cultural conquest. Irish traditional music can be listened to today all over the world – not merely in the usual strongholds of New York, Boston, and Sydney. Courtesy of the phenomenon of the Irish pub, you can arrive in Bangkok or Beijing too, grab a cab and tell the driver to take you to the nearest Irish bar, and the chances are that you'll be clutching a pint of Guinness before too long and listening to a visiting band playing a session in a corner. There is even a business in Dublin – the Irish Pub Company – that exports entire pubs in long panels, complete with mirrors, wooden counters and ornamental knick-knacks, to be bolted together and assembled instantly. Ireland – arriving in the back of a trailer. The existence of hundreds and hundreds of these Irish bars says everything you need to know about the remarkable power and marketability of Irish culture. Add to these the presence and visibility of Irish music stars on the world stage – U2 and Van Morrison, Enya and the Riverdance extravaganza – and you have a phenomenon indeed.

INDICATORS of music, symbols of music – these cluster together to greet the ferry as it slows down and prepares to dock. Dublin seems to stretch out to welcome the visitor; long before the ferry arrives at its berth, the long arching coastline has embraced the ship and the traveller, the Dubliner coming home. On the port side of the ship, the high frowning wall of Bray Head gives way to the shelving shingles of Killiney beach, the spectacular houses at Sorrento Terrace and the medieval village of Dalkey on its rocky headland. In front of the village, wild goats roam on Dalkey Island and shelter in the shadow of its Martello tower. This stretch of coast is the home of Dublin's musical superstars, and the homes themselves are clearly visible from the ferries as they ply the route between Ireland and Wales. On this still evening, I can see the lights coming on over there too: in Bono's house which faces east on the edge of the sea, in the castellated mansion next door where Enya lives, well tucked out of sight. Lisa Stansfield has settled in Dalkey and drinks in Finnegan's pub beside the train station; I saw her there one warm night. Today, Dalkey's High Street is crammed full of restaurants, bars, delicatessens and expensive cars too. Housing in the area is firmly out of reach of most Dubliners, so they settle for visiting on a Sunday afternoon instead. I visit too sometimes, fancying myself quite the cosmopolitan as I brunch in a gastrobar called IN on the main street, browse in the Exchange bookshop, fire down an espresso in the Queen's, or gaze in staggered astonishment at the prices listed outside the über-trendy Kish restaurant. After all, there are limits to trendy living, and I was brought up to be sensible with money and not throw it away on fripperies.

Above the lights of the village is Killiney Hill, which has been preserved as a wooded open space and which is dark tonight in the twilight. Just along the coast are the two great stone arms of Dun Laoghaire harbour, built by the British in the middle of the 19th century, when Dun Laoghaire was called Kingstown and was the railhead for all services to Ireland. Queen Victoria landed here on her way down to County Kerry, though history doesn't recall if she was amused. The vast piers were one of the engineering marvels of the 19th century and today, Dubliners pace them as part of a bracing Sunday constitutional. The ferries dock here too and I can see one in port, glimmering hugely white in the lights from the town and from the new Pavilion Theatre that overlooks the water. Beside it is another Martello tower at Sandycove, beloved of James Joyce. The lighthouses shine out along this entire rocky coast.

On the starboard side of the ship, the land is even closer. The shipping channel skirts the pounding shores of the high Howth peninsula and the Bailey lighthouse at its tip: it shines straight onto the ship for an instant and then moves away. Joyce got here first too; Joyce got everywhere first: even the ferry I am aboard is named *Ulysses*, and he put the evidence into the opening lines of *Finnegans Wake*:

> riverrun, past Eve and Adam's, from swerve of shore to bend of bay, brings us by a commodius vicus of recirculation back to Howth Castle and Environs.

These words formerly were reproduced on the back of the old Irish £10 note, which I think says a good deal about Ireland's ability to market itself with a certain style. But the days of the £10 note are gone now: when the euro arrived, it put an end to such cultural nationalism and brought a tinge of regret even to a committed Europhile like myself. The sight of Howth has always made my mind leap, like one of the goats on Dalkey Island, from *Finnegans Wake*, which I have never read, through to *Ulysses*. Now I have never read *Ulysses* either, although I have more than once pretended to have absorbed it from cover to cover. But my mind tends not to linger here for longer than an alarmed instant and instead jumps smoothly once more, this time on to Kate Bush. There we have it: from *Finnegans Wake* to Kate Bush, in one economic and shameless movement. This is the sort of admission that makes the Joyce purist blanch and weep, of course, but generally there is method in the lurching of the human mind, and so too in this case. Bush used Molly Bloom's soliloquy that ends *Ulysses* in fashioning the lyrics of 'The Sensual World'. Molly Bloom says,

> ...and then I asked him with my eyes to ask again yes and then he asked me would I yes today yes my mountain flower and first I put my arms around him yes and drew him down to me so he could feel my breasts all perfume yes and his heart was going like mad and yes I said yes I will Yes.

And Bush? Well, she says,

> Mmh, yes,
> Then I'd taken the kiss of seedcake back from his mouth
> Going deep South, go down, mmh, yes,
> Took six big wheels and rolled our bodies
> Off of Howth Head and into the flesh, mmh, yes,
> He said I was a flower of the mountain, yes,
> But now I've powers o'er a woman's body, yes.
> Stepping out of the page into the sensual world.
> Stepping out of the page into the sensual world.
>
> And then our arrows of desire rewrite the speech, mmh, yes,
> And then he whispered would I, mmh, yes,
> Be safe, mmh, yes, from mountain flowers?
> And at first with the charm around him, mmh, yes,
> He loosened it so if it slipped between my breasts
> He'd rescue it, mmh, yes,
> And his spark took life in my hand and, mmh, yes,
> I said, mmh, yes,
> But not yet, mmh, yes,
> Mmh, yes.

Howth falls behind the ship, Kate Bush's bells clang in my head and the sirens suddenly bellow to urge us to our cars. The ferry pulls up to the dock. I remember my ENETRI wall units, BONDE bookcase combinations, KAJAK storage cases and rush below. Someone might steal them. Such things are like gold dust in Ireland.

ONE OF my favourite walks in Dublin is from the docks out to the Poolbeg Lighthouse. Surely, few capital cities can boast such an exhilarating walk: along the long, low South Wall breakwater, across which waves can pitch and wash in windy weather, from the mouth of the Liffey to a red-painted lighthouse which seems to stand suspended on the sea. The city vanishes behind me and all I can see is the lighthouse ahead, Howth stretched to the left, and an immensity of sky. There are great signs at the entrance to the walk warning against 'Danger', and warning me that I pass 'At My Own Risk'. But it's a risk worth taking, I think: as I walk into the horizon, the water laps and breaks on either side, and the air is full of a tang of salt. It is like being on a boat.

I reach the lighthouse and turn to go back: Dublin suddenly, startlingly opens up in the distance. The bend of the bay is even more pronounced from this angle and the land seems suddenly to envelop me. The view now is uncompromisingly industrial, but stark and beautiful still. Straight ahead, the red-and-white stripes of the Pigeonhouse power station chimneys loom up into the still, expansive sky. The Pigeonhouse stands in the estuary of the River Liffey and has become a de facto emblem of the city. Beyond it the dockyards and depots tread across the landscape for what seems like miles. From here, it seems as though the only way into Dublin is by water – up the Liffey to the quays of the city.

Even on this margin of civic life, there are strong musical associations. On the south side of the Liffey and on the edge of the docks stood Windmill Lane Studios, where U2 and many others recorded their music. The studios became a kind of mecca or pilgrimage for fans, who arrived and added their own contribution to the layers of graffiti on the walls surrounding the building. But the studios are gone now, demolished in the teeth of protest to make way for the ongoing development of the city's docklands. U2 have ambitious plans for a landmark building and recording studios in the area.

A little further up the Liffey, pushing against the river's flow as it empties into the Irish Sea, is the city centre itself. It's heralded by the choking traffic on the quays and by the Georgian perfection of the

Lonely Sentinel: The Poolbeg Lighthouse, Dublin Bay

Gandon-designed Custom House. There are glimpses of other buildings further from the water too: the Abbey Theatre on its shabby corner, close to the northern embankment; and the classical columns of the General Post Office a little further away on O'Connell Street. The curving façade of the old parliament building – now the Bank of Ireland – gleams near the southern bank of the river; beyond it is the austere West Front of Trinity College, its main adornment being the two statues of Burke and Goldsmith that flank the main entrance. Students and tourists swirl past these two statues by the thousand each day and probably few stop to think of their association with Dublin's 18th-century heyday, when they rubbed shoulders with other musicians, philosophers and writers – Handel and Arne and Swift – in the tiny city centre. I passed them daily for years and I scarcely so much as glanced at them.

However, the tourists certainly notice the other statue hereabouts: just beyond Trinity and a little further from the river stands Molly Malone herself, wheeling her wheelbarrow and sporting vast breasts that resemble a brace of butternut squash. Dubliners seldom notice her, of course, and maybe those that do are a little mortified at this monstrously well-endowed girl exposing herself so shamelessly at one of the city's busiest junctions, but visitors love her – and why not.

The Clarence Hotel, Temple Bar: Bono will be along later.

After all, this is not a city that has much time for abstract art, so it makes sense to really go for it, and to err on the side of realism.

Under O'Connell Bridge and still pushing west is the Ha'penny Bridge, which is as iconic a symbol as the city possesses. A few years back, with the bridge beginning to look its age, it was taken apart and brought up to the Belfast shipyards to be repaired. Now it looks brand-new again, and is not put to shame by its companion, the Millennium footbridge, which is low, minimalist, sleek and just 100 metres further upriver. The Liffey boardwalk gleams silver, slung over the water from the northern embankment and with optimistic coffee kiosks dotted along its length.

Facing the boardwalk is Temple Bar on the southern bank. If dastardly plans hadn't gone awry, this whole old quarter of the city would have been levelled in the '80s to make way for a huge bus station. That was the plan and as it had been all drawn up and arranged, any self-respecting business got the hell out of the area while it could, leaving tiny shops to mushroom, and musicians and artists to colonise the area, by taking advantage of cheap rents and joining the old bars which had existed for generations in this district of tangled and cobbled streets. Soon enough, Temple Bar developed a distinctive energy of its own: the artists and musicians were joined by others and soon enough again, the government saw what was going on and resolved to create Dublin's very own Left Bank, right there. Right here. The cobbles were taken up, cleaned, and laid again. The buildings were cleaned and repaired on the outside; inside, stucco work on magnificent Georgian ceilings was restored gorgeously, old timber was sanded and varnished, stained glass windows were removed, repaired and reinstated. The whole fabric of the area was taken up and replaced, in fact, and Temple Bar set about reinventing itself creatively too.

But it has only worked up to a point: the artists are still there, or some of them are, hanging on by their fingernails as the rents spiral. The smoky old bars were soon demolished to make way for superbars which seem now to stretch for miles and which trample on the very idea of character and vibrant life. On the other hand, some studios and galleries thrived, and exquisite cafés opened. People returned to live in the area and were joined by the Irish Film Centre, which took over the old Quaker Meeting House and fashioned two cinemas, a bookshop, and a café out of its ruins, and grouped them around a glazed plaza. Open-air food markets moved in too, taking over the new public square that was created in the heart of the district; they sell organic vegetables and meat, focaccia, and cheeses each Saturday. The Project Theatre rebuilt itself and the Contemporary Music Centre took over a tall, thin Georgian townhouse and set up a focus for art music in Ireland. A pastry shop and café called Queen of Tarts was set up on the edge of the area, introducing a whole new aspect of pleasure to my life. And U2 moved in too, buying up the old Clarence Hotel, shunting on the hookers who had seen the old ramshackle building as something of a home from home, and creating in the process the city's sleekest hotel. The Clarence sits directly on the water: it is higher than any of its neighbours, chic, elegant and beautiful, and full of beautiful guests, too. Today, you can sit in the Octagon bar and eat designer crisps all afternoon, if you like, and fancy yourself quite the celebrity – if you can be bothered.

On Essex Bridge, other kiosks are being set up in preparation for the permanent book market which is now being established on this spot. Temple Bar falls away and the Four Courts appear on the northern bank. Like Custom House, they are Gandon-designed and classically beautiful; unlike Custom House, they were burned during the Civil War, taking with them a large proportion of Ireland's national archive. What we see today is a painstakingly recreated building. Behind it lies one of the oldest parts of Dublin; Smithfield was once famed for its horse market, its fish and meat and flower markets, and its old pubs with their interiors of polished wood and mirror. But today, the horse market is gone and a new plaza has been created in its place: vast gas braziers march down one side, and new apartments buildings and cafés have colonised this deeply, dense urban space. The famous Cobblestone bar still remains and traditional music is played there each night – though not for much longer, because newly announced development plans may mean the Cobblestone vanishes just as so many other old Dublin pubs have before it, to make way for a new building, new apartments – a new city. However, the fish market remains and has been newly repaired; fresh fish gleams on marble slabs daily.

On the southern side of the Liffey, the ground rises sharply to a height above Wood Quay. This is where the original Viking city once stood, although much of the ground has now been covered by the extravagantly ugly Civic Offices, built amid howls of protest for Dublin City Council. Above this monolith sits Christchurch Cathedral: a cathedral has stood on this site since the foundation of the city a thousand years ago, although the fine building we see today, all flying buttresses and neo-Gothic arches, is largely a Victorian construction. But the great bells of Christchurch in the cathedral belfry are a Dublin institution: they have been around since the mid-1700s and so are even longer established than U2. Each December, the bells ring in the New Year to crowds in the street below; and the choir is famous in the city too. Each Sunday, the bells ring out at 10am for an hour, pealing across a still sleeping Dublin.

Next to the cathedral, on the same long ridge of high ground, is the Liberties, the name given to the old working class district which grew up outside the medieval city walls of Dublin. The street markets here are a different shape, and a different sound and smell from the ones in Temple Bar. You'd be hard pushed to find a round of Gubbeen cheese or a venison sausage here; instead, it's all teetering

Anna Livia: Dublin Riverscape

pyramids of toilet paper on special offer and giant bars of Toblerone selling at four euro a pop. At the heart of the Liberties is the Guinness brewery, first established in the 18th century, and holding a one-thousand-year lease on the land. This is the real trademark of the city and the country: this is the brew taken abroad by the emigrants and now drunk in the thousands of Irish bars scattered across the globe. But the company is now owned by a faceless multinational; and maybe this is appropriate too, since Ireland is now officially the most globalised country on earth. Ask most people what they mean and they will shrug. Does it mean that Ireland exports its culture more successfully than any other country in the world? No, it doesn't mean that, but it could, because Ireland does export its culture more successfully than any other nation – aspects of it anyway. The rich, coffee-like smell of roasting hops hangs over the Liberties permanently.

The Liffey is not a great river and already it is beginning to narrow as it nears its source in the mountains, to assume the proportions of the country stream it really is. Of Ireland's rivers, only the Liffey is imagined as female: its goddess is Anna Livia, smooth and ladylike among a crowd of thrusting, macho river gods. At Kilmainham, the river flows below the gloriously restored Royal Hospital, which now houses the Irish Museum of Modern Art; and Kilmainham Gaol, where the heroes of Ireland's struggle for independence were incarcerated over the years. Here, suddenly, the city seems to stop: the river flows between green fields and parkland for a while; a weir branches out, flowing along the edge of the austerely beautiful, Lutyens-designed War Memorial Gardens. The vast Phoenix Park opens up on the northern bank and then suburbs stretch on for miles beyond, but the Liffey seems just like any old river now. It's only when it hits Dublin that its significance balloons dramatically – or so Dublin likes to think.

THE FERRY is at rest and the sirens have stopped squawking when I return to the car. My IKEA booty remains intact; my friends are already waiting. After this long day, they are in no mood to wait around for anyone, and I have the car keys.

'Thought you'd fallen overboard,' grunts one.

'I was looking at the view. I got carried away.'

'Get into the car, will you? They'll be opening up in a minute.'

I interrupt eagerly, flushed with my view.

'Dublin looks great from the water – really great.'

Tuts are followed by silence. It really has been a long day. I get into the car, just as the great doors open, and we drive off. Dublin really did look great, I think, but even so, I'm soon obsessing about IKEA again.

1

An Angel At My Table

Dublin's New Rock Generation

IN DUBLIN today, as in most cities, good coffee is seen as a barometer of sophistication. Coffee, in fact, is now the ultimate cliché: good coffee equals lots and lots of sophistication; bad coffee, so the theory goes, means none at all. It's as simple as that. But this means that, until about the mid-'90s, Dublin possessed no sophistication at all. Back in 1990, when I first came to the city, my friends and I would nip out of

Whelan's: At the Heart of Dublin's Music Scene

Trinity College for regular pit stops in the streets round about. In those days, coffee came in thick, heavy mugs and had the consistency, colour and approximate taste of liquid tar. We drank it all the same, wincingly; it swilled around inside us all day and our nerves were shot. It seemed never to occur to anyone that coffee need not taste this bad – indeed, that surely it never did taste this bad in, say, Italy or France. No: we simply hoisted our crucifixes a little further up our backs and carried on drinking.

Then, aged 23, I went to Seattle in the summer of 1993, just as the city was going crazy for Nirvana, grunge and skinny lattes. My friend Jane was with me: she dreamt up the idea of coming back to Dublin in the autumn and opening up an espresso stand on Grafton Street. 'It's never been done before!' she told me excitedly as we walked down towards Pike Street Market and looked out over the water. In hindsight, she was right there, but at the time, as I recall, I simply peered out over the top of a pyramid of prawns and pulled a face.

'Dunno about that.'

She looked put-out.

'I could make my fortune!'

She was right there too, but alas! the moment passed. She went to Costa Rica instead, where they have more coffee than they know what to do with, and where there are certainly no fortunes to be made in selling it. Meanwhile, I went back to Dublin and sniffed a change in the air, but left the business of opening coffee houses to others.

Just like in The Carpenters' song, those times were not so long ago, but it's a little more difficult to find such disgusting tarred coffee in Dublin now. Tastes and times have changed, though sophistication only goes so far: the Dublin fashion sense, for example, is as hit and miss as ever.

I think about all this – espresso stands, Seattle, grunge and prawns – all whirling through my mind in an instant, while sitting in **Busyfeet and Coco**, a small and noisy café just off Grafton Street in Dublin city centre. Chairs scream as they are dragged across the terrazzo floor. Busyfeet does good coffee and good tea – Fairtrade all the way: it attracts a fashionably arty clientele, after all, so it can't be seen to be blatantly fleecing Guatemalan coffee growers. Instead, it steers itself and its customers away from that wicked road to hell. People seem happy enough, especially if the product is good. I eye people over the rim of my cup: I'm early for my appointment and my friend John Hegarty (no relation) hasn't arrived yet, so there's nothing to do but wait and watch the scene and scrape away with a spoon the disconcerting mountain of froth from my latte.

Dublin is still a young city, though not quite as predominantly youthful as it was. Other European societies are rapidly ageing, with all the attendant hand-wringing over pensions, elderly bulges in the population and economic collapse. Ireland hasn't reached this point yet: the influence of the Catholic Church ensured that the country's post-war baby boom sustained itself longer and until the mid-'70s, five and six children in a family remained the norm. But today, family sizes are dwindling in Ireland as they have dwindled everywhere else in Western Europe. Ireland was behind the times demographically as it was economically, socially, and culturally, and so Dublin is still remarkable for its crowds of 20- and 30-somethings thronging the city's streets. And today, it seems to me that they are all gathered in Busyfeet and Coco, all dragging the wooden chairs around clatteringly. I finish my cup of froth, John arrives and we leave them to it.

This is a discriminating generation: more or less informed, more or less educated, and more or less interested in culture in its widest sense. You catch a sense of this in many areas: in Busyfeet and Coco at any time of the day, in the street corners jagged with new shops and coffee houses, and in the bookshops and theatres. But maybe this energetic cultural moment finds its most direct expression in Dublin's extraordinarily diverse and energetic music scene. On this

Busyfeet and Coco Café, 41–42 South William Street, Dublin 2 (671 9514)
The small and, yes, busy café is located right in the heart of town and offers generous sandwiches, fresh salads and feel-good organic and Fairtrade coffee all day and into the evening.

chilly January day, I'm on my way to experience it for myself. I'm on my way to **Road Records,** the city's most influential independent record shop. 'Record shop,' I say to myself, but that doesn't really cover it. John, who is a musician himself and knowledgeable about these matters, is going to introduce me to the owners.

As far as shops go, Road Records is fairly standard from the outside. It's on a small and narrow road, and is itself housed in a small and narrow building. Sometimes, it seems beleaguered, hedged in by super-pubs: to my mind, a symbol of all that was appalling and crass about '90s Dublin. Hogan's bar looms across the road; the Capital is just down the road; the vast Market Bar has just opened a few doors up. The Market has high ceilings and uncomfortable banquettes, and sells marinated anchovies, artichokes and stuffed olives as nibbles. There are no peanuts and no fat bags of cheese'n'onion crisps here. Sometimes, on those rare occasions when I'm not feeling too judgemental, I grudgingly admit that the Market is not bad, as vast bars go, in fact, it is almost cool. The food has redeemed it to my mind. But Road Records, while it certainly doesn't sell marinated anchovies, artichokes or stuffed olives, is undeniably more cool. It is cool without even trying. We go in.

Browse, Buy, Listen at Road Records

Inside, CDs are on sale on one side, neatly tied in little plastic bags; vinyl is stacked on the other side. There is lots of music by Irish bands and singer-songwriters: The Frames, Damien Rice, The Thrills, Gemma Hayes are all there, I see as I flick distractedly, alongside Elvis Costello, Tom Waits, Nick Cave, and The Beach Boys. The walls are bright canary-yellow.

Julie Collins and Dave Kennedy run Road Records and they are both here today. Dusk is falling: we have a look at the music while Julie and Dave shut up shop. Dave has a spot of paint on his nose: the basement is being painted, they tell me, in preparation for a Road Records expansion in a month or so.

'I hate painting,' I say. 'I always feel I want to kill someone.' I feel tense just thinking about it; and I don't offer to help.

Dave shrugs; he is too polite to complain, but I can tell he hates painting as much as I do.

Painting apart, however, Julie and Dave radiate the kind of serenity that comes from doing exactly what you want to do. Road opened in 1997 and has been going strong ever since.

'And you set it up?' I ask.

'Yep, we set it up. September 1997,' Dave says and there is a note of justified pride in his voice.

'We both worked in a record shop here in town,'Julie says, 'and we simply decided we could do it ourselves. We felt that there was a gap that the big shops weren't filling, a gap that a small, versatile shop could fill more easily. And we also had a clear idea of what we wanted.'

'And what was that?'

'We simply wanted a shop that could reflect the indie scene and that understood what was going on at the grassroots.' She shrugs. 'Simple as that.'

They finish what they are doing and we leave Road, pull down the shutters with a roar and go around the corner to the Central Hotel. I've always had a sneaking regard for the **Library Bar**, which is on the first floor of the building and overlooking the road. It is styled like a gentlemen's club in Pall Mall: all leather armchairs, roaring fires and book-lined walls. It's a good place to come on a wet afternoon, but I always had the idea that it was somehow secret and certainly not fashionable. Now, however, I look around and wonder. The people sitting in the wing-backed leather armchairs are not little old ladies and besuited gentlemen, but people in their 20s and younger, supping their pints of Guinness, fiddling with laptops, and talking earnestly about music and music software against a backdrop of shelves lined with burgundy-spined books.

'I thought we'd have the place to ourselves.'

'Hardly,' Julie says and laughs. 'People seem to like the fires.'

It's true: everyone looks snug as bugs. We take a table near the fire and snuggle in too. Soon, my friend Ann-Marie Hardiman joins us. I asked her to come along: her knowledge of the Dublin music scene is prodigious and so I thought she would enjoy the conversation. Together, we make a cosy group around the fire.

'It was always important for us to stock new music,' Julie says, 'to keep an eye on what was going on in the music scene and give new bands and new musicians a chance to sell their records. I suppose you could say that we knew a lot of bands at the time and we made a,' and she pauses for a moment, 'a conscientious decision to try and stock this stuff. With all the changes in technology, a lot of bands are able to record at home, and get stuff produced very cheaply. So we made a conscious decision to stock this music. We were surprised at the sheer number of bands who took advantage of the service and how big some of them have gone on to be. Sometimes, bands really take you by surprise at how good they are.'

Dave nods.

The Library Bar
Central Hotel
1-5 Exchequer Street
Dublin 2 (679 7302)
Upstairs in the Central Hotel you'll discover the Library Bar, got up in the manner of an old gentlemens' club, with thick carpets, winged-backed leather armchairs and leather-bound volumes on the walls to boot. It's usually quiet(ish) when other bars are thronged and boasts a vast fire and waiter service – perfect and luxurious on a wet Dublin afternoon.

'When we opened in 1997,' he says, 'bands were beginning to make their own records and not wait for record labels. Of course, there had always been a DIY scene concentrated on punk rock in the city. About six or seven years ago, though, other bands began to realise that they could save up some money and make their own records. It was easy and cheap, but then what happened was that they had 500 copies and no shops! Unless you have distribution, the shops won't take in copies. I knew that: I had been involved in music, though none of it,' he adds drily, 'had been very successful. So we knew how hard it is for unknown bands to actually get shops to sell your records. And we noticed as soon as we opened that we suddenly had a dedicated Irish section for independent music with no label. Within a couple of weeks, we had maybe 50 records and now we have 200 at any one time.' He shrugs. 'You know, even now, there are only a few shops that will stock that kind of music. The big shops just don't.'

I think about the news this morning: Tower Records has just filed for bankruptcy protection in America. Dinosaurs come into my mind: great lumbering dinosaurs, with the independent shops and supermarkets running rings around them – Dinosaurs and mammals. Maybe this is the case, maybe it isn't, but it makes a good image. I edge closer to the fire.

'Unless they cotton onto the fact that a band is on the cusp,' Julie says, 'then they buy them in quickly enough. They can be quick off the mark when they want to be.'

I frown to myself – so much for my dinosaur image. Damn.

'For example, when The Frames released their last live album *Setlist*,' Julie goes on, 'it was all over the big shops. The big chains got into them right away. I'm very pleased to say we always stocked The Frames' music, but it's only when something's proven that the big shops jump on the bandwagon. And that's what makes an outfit like Road so important.

'And the interesting thing is that the big chains don't order locally; they order centrally from London. They have no idea how music sells in Ireland: that what sells in Dublin mightn't sell in Cork, and what sells in Belfast won't sell in Galway. So it's only

Top Five Record Shops

Dublin is a good music-shopping city, not least because the usual combination of mega-chains and small independent shops is spiked by specialist Irish music stores – and because Dublin city centre is so compact, you can source all this music in the course of a ten-minute walk.

Road Records
16B Fade Street, Dublin 2 (671 7340)
Road is the best independent music store in town. The owners are knowledgeable, the clientele equally so and the walls are painted as bright a canary yellow as could be wished for. Come here for tickets too.

Celtic Note
12 Nassau Street, Dublin 2 (670 4157)
The windows of Celtic Note usually feature all manner of Celtic lovelies, including The Corrs [the sisters, at least] and Enya. But you should venture inside even so: the shop stocks an impressive range of Irish music. It's a Ticketmaster outlet too.

Tower Records
16 Wicklow Street, Dublin 2 (671 3250)
Tower Records is the best of the big stores, stocking an impressive and varied stash of music, as well as the usual publications and accessories. Tower is fairly responsive on the new music front too, and its Irish section is worth checking out.

Big Brother and Selectah
4 Crow Street, Temple Bar, Dublin 2 (672 9355/616 7020)
As you push dismally through the hellish soup of a Temple Bar Saturday afternoon, stop by Big Brother and Selectah, which occupy adjoining premises in one of the district's cobbled lanes. Selectah is at street level and specialises in techno; Big Brother has just moved from Road Records' basement into its very own basement and offers a good range of techno and hip-hop.

when something is proved will they jump on the bandwagon. We always give people a chance; and that's where we have the advantage too.'

John says, 'Road works as a focus for the Dublin scene. People just drop into Road to find out what's happening...'

'They drop in for cups of tea and chocolate!' Julie laughs. 'The Dublin music scene – it's seriously hard-core; it's tea and Toblerone all the way.'

'...and it's a funny thing,' John goes on. 'When Road opened, it seemed to put a face on a scene that was already there. Road is the place where everyone meets.'

'I suppose it's essential,' I say, 'to have that focus.'

John hesitates a moment and then says: 'Well, not really. It is essential to have a focus, yes, but on the other hand, everyone knows everyone else. You have The Frames and a whole set of bands who know them; and then you have The Redneck Manifesto and David Kitt and Damien Rice; you have a whole set of bands and singers who all know each other. And they all play together – the music scene in Dublin really is very interconnected. But I agree that it's good to have somewhere apart from pubs and music venues to meet.'

I can imagine, I think to myself. Dublin life swirls so utterly around pubs and pints of Guinness that a place where you can get a cup of tea and a Toblerone would sound devastatingly attractive.

But Julie says, 'Well, Road is good – of course it is – but the music venues are great too. Whelan's is a great point of contact. We've met people just starting off who have just turned up at Whelan's with a guitar and were invited to play a couple of songs at a gig. The Frames are very good at letting people do that too. And Whelan's is a great place: John Hennessy took over the management and he started having bands launch their records there; he took on The Frames in a big way and he set up late-night sessions too...Whelan's is just very important, and very recognisable. If people see you're playing at Whelan's, they reckon you've made it. You get recognition. It's like a seal of approval.'

John says, 'And so with Whelan's and Road Records, you have a kind of nexus.'

IT IS quite dark outside now and a chilly-sounding wind rattles the sash windows. I ask my friends about the music scene in the '80s, the whole curious, disturbing era. There is a pause and a shaking of heads and then John says, 'That whole thing: selling the city as a music capital in the '80s – it just really backfired.'

Julie murmurs, 'Because it wasn't a music capital!'

'It was really counterproductive.'

'You see bands trying to come back now,' Ann-Marie says, 'and so embittered by the whole experience.'

Julie shakes her head again. 'I don't blame them. They really did get shafted. They got huge advances: they didn't realise about the small print where you had to pay for the recording studios, the producer flown over from New York and all the rest of it...prohibitively expensive, the lot of it.' She stops for a moment and then says, 'But you know, it all came out right in the end. Everything corrected itself and maybe it happened for the best.

'The '90s came and then the boy bands arrived and everything else faded; the big labels had the Irish product they wanted and so they got out. Sony left Dublin, and we were left to set up another way of doing things. Everything that happened seemed to take the pressure off. Didn't it?'

'It did.'

'When Boyzone appeared and the boy band thing happened in the mid-'90s,' Julie resumes, 'the whole emphasis was placed somewhere else. Record companies stopped coming here or just shut up shop and so you had a group of things happening: the singer-songwriter thing took off at the International and the DIY thing was happening with The Hope Collective and a lot of new young bands starting up; and what we got then was that Road opened in September 1997 and Whelan's started getting new bands in...'

This is a lot of information to take in. I know about the International, of course. It's a lovely pub just down the road from here, with an old bar on the ground floor and a performance space upstairs. I've been to plays here, comedy improv, the old gig. But what was The Hope Collective?

'WHAT WAS The Hope Collective?'

John takes a sip of his pint and says, 'It was real quintessential early '90s Dublin. It was a punk scene run by a guy called Niall McGuirk. It was a real DIY scene: it put on a lot of gigs, supported a lot of bands – and it really set an example for what people are doing now. It was almost like people were looking after each other. And it's probably the main reason, the single best reason, why the scene is so good in Dublin now.'

Julie chips in, 'Niall wrote a book last year called *Document: A Story of Hope* and he got all the bands he worked with together and he got them to provide a vegetarian or vegan recipe. It was very right-on: if you played at a festival sponsored by a big company, for example, you were cut out of the loop. It was very clear, very clean.' Then she smiles. 'And the book! The book really is great: it's a history of music in Dublin too and Niall is a really great guy.' She glances at Dave. 'And Dave has a recipe in the book!'

'Oh?' I say and turn to Dave. 'And what's the recipe for?'

Dave says solemnly, 'It's a recipe for vegetarian chilli.'

'How long did it last?'

'What – the vegetarian chilli?'

'No – not the vegetarian chilli. The Hope Collective.'

'Oh – about five years.'

'About five years,' repeats Julie thoughtfully. 'Not bad for an organisation like that. They never made money. It was never about making money: any cash that was generated went into a fund and people could borrow small amounts when they needed it – say, for a fanzine. It was incredibly admirable: nobody had ever considered doing it.'

'It just brought on a lot of bands and people who otherwise would have found it very, very difficult,' John tells me. 'The Waltons, for example, who became The Redneck Manifesto, and this was at a time when other people could be unbelievably bitchy on the scene. The difference in mentality was amazing and you can see this now in the people who came out of the Hope scene: they are just a different generation of musicians; they don't sit around complaining; it is amazing.'

1

Dublin's New Rock Generation

Dave chips in, 'And it had a natural lifespan. Collectives are so difficult to keep going and this one ran its course.' He added ruefully, 'The whole punk rock scene is young people's music, really; after a certain age, it's difficult to maintain interest in it. So I suppose it was inevitable that the Hope would last for a while and then stop.'

There is a silence; the fire crackles.

I glance towards the windows of the Library Bar. It's sleeting outside now, and the sight makes me even less inclined to leave the hearth and go home. Thankfully, everyone else seems to feel the same way: before I know it, another round of drinks is ordered.

'It's just curious how music changes,' John says. 'How the culture changes. A few years ago, people wanted to go to England and make an album for a hundred grand; and now people want to make their own music, do their own thing, work during their day and keep their freedom and control their music without any financial constraint. The great example is The Redneck Manifesto, who went off to Texas.'

My concentration snaps at the word 'Texas'. George Bush's ranch in Crawford, Texas, leaps into my mind. Dick Cheney, Laura Bush's unnerving smile, environmental degradation, electric chairs, a documentary about fat people in Houston which was on the television lately. 'Texas?' I squeak. 'Why did they go to Texas?'

Julie sees my expression, seems able to read my mind too. 'Well, not Texas really,' she says reassuringly. 'Austin, Texas – it's not really Texas at all. The South by Southwest festival in Austin.'

'Oh. Right.' I take a large slug of Guinness to steady my nerves.

'It's a brilliant festival – very important. The Rednecks went there this year. It isn't a big corporate thing – instead, you get lots of smaller companies. It's really laid-back and friendly. The Rednecks had a publishing deal but BMX Bike loved their music so much that they put it on their publicity videos!'

There is delighted laughter all round.

'It's the whole travel and exposure thing,' Dave says. 'I'm always amazed when we get mail order from Salt Lake City and places like that, saying, "Oh, we heard this music; it's great! Send us some more." It shows how things can work when you can travel. The Rednecks just saved up and went there under their own steam; they didn't get a grant or anything – but they really are a big success story. It means that if they ever went back to the States, they would slot right into a scene that would be really supportive.'

'And it shows too that Dublin is becoming a music capital by default,' adds Julie. 'Not in that inflated bubble way – in a real way, from the bottom up. The Rednecks are the evidence of it: a real band, making real music and slowly building up a reputation.'

There is plenty more where that came from too, I think, as I look out at the sleet falling in the lamplight: Damien Rice, Gemma Hayes, David Kitt, and the whole crop of singer-songwriters, and the ones claimed from abroad too, like David Gray. The list is as long as your arm.

John says: 'People saw that they could sell their music in Road Records, play a gig in Whelan's, and build it up from there. Now David Kitt plays Vicar Street and Gemma Hayes the Olympia – bigger venues in Dublin...'

'Not to mention the bigger venues abroad,' adds Ann-Marie and everyone laughs: David Gray and Damien Rice have just begun their European tour.

'I remember Damien Rice coming into Road with home-made tickets for a gig in Whelan's!' Julie says. 'He'd be delighted if he sold 40 tickets. Now he can sell out Vicar Street in a minute! It's fantastic. We haven't created a superstar in Dublin yet, but Damien is doing really well in America: he's taking The Frames with him on tour over there later this year. So hopefully, that will help to bring on Dublin acts in the States.'

I HAVE noticed – I can't help but notice – that people talk a good deal about America. Where 15 years ago, the idea was to break Britain, now it's all about breaking the American market. In one way, of course, this is a pretty good sign: certainly, nobody could say that the Irish music scene was hopelessly in hock to the former colonial oppressor. And it's clear too that the reaction against the excesses of the '80s is still going on: bands and musicians have educated themselves about the music scene. They know that the big deal and the instant careers are a poor choice in the short term. The intelligent move is to build it up, play at home, establish a base in Dublin and in Ireland and then move it on.

All the same, I've been struck by the emphasis on America. It isn't only Robbie Williams, it seems, who wants to break the States. Musicians in Dublin want to move it all towards America now too. It seems to me that this chimes with a greater cultural debate going on in Ireland, which can be neatly summed up in one short question: Should Ireland be more oriented towards Boston or Berlin? This was the subject of a now-famous – some might say notorious – speech given by a high-profile Irish politician a few years ago. Should Ireland embrace the low-taxation and low-spending economic model offered by America; or go for the system of high taxation and better services common in the EU? So far, it seems that the Irish instinct favours the former: direct taxation in Ireland is relatively low, although indirect taxation is punitive.

But it isn't simply about taxation. The Irish were always considered good Europeans. The Irish state may have benefited enormously from the EU, with roads and infrastructure rebuilt using European money, yet there is a sense that the Irish state has always been oriented more profoundly towards America culturally and emotionally. Even during the Iraq war, Ireland violated its cherished (albeit never quite defined) neutrality by allowing American planes to cross Irish airspace, and land and refuel on Irish soil. The reason given was that as a nation, we could not afford to anger America. All of this had passed through my mind lately and I wondered if Irish music had simply exchanged one external focus for another. As for Britain, it's scarcely mentioned.

Or maybe they have learned by experience. The big irony is that U2 were making it in America but sinking in England. So their management brought them to America and that's what saved them.

'What about Britain?' I say, as the fire glows and flickers. 'I never hear anything about the UK these days... Is it too much of a generalisation to say that bands aren't concentrating on Britain any more?'

Dave says slowly: 'Well, it's true that you never hear about people packing up and moving to London any more. You just never do.'

'And they never get a good reception when they do go,' Ann-Marie adds. Everyone nods in agreement and Ann-Marie goes on, 'I think the British audience is a more difficult audience to please. The American bands on tour who play in London always find it difficult; then they come here and can't believe the reception they get. In London, audiences say: 'Impress me; can you impress me?" In Dublin, people say: "I'm here to have a good time"; there are fewer judgements.'

'I suppose David Gray is a good example of that,' I pipe up. Everyone in Ireland knows about David Gray, so I feel on safe ground.

'He really is.' Dave sips from his pint. 'He had three massive albums here in Ireland but he couldn't sell a record in Britain. The first single that sold there was a re-mix. Over here, he was able to make a living.' Then he adds: 'But he kept plugging away in America and he eventually made it. That's what helped Damien Rice break America too: he had David Gray's management team, who really knew their stuff – plus his music was good. But David Gray couldn't have got arrested for years in Britain, while over here, his music was being played and played on the radio, and his videos on the TV. Eventually, the buzz caught on in the UK. And as for Damien Rice: well, he's on the Leno and Letterman shows; he's making it big.

'The difference is that over here, bands can build up support just by playing gigs all the time; small is beautiful. In London, you really need to get on the front of *NME*, otherwise, people won't take chances.'

'Dublin is like Glasgow,' I say wisely and Ann-Marie flicks me a glance. She has known me for years; she knows I have never been to Glasgow.

'Similar cities, for sure,' Dave agrees and I glance back at Ann-Marie. 'People are willing to take a chance. It's an interesting phenomenon.'

Dublin's New Rock Generation

1

'It shows that Dublin has changed so much over the last few years,' says John meditatively. 'The way people make music and the way they listen to music – these have both changed. People have realised that Dublin is a small city and quite central too, and this is a virtue. You can go drinking at Vicar Street and catch anyone playing. And attendances have rocketed over the last few years. So

Top Five Venues for Live Rock

The Village (map: 2)
26 Wexford Street
Dublin 2 (475 8555)
The Village is large and slick and offers live music nightly. There's room for 500 or so punters and, because The Village self-consciously caters for broader tastes, the programme is wider and more varied. There's food and a chilled-out bar area too – both open all day.

Whelan's (map: 1)
25 Wexford Street
Dublin 2 (478 0766)
The greatest of them all in some eyes, Whelan's is a long-established and treasured live music venue on the Camden Street–Wexford Street strip, just next door to the Village. It's surprisingly small, with room for no more than 300 or so, but invariably offers a great atmosphere and better music. Come here for newish bands, for Road Relish launches and for the occasional more unusual feature too.

Olympia (map: 25)
72 Dame Street
Dublin 2 (679 3323)
If your grandmother is a hooker, you'll be at home in The Olympia: the venue is got up in lashings of red paint and gold, is distinctly Victorian vaudeville in tone and at first sight seems an unlikely music venue. But in spite of – or perhaps because of – these associations, The Olympia is one of Dublin's most successful venues and plays host to the city centre's biggest concerts, as well as regular theatre.

many bands are being brought over from America – The Palace Brothers, Tortoise – and this helps to change music here. It's like a direct exchange of ideas.'

Julie says: 'The bottom line is that we have a discerning gig-going crowd here. People would rather see a good band rather than some flash-in-the-pan *NME* band. They aren't ready to believe the hype:

Vicar Street (map: 11)
55–59 Vicar Street, off Thomas Street
Dublin 8 (454 6656)
Newish but already firmly established as one of the city's best live music venues, Vicar Street is a little larger again than The Village and excellently kitted-out. The venue recently played host to the Planxty reunion concerts and offers a wide range of international music and comedy every night.

Liberty Hall (map: 19)
Eden Quay
Dublin 1 (872 1122)
Liberty Hall is the tallest and quite possibly ugliest building in Dublin, but don't allow this to distract you ... the newly revamped venue here offers a good and varied diet of music.

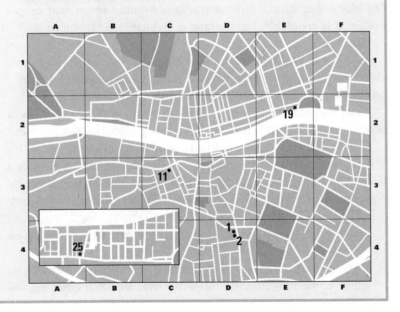

they want to see people making a bit of an effort; and they really want to support local music and good music.

'I remember the Glasgow band that came over here – The Cosmic Rough Riders. They came over here and played in the Sugar Club and only got 40 people or so. They said, "Why did nobody come?" And we said, "You should have gone to Whelan's." There is a feeling like Whelan's is our venue, while the Sugar Club really isn't. People are sensitive about things like that. They hate to feel like they are being taken for granted.'

'There's a terrible dearth of good venues.' Julie shakes her head. 'A real lack of infrastructure and a real lack of smaller places. Whelan's has a 400-person capacity and you can fill that if it's Redneck Manifesto or The Jimmy Cake. But new bands really can't fill it – you can see the tumbleweeds rolling through.

'And so many small places have vanished. The Funnel on the quays is gone, so is the Music Room on Abbey Street – it was small and old-fashioned and great. And the Cobblestone is going.'

People sit up at this; they haven't heard this piece of news. The Cobblestone is such a famous traditional music venue that people assume it is inviolable, but nothing is inviolable in Dublin today.

'Really?'

'So they say. Of course, it'll be rebuilt, but with apartments built above, so you won't get the bands coming. Late gigs will be knocked on the head because of complaints and that'll be the end of that.'

'And the poor Baggot Inn,' Ann-Marie sighs. 'Gone too. Just a hole in the ground now. It'll be rebuilt too, I suppose – but as what?'

The Baggot Inn was demolished just before Christmas: today, it's a void surrounded by hoardings. The venue, we all agree, was a fleapit of the highest order, but it had a certain je ne sais quoi. U2 played here in the late '70s; so too did Christy Moore, Paul Brady, and The Undertones.

I ask about straws in the wind. 'Are any new places coming on stream?'

Dave shakes his head. 'Costs are too high: insurance is prohibitive, the buildings are too expensive, and staff costs are too

Vicar Street venue (no vicars here).

much. It just isn't viable. You just cannot make money. Instead, every couple of months, a small venue will open up over a pub and stick around for a few months before vanishing again.

'The reason is economic; it always is.' This is all getting very Marxist; and another brief silence falls. I feel guilty: I hadn't intended to make everyone suicidal.

'It's a question of a marriage,' says Ann-Marie. 'Someone who knows about venues and economics; and someone who knows about music; put it all together, then it might work.'

Julie says dreamily: 'Do you remember Jute?'

Ann-Marie and I exchange another glance. We remember Jute. Jute appeared for a year or so while we were students, before vanishing again. It was the Brigadoon de nos jours. Jute was a very, very cool bar and very quirky, with a room upstairs where people always played music. It had big sofas, where you went to have a drink and loll around pretending to be the last word in cool. I frown suddenly: I realise that Jute is now the Capital – right opposite Road Records – an outrageous imposter. We all sigh for simpler times; we all take another swig.

'Charlie's on Golden Lane is gone too.'

'You couldn't get in there if you were over 18: they'd stop you at the door.'

'Slattery's on Capel Street.'

'The Fox and Pheasant.'

'Barnstormers. When you stop to think about it, you realise how many places are gone.'

'Or worse, turned into a lapdancing club.'

Listening to this catalogue of disasters, I realise that the amount of musical energy and talent in the city simply isn't matched by the infrastructure and the know-how. It seems there is no framework that might help showcase bands and provide some cash; a body to enable bands to go to, say, South by Southwest by giving them a few euro. These things are out of most people's reach.

I ask: 'Is there some attitude: "you should be commercial or you should be quirky"?'

'Yes,' replies Julie firmly. 'And most bands don't fulfil either criteria.'

'The frustrating thing,' Dave says, 'is that it wouldn't cost much to send a band to Austin, for example: they would have friends there, and they would have a network. They only need their airfares paid for, but even the airfares are too expensive for most people. That's why I think we need a dedicated Music Network that will be able to respond to our particular needs. We have a few websites where people can chat to one another, but there is a dearth of that network of support. Years ago, we had Temple Lane Studios, where people could just hang out during the day…'

'And the Garden of Delight,' says Julie. 'Remember that? It's an apartment block now. When we were in Glasgow, we went to the Thirteenth Note: a venue, a bar and a vegetarian restaurant. All the bands went there and hung out – Dublin has no venue like this at all.'

'And that's the strange thing: Dublin is a provincial city and remote from London. And that means it's like Scotland and Wales: there is a separate energy. So we really need the infrastructure to cope, and we're not getting it.'

When I ask how they expect the scene to develop, there is a moment's thoughtful silence. Then Dave says, 'You expect things to go in circles. Ten years ago or so, the big labels were here and then they left; and in the future, labels will be interested again and they'll send people over again. The difference is that bands over here have grown up and aren't so interested in the quick buck. People are more cautious and also more genuinely interested in the music itself. And also people are less desperate now: people have jobs and play music at night and so they can afford to be more strategic and thoughtful about it. They'll bide their time now; they can afford to wait.'

Julie says, 'I think the big labels don't need to go looking for new music so much: they just get the Popstars to come along and record a song and the labels make an absolute fortune. The quick buck – why should they invest in new people?'

'The last big signing in the city was Paddy Casey,' John says, 'and he was signed by Sony; Juliet Turner by East West – and they got big bucks. But these bigger companies aren't coming any more and the big deals are gone; and Irish acts really want to sign up for smaller outfits. They're just getting more clever really.'

Julie adds, 'And that's something else: people are maybe less distinctive. You used to be able to tell if a band was from Dublin or Cork – there was a definitive sound. But The Thrills sound American, which I think is probably good: bands don't box themselves in.

'But there is still a pretty bad bottleneck just because of the lack of good small venues. All these really good bands are just not getting out there. Dublin really could do better. Bands like The Jimmy Cake and the Rednecks – they really have to get out there, but it's difficult. And they could be huge.'

Julie tells me, 'There are nine people in The Jimmy Cake and they all do other things. Jürgen Simpson is the accordionist with The Jimmy Cake and he writes opera and is into electronica too –

1

you should talk to him. They are all working in about three different forms: electronic and dance and other stuff. Nobody ever keeps to the genre you might expect. And people from bands from a few years – people like The Plague Monkeys – are all still around doing lots and lots of other things. And it's all incredibly intertwined. And all the independent labels: Independent, Scientific Laboratories, Volta Sounds, Volta Beats which does dance. Labels that specialise in hip-hop in Dublin, which is a big thing. And Dave does Road Relish.'

'Road Relish?'

'It's a – it's best described as a not-for-profit record label,' Julie says.

'We – three friends and I – set up Road Relish three years ago,' Dave tells me. 'We wanted to form a sub-pop singles club: limited seven-inches, one band on each side, split seven-inches. One of us was in a band, three had been in a band, so we knew how the scene worked. We wanted to do something for bands who didn't have the time or money to release their own records. Labels tend to notice when you can produce your own music, and also, there was simply a lot of really good music in Dublin and we wanted to provide a platform for it.'

I think this sounds admirable, but when I say my thought aloud, Dave shakes his head.

'There was really very little risk: pressing 500 copies is no big deal and we stick to singles and we go with vinyl too, which is a bit of an indulgence. It has to be vinyl: we were all of the opinion that vinyl is the way to go.'

Julie laughs. 'A girl was in Road a while ago and she bought the Road Relish seven-inch by Glen Hansard from The Frames. I packaged it up for her and she looked at it and said, "I won't fit that into my CD player!" I said, "Well no, you won't – but it isn't a CD." She said, "But how can I fit it into my CD player?" I said, "You don't! Don't even try!" She just didn't understand. And she's never been back.'

'I remember the first coloured vinyl record I ever saw,' I say nostalgically. 'It was a single by ELO and it was bright purple, really shiny.'

'Well, the cool labels will release some records on vinyl now, just because it's cool,' Julie tells me. 'And it's cheaper too. Spare change, so people will risk it. A company in England, Shellshock, told us that people buy coloured vinyl and file it accordingly – blue, green, yellow...'

I think: I would do that too.

'...and Road Relish's last release, by The Chalets – it was white.'

The Chalets
(The Milky Bar Kids)

'White!' I say. 'Like a Milky Bar. You could eat it.' Then I say: 'I suppose vinyl is so pure. And since people have to compromise in every other aspect of their lives, why compromise on this too?'

'Exactly,' Dave says enthusiastically. 'And besides, vinyl sounds better! Five years ago I didn't even possess a CD player – I have one now, but I still love vinyl. I think there's something collectible and just nice about vinyl. And also: people will buy a vinyl seven-inch, but wouldn't buy a CD single.'

'So really, Road Relish is a labour of love?' This time, Dave nods.

'Yes, it really is a labour of love.' He laughs. 'But great too. We put money in which we'll never get back – but we never expected to get it back. We have shows at Whelan's to go with the seven-inches. We don't pay bands, we give them some copies to sell at the shows. And there's no contract – nothing like that – people are free to release the record again. We distribute a few in the UK too and John Peel plays them.'

Julie says, 'He always plays them.'

'We simply know how things were or are in bands,' Dave replies. 'We all know what the situation is for new bands, we all know how difficult it is – and really, it's worth it. And the records always sell out, you know? People are collecting them now, which is good.

'We always like to see a band live and we only release music we like: we don't like to release music simply because it will sell; and

Julie and Dave's Essential Dublin Discs

The Redneck Manifesto, *Thirty Six Strings* (Red F Records) – An eclectic and riveting mixture of guitar instrumentals.

Large Mound, *Raised On Rock* (Julius Geezer Records) – 11 furious tracks in 20 minutes. Includes 'Whoopass' and 'If Only I Hadn't Been Born'.

Decal, *404 Not Found* (Planet Mu) – A subtle, ambient album that reveals itself slowly. Tracks include 'Somewhere Worth Living'.

The Tycho Brahe, *This is the Tycho Brahe* (Konstantin Records) – An intimate, lo-fi – and self-produced – record from the celebrated Dublin trio.

The Last Post, *Dry Land* (Bright Star Recordings) – A beautiful album of lost love and heartbreak. Includes 'Something Tells Me…'.

Dinah Brand, *Pale Monkey Blues* (Perilous Magic) – Melodic country rock sounds.

we generally invite bands. And we try to cover various areas: electronic and rock and the rest. There are no hard and fast rules, although we usually like to keep it Irish.'

'I suppose you're always a little ahead of the game? You get the music out there just before it gets a head of steam.'

'Well, yes – we like to hear the music live, so we can get out there first. But we're always going to gigs, you know, so we simply do get to hear them first and get in before they are contracted to someone. Up next is Give A Man A Kick from Limerick; and The Waiting Room from Cork – both great, punky, fresh. They have verve; and the record will be out in April. We'll have a launch night in Whelan's: we'll try and sell as many records on the night as possible and if any profit is made at the gig, the band gets it. People trust us: we don't release bad records and there's usually a good atmosphere at the gig – a bit of drunken fun.'

I ask them if the selling profile of Road has changed much over the years and Dave nods.

'Hugely. We started off with indie and punk but it has altered a lot. People want different things and the customers dictate what we sell.' He pauses. 'To a degree anyway. Still no Beyonce.' There is laughter and he goes on: 'We have to be careful because it's a slippery slope from there down to Justin Timberlake.'

My mind lurches again and alarmingly – this time away from Justin Timberlake and towards Janet Jackson's exposed breast. Once more, my concentration snaps: I shake my head a little to dislodge this alarming thought.

'And in the future,' John says, 'people will do what The Frames have done: they'll record an album and bring it out themselves. There will be just a lot more flexibility. And the Internet will help so much. People who have never met can swap files and record albums that way. It just helps cross-fertilisation, it builds support, and it means you know people everywhere; support and ideas can criss-cross, so that you get the sense of a multi-polar world. It's in this way that London doesn't matter so much any more.' Then he says, 'And Road helped that too. It stocked records that you couldn't get anywhere else in Dublin. And that helped spread ideas as well as the records themselves. So in that sense, Road has been pivotal. They take ideas and do their own thing with them.'

Julie and Dave look modest, say nothing.

'Kind of like the positive side of globalisation,' I say and Julie says: 'Yes! It isn't just about raping virgin rainforests.'

Dave shrugs. 'We'll take in anything at Road: if it doesn't sell, we'll give it back, but we'll always give people a chance. If a shop is open-minded, then all sorts of avenues open up as a consequence of that. Music gets made and distributed which otherwise wouldn't get made. And quality has improved too: people know we won't lie to them about how good or bad their music is, so they think and work harder. So it's all good.'

And with that, it's time to call it a night. The sleet has stopped, but it's freezing cold as we break up and go our separate ways.

I'm chilled through by the time I get home. I make tea and settle down with the new edition of *Foggy Notions* that I picked up in Road Records. *Foggy Notions* is a music magazine, but not like most of the others you find in the shops. Instead of the usual formula of glitz and millions of photographs, *Foggy Notions* is printed on thick, luxurious paper and is positively scholarly. There are long, in-depth reviews and articles. It is a magazine that demands attention: and it gets it from me. I read a long piece about Nick Cave and forget the time; it's late before I make it to bed.

The Frames

A FEW days later, I receive an email from a friend in New Zealand. 'You should talk to The Frames,' Niamh writes from Wellington. 'My brother says The Frames' last album [*Setlist*] was the most under-rated in the industry. He carries a tape of it with him at all times and has converted many a globetrotter along the coasts of the Antipodes.' A little later, she goes on, 'But mostly I remember The Frames as the band who hovered on the wrong side of greatness for so long that eventually they became successful without ever being a success.'

I'm just about to frame a sarcastic reply to this, but decide to make some coffee and read the BBCi website instead. Amid a plethora of financial scandals and collapses, I read the news flashing up on the top of the screen. 'New Zealand author Janet Frame dies', it says. I blink at the monitor. There are too many Frames going on at this hour of the morning. I drink my coffee, and draw my dressing gown a little closer. Altogether too many Frames – and Janet Frame was one of my favourite authors. I went through most of her books a few years ago, and watched Jane Campion's film of *An Angel At My Table* at the old Light House cinema in town – now sadly defunct. And I'm meeting Glen Hansard, The Frames' leading light, later in town. Such a day, crowded with Frames, seems more than a little coincidental.

As I sit there at my desk, I remember something else. The Frames had a song a few years back, also entitled 'An Angel At My Table'.

Surely more than coincidence too; I make a mental note to ask Glen about it.

The Frames have been around Dublin for years. They are all in their 30s now, and have seen a thing or two: as one friend has told me, they're 'battle-hardened'. Glen was in the film of *The Commitments* a few years back, but the same friend has said that he doesn't like to be asked questions about it. I can respect this. I decide, and resolve not to ask him about it. The morning passes fretfully: I read a few obituaries of Janet Frame, which have been produced and published with indecent haste; listen to some music; and get very little accomplished.

I meet Glen in **Simon's Place**. This café has been something of a fixture on the Dublin scene for years. It was originally on another site; it was called Marx Brothers and was rather stylish, with lots of wood and posters and thick, chunky sandwiches. I went there a lot. There is a Mexican restaurant on that site today: Marx Brothers has become Simon's Place and has migrated up the road. The surroundings are not so salubrious and the place is not so comfortable, but I still go for the sandwiches and soup and for the cinnamon buns which arrive, still warm and chewy, at mid-morning. And it is still a very funky place. It's located at the end of the George's Street Arcade, which is the nearest thing Dublin has to a covered market. The arcade sells jewellery, second-hand books, Indian

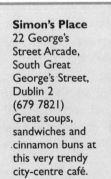

Simon's Place
22 George's Street Arcade, South Great George's Street, Dublin 2
(679 7821)
Great soups, sandwiches and cinnamon buns at this very trendy city-centre café.

necklaces, chips and bagels and candles and is at the centre of one of Dublin's most fashionable shopping areas. Across the road is La Maison de Gourmets which sells good – and fabulously expensive – French bread; and the Harlequin, where supermodels reputably come to buy vintage gear. (I've never seen one.) Road Records is just around the corner too – in Dublin, everything is just around the corner – and so too is the Market Bar and its marinated anchovies. But Simon's Place is good enough for me today.

I arrive bang on time. There are no seats in the main café and so I make my way downstairs, where it is quieter, and I drink my coffee. The walls are festooned with posters. I see Camille O'Sullivan's latest tour advertised and I remember that I have to phone Camille and meet her for an interview; I make a note in my book. There are posters for the last Road Relish party too and for anti-racism demos in Belfast. The city has just been nicknamed the 'Hate Capital' of Europe, on account of an upsurge in racist attacks there.

The air in the basement café is thick with smoke. The Irish government has recently announced a ban on smoking in the workplace, which will outlaw all smoking in bars and restaurants. It is a surprising development in Ireland: such legislation is more Californian or Scandinavian than Irish, marvels the media. Will it work? It is clear, of course, that the government is more concerned with future lawsuits than with protecting the health of its citizens. But whatever the reasons, public reaction has been by and large positive.

As I look around Simon's Place, I think that it is places like this that will really notice the difference. Nearly everyone is young and cool and nearly everyone is smoking. The atmosphere, I think, really will change when the ban comes into effect in March.

At the next table, three lads in their 20s are discussing setting up a band. One of them tilts back in his chair, another taps the cover of his guitar case, they all talk loudly and enthusiastically. They all glance at the man now clattering down the stairs and then stare intently but covertly as he makes his way across the café to my table.

'Is this the guy I'm looking for?'

'Glen?'

'That's me.'

I order another coffee and – 'a cinnamon bun?'

He nods. 'Sounds good.' And we talk.

Glen Hansard is my age – 33. He looks younger than his age (I hope I do too) and bursting with health: his eyes are bright and his skin glowing. He begins to talk about Dublin, and about the band's relationship with the city. The Irish are famous for being begrudgers, of course – it is an Irish trademark, an Irish cliché – but Glen says that The Frames have never experienced any of this.

'Of course we want to make it big on the world stage,' he says, 'but we're also a community band. When we walk on stage, we know we're engaging with Dublin. That's why we've always tried to be honest and transparent with the audience. And besides, the idea of an ego is a comparatively new one. Painters only started signing their art at a certain time in their careers; before that, it was a service, like baking bread. The idea of an ego is comparatively new. And The Frames finds this appealing.

'I think our attitude comes from a certain paranoia about the business. Ireland is sandwiched between two big cultural heavyweights: we love America and we want to break them; and we have a colonial hangover about England.'

My ears rise up like antennae at this. It's the England–America thing again; and I ask him what he means.

'Well, we're so culturally different from England – that's diluting now, of course, but there are still fundamental differences. And at every point in The Frames' career, we signed contracts with English people– I'm not a nationalist, but part of me rebels against this idea of taking the Saxon shilling. "You're working for the English."

'It comes from family history, I think: my mother brought me up on stories of my great-grandfather being in the British Army and his wife in the IRA; and my uncle was a nationalist working for the Brits. So it's a cultural thing: in all our histories, we dislike the idea that the English are our employer.'

I know, of course, about The Frames' difficult relationship with the corporate side of music. It had always been fraught and is clearly fraught still; and I'm interested in what seems to be the sense of a mingling of the corporate and the English. Again, I ask him to go on and he does, sketching out his background in Ballymun in north Dublin and the origins of the band, contextualising his argument lucidly and fluently.

'When we started off, I had no idea of the underground punk scene. We were very corporate, I suppose, from the word go. I started off as a busker on Grafton Street and was spotted and signed up to an English label. I was greener than anyone I know when I first started – didn't know a thing. I simply had a Holy Trinity of heroes – Bob Dylan, Leonard Cohen and Van Morrison – and they all existed for me in another universe. Culturally, I hadn't a fucking clue. I wasn't stupid, I think I was just very naïve.

'So I signed a publishing and record deal when I was 18. All my instincts – that had brought me from Ballymun safely – were going against this deal. When I look at the deal now or show it to anyone, they say: "I can't believe anyone let you sign this."' He pauses. 'I think my advice now to any band would be Beckett's advice: "Go out, fail, do it again, fail better".' He stops and takes a bite from his cinnamon bun and says: 'That way, you'll understand.'

I like his reference to Beckett; it shows a certain style and I nod appreciatively. I remember what someone said to me a few days ago:

'The Frames: A lot of people dislike The Frames. Their gigs are a bit overblown. It's all very spectacular. The music is great, but some people get resentful.'

This was the nearest I had come to picking up any begrudgery about The Frames. I can understand it, up to a point. The lead singer is quoting Beckett and this might vex a listener. But I don't feel vexed; I'm enjoying Glen's fluid and articulate conversation. Besides, I think, people are surely entitled to quote Beckett if it's relevant? I would be quoting him too, I suppose, if I knew any quotations.

Glen continues: 'But we're in control of our destiny now, for the first time in years. We were in a relationship with a man who didn't have his facilities together. We said: "Please, please let us go. We're not selling the records. This isn't working and we're not changing our songs to make them more radio-friendly."'

I notice his discretion and unwillingness to criticise anyone by name, and I appreciate his delicacy. I ask: 'I suppose you could have changed your songs when you were 18?'

'Yeah – I suppose we could,' he replies. 'But my attitude now is that compromise is cancer. If you compromise, then anyone can push you around. You just can't sell your soul. You see people doing that all the time. And I didn't want to get sick. I was watching people smoke their brains out and going nuts in the business. I wasn't going to go there.

'But you know, fair play – the label let us go. They could have held on to us – and instead they let us go, let our career go. We've seen people locked into deals with labels and their career just runs into the ground. I knew this one guy who had been working on an album for six years and the label still wasn't happy.' He stops and then says: 'But that's his story.

'I find it hard to talk about The Frames' history without feeling instinctively angry about England. When we were 21, we were dropped by Island. The Cranberries went on tour instead of us and their album was fantastic. They had success and so Island had the success they wanted. We were naïve, thinking we would be successful too, but the label didn't see it that way – we were dropped.' He shakes his head. 'It was crushing at the time – a crowd of young men. You lose all your self-belief. Of course now I see we're only a band, a song, an album, but at the time it was terrible – really, really terrible.' He shakes his head.

'My dream was never to be on *Top of the Pops*. My dream was to play in really cool bars – to go to New York and hang out in Central Park.' He waves his hand and says: 'To be a troubadour. My guitar would be a key – or my surfboard. And suddenly we were dealing with shattering pain instead.'

'Did you ever feel,' I ask him pryingly, intrusively, 'that it wasn't going to work as a band? Did you ever feel like stopping?' I feel like a tabloid journalist.

1

'Well, that was my job,' he replies and shrugs. 'I was the songwriter, so I would decide whether we floated or sank. At the time, we gathered and rehearsed, and rehearsed and stayed together. Then I went to New York: ironically, Island had given me money to go and stay in the Philippe Starck hotel in New York and meet some songwriters and "learn" from them. So I wrote loads of songs – though I was careful not to meet any of the songwriters! I went to the Park every day and didn't say a word to anyone for a month. And in that time, I got very close to my own head.

'And so I got the poison out of my system. I went to an exhibition about shamans and wrote about it and cleansed myself. Then I came back to Dublin and said to the band: "Right, let's do this." And then I met Donal Dineen, who was then doing *No Disco*, and he said to me: "You know, you don't actually need a record label to make records. Your band can do this on your own and besides, you don't want to get into a relationship with a label at the minute." He said: "Look, I'd like to propose that you make a record. That song, 'Revelate', would make a really good single" – we'd just made it – "so let's borrow lots of money, make a single and put it out as a single. We'll make it for nothing and it'll make a bit of money and that'll be enough to get you to the next album." It was a great piece of friendship – and so we did it. It did really well: we shot the cheapo video in a post office; that helped to sell it, and Donal showed it on *No Disco*. Within a couple of months, we were on the chat shows, on RTE and on MTV's Alternative Europe Music Awards. That was our venture into the idea of an independent approach – and it really worked! The band got a lot of energy out of that.' He smiles, seems delighted with the memory.

'At that time, I didn't know much about Irish music. I was never heading off to the Baggot Inn every night listening to bands. I never knew any of the journalists and never knew what was going on when I read the music press and read them slagging everyone off. I couldn't believe it. It was all so paranoid and it didn't trust itself. Bands were being abused by the music press: they were built up and then kicked down, and you know, that's not what musicians go into the industry to do.

'We had our chance early on – had an interview in *Melody Maker*. I was sitting there and I was thinking: "This is just shit. This'll make me depressed for a week."

'With our first album, we toured England. Radiohead would be on and so would Blur; and afterwards we watched those bands just go stratospheric while we didn't. Then we watched The Cranberries too: their energy rose and then was just dissipated. It makes you think that the nature of things has its own law completely. That it really is chaos – although the media really thinks that it controls everything. It really doesn't though – not at all.

'So we made a record with Pete Briquette from The Boomtown Rats. He said he wanted to record us, and we thought it was great. We called it *Fitzcarraldo* after a Kinski film: this guy has to drag a ship across a mountain and he gets the locals to help; they think he's God, because he has blond hair and plays Caruso. And I thought: "This is me: I have to pull The Frames, like a great big whale, out of this hole – and I'll do it!" So I called the album after the film because it just blew my mind.

'Then we played a gig in England and ...' Glen pauses and then laughs aloud.

'What?' I ask.

'Well, we made the mistake again!' And he laughs again. 'We were approached by a label and we signed on, even though the alarm bells were ringing louder than ever. And then, for the second time, our careers fell down a hole. First with Island, which involved touring England – that tour nearly broke up the band. England has never worked for us and eventually we decided that we'd never tour England outside of London again. And then we signed a second deal and it all went to hell again. Everything stopped. We spent two years making an album, it came out, and they immediately wanted another one. Then we made another album, it came out, and they wanted another one straight away.'

I say brightly: 'Like a hamster.'

He looks at me. It's not a very flattering comparison but after a moment he says: 'Yeah, in fact. Just like a hamster. It was terrible.'

The Frames

The Frames was formed in the city by Glen Hansard in 1991 and since then has signed on to top record labels, released albums, been dropped, signed up again, released more albums – and never quite made the breakthrough. It's a sign of the band's unique quality, therefore, that they are still around more than a decade later.

Photo courtesy of Redferns

Early Frames albums – and in particular the powerful and textured *Fitzcarraldo* – made producers sit up, but it is only in the last few years that the band has managed to disentangle itself from various record deals and re-established a momentum and coherence. In 2001 the Albini-produced *For The Birds* signified the beginning of a new journey; and this was confirmed by *Set List* (2003), hailed as their most eloquent and polished album so far.

In 2004, the band began touring to North America, Europe and Australia and signed a new deal with the indie label Epitaph – and this time, the omens look very good indeed. And in the meantime, The Frames' Irish support has kept passionate faith in a band that has put itself and its fans through the mangle more times than enough.

Line-up:
Glen Hansard: Lead vocals; Joe Doyle: Bass; Rob Bochnik: Guitars; David Hingerty: Drums; Colm Mac Con: Violin

But I make a mental note not to use this simile again. Nobody likes to be compared to a hamster.

'You know, I look at someone like Damien Rice. He's the most normal and unassuming person I've ever met. He just wants to do music. He has never gone to a songwriter: he is always grounded, he writes all his own songs, owns all his own songs and all his own albums. He makes decisions for himself. He has never been broken: he just does his own thing, and trusts his own instincts. Eventually he signed to an indie and look at him now – it's beautiful, really beautiful. And we're trying to do our own thing now.

'We came out of the second record deal and we played it cautious; now people are coming to us asking for advice. We've never been cynical; we're not as naïve as when we started but we're still optimistic. And we've played with our heroes, so it's a charmed life. We've met Dylan, Van Morrison – all the people I admire. Creatively it's a charmed life; on the business front: a few problems with the engine, but it's a sound car.'

The cinnamon bun is sitting neglected on the plate. I wish I could take it and eat it, but this wouldn't be polite. Glen laughs again: the best is yet to come.

'But you know what? After all that, we've signed a new deal. The third time!'

'Really?' I say and stare. It doesn't seem to fit.

'REALLY. But this is a good deal.'

He tells me the story, and I am startled to hear that it involves Austin, Texas, too. As I listen, I realise that I really must get rid of my prejudices surrounding Texas.

'You could get our music anywhere in the world,' Glen says, 'if you looked hard enough; we were always depending on word of mouth and on good energy. But then we were in Austin one night, playing in a club. The PA broke and I was singing a few Van Morrison songs on my own. Then this dude came up to me at the end and said: "I work for a label called Epitaph." I knew that Tom Waits was signed to Epitaph and so I was interested. We talked for a while – ended up talking for a year! Then the guys from Epitaph came to Dublin and saw us playing for a home crowd. They were just blown away. Then we played in Austin again...'

I interrupt. 'At South by Southwest?' I ask excitedly.

'Well, yeah,' says Glen and he looks a little puzzled. After a pause, he goes on. 'Anyway, we shook hands on the deal and we checked the contract for five months and were happy with it. We own the music. We get no advance but start making money on the first sales. And we're lucky: we're an indie band, signed to an indie label and we know our fans won't shaft us or MP3 us.'

He stops again. 'And you know what?'

'No. What?'

'It's opened up the whole American indie culture to us. It's like…'

Again, he pauses.

'Like opening the door of the wardrobe and finding Narnia,' I say and he laughs.

'Yeah, exactly like that – a whole new world. People like Mercury Rev. hadn't been on my radar, and it meant I finally met Steve Albini in Chicago. I'd always been a Pixies fan and I'd always thought: I have to meet this dude. I did lots of solo tours in America – trying to build up the grass roots support there, which is what you have to do there, if you want to make it big. And so I got to know about The Pixies and Steve Albini.'

Steve Albini is massive in the indie world: a producer of rare integrity and skill, who makes gorgeous albums in his Chicago studios.

'I finally got him on the phone – this was years ago,' Glen says. 'He said: "Who are you?" and we spoke on the phone for 20 minutes and then he said: "I'll meet you in April at Abbey Road. I'll book it." And I couldn't believe it.

'Then we signed to a label and we told them about Albini – and then the deal fell through. But we never found out for another ten years what happened…'

I look at him – the cinnamon bun is for the moment forgotten. 'What had happened?'

'Well,' Glen says, 'ten years later, I happened to be introduced to Steve in Chicago. We had a cup of tea and after about 20 minutes, he said: "The Frames. I know you: I was supposed to work with you years ago and you let me down. So what happened?" And after this long and confused conversation, we realised that the record company had phoned *him* and said we weren't interested; and told us *he* wasn't interested. I suppose,' he says sanguinely and shrugs, 'that's just the way it works.

'Anyway, that's when Narnia kicked in. He introduced me to all these indie bands in Chicago, because Chicago is the capital of the indie scene in America. His studio is the best, he built it himself; and he's the best too in my opinion.'

We stop for a moment: The Frames have come on in the background. Glen rolls his eyes.

'And then he booked us for ten days and I rang the boys at home and they could hardly believe it! He loved just sitting listening to us: I think he's intrigued by this sense that we're the only band to have recorded with Trevor Horn, then gone to Steve Albini – from Johnny Pop Pants to the most straight-up independent geezer in the world. Clean and clear guy. I wonder why he doesn't take a bigger cut – his studio is always within weeks of closing down – but he never does. He says: "It's not about me; it's about the music." His ideals are as clean as they have always been. He says: "I exist because bands need me. I'm not a charity; it's just a fact."

'And for us, he has been instrumental in building us up in America: he provided the building blocks. We're heading to Chicago tomorrow, in fact, to record our new album. And this is the great thing too – this is how our relationship has developed. There is another engineer in the studio, Rob Bochnik, who Steve works with all the time and who knows electro-audio better than anyone. When we were stuck for a guitar player in America, Rob came on tour with us and so we asked him to join The Frames. Rob was really taken aback, but Steve said: "Take the job or I'll fire you! And your job will always be here for you." It was amazingly generous of him. Hopefully,' Glen says absentmindedly, 'the new album will be out in June. Don't have a name for it yet.'

The conversation is winding up now; it's getting later and he has to meet someone; and I'm starving. As he gathers his phone, his coat, and his bag together, Glen says, 'I was talking to Damien Rice the other night – we're going touring with him later this year – and I was talking about how brilliantly it has all been going. And I realised how conscious I had been of the struggle, how used I was to just struggling all the time, for 14 years. You just get used to it. It's a sad thing to say, but you hardly know how to not struggle. I feel great, but I'm also conscious of all those other feelings too.

'I know I'll always live by playing songs, by making music. I hope, of course, I'll have a house in Dublin and lots of friends and travel the world. All we are is a bunch of men travelling the world in a way, with one goal in common: rock and roll. It's like the Hare Krishna: the message is always the same, or at least you work to make it like that.

'I've lived a nomadic life; I always have and I couldn't go back. I want some stability back here, but I want the nomadic life too. The Frames have experienced it all – everything except for getting rich and growing fat. We haven't done that yet.' He laughs again. 'I hope we never settle, never put on weight, and never get comfortable in our armchairs. I hope I never come to a conclusion. I think the struggle we had seemed to keep us grounded. When I did *The Commitments*, I had some money in the bank and I felt so unfocused and wasn't feeling life. It's an awful affirmation, but I remember saying to my mate that I was glad when I was finally broke again. Financial security is great, but it's numbing too. And of course I hate being seen to be above anyone else.'

And this is wise, I think to myself: Irish people certainly don't like people getting above themselves or anyone else. And we got through the interview without my mentioning *The Commitments* once.

He is about to go now, but then he pauses and sits down again.

'I got a piece of advice a year ago – from an authentic rock star. I can't say the name. He said: "You could be huge, but the shaman lives outside the community, because his energy is based on respect and fear. People should never see you eat, and never see you live." He said: "You go into town and people see you hanging out in cafés and eating sandwiches and swanning about. You need to move out to the country, be seen less." Which is fair enough. But I said: "I hear what you say, but that's not me. I'm not interested in the respect – only in the music. I don't want that kind of respect." What this dude didn't realise was that I already had a teacher in Steve Albini, who talks the truth and speaks straight and is immaculate with his language. "To thy own self be true.'"

I am so desperately curious to know the identity of this authentic rock star that I hardly listen to what Glen is actually saying. But Glen really does have to go now. We shake hands. He heads back up the stairs and I hoover up the rest of the cinnamon bun as though I haven't eaten in a week.

A FEW days later, I remember that I never asked Glen about Janet Frame. I take out *Fitzcarraldo* and listen again to 'An Angel at my Table'.

There's an angel at my table
And she broke her wings
She's packed her things
She said I'm the only one she'll turn to...
Will you be my anchor
When there is no-one around to hold me down
Will you be my anchor
I know you're not the answer
There's an angel at my table
She said I'm the only one she'll turn to.

Then, impulsively, I send Glen a text message. Was there a connection? – I'm assuming there was. And had he heard that she had passed away?

Back comes a text a minute later: 'Jesus! I didn't know that. Yes, there was a connection. She was partially behind the naming of the band too...I always liked The Frames sounding like a family name.' After a minute, there is another message: 'I just told the boys...she was a powerful woman.'

2

The Triumph Of The Will

Dublin's Rock Icons

THE BEST way to see Dublin on the cheap is to take the DART train. DART stands for Dublin Area Rapid Transit and it is that rare feature of life in this city – public transport that works more or less as it

Lynott may be gone ... but the Pembroke remains.

2

Dublin's Rock Icons

should. The DART hugs the long curve of Dublin Bay, from Malahide in the north to Greystones in the south, and it offers unbeatable elevated views of the sea and of the city centre. It isn't so savoury at rush hour – you can imagine the staff rushing up and down the station platforms with cattle prods, forcing people into already packed carriages – but you can't have everything.

On a bright morning at the end of winter, I walk along the towpath of the Grand Canal towards the nearest DART station. The swans are out in force: great flotillas of them float on the water and a few sleep on the bank; their eyes flicker open and stare at me menacingly as I skirt them. I pass the copper statue of Patrick Kavanagh sitting on his bench at Baggot Street Bridge and pause a moment.

Patrick Kavanagh and Groupie, Grand Canal

On Raglan Road on an autumn day I met her first and knew
That her dark hair would weave a snare that I might one day rue
I saw the danger, yet I walked along the enchanted way
And I said: let grief be a fallen leaf at the dawning of the day.

The author of 'On Raglan Road' liked to hang around hereabouts
and this statue was unveiled ten or so years ago by Mary Robinson
when she was President. I loiter a moment, then walk on along the
towpath and down to the DART station.

I'm meeting Barry Devlin, formerly of The Horslips, and now
scriptwriter and producer. I knew he had had quite a career and
people had encouraged me to talk to him. 'He knows all sorts of
people; has all sorts of stories, has all the history.' I was glad I had
called him.

The DART rumbles through the city's salubrious coastal
neighbourhoods: past the marshy bird sanctuary at Booterstown, the
long strand at Sandymount, and the pincer arms of Dun Laoghaire
harbour. I get off at Dalkey and Barry meets me off the train, and
drives me along the main street of the village and up the hill to his
house. It's a fabulous house – with Joycean associations, like
practically every other house in Dalkey – and I make no bones about
my envy.

'If you ever want to sign it over to anyone,' I tell him, 'you know
you can always call me.' He laughs, and makes tea.

The Horslips were around all through the '70s, touring and
producing their own brand of Celtic rock, and designing album
covers that remain distinctive. Their music ought to feel distinctly
passé – indeed, I suppose it is in many ways distinctly passé – on the
other hand, a Horslips exhibition is presently being installed at the
Orchard Gallery in Derry. I saw the poster for it a few days before
and so there is clearly something going on – something zeitgeist-
esque. Besides, I have always imagined the band as, in some ways,
ahead of its time. After all, The Horslips blended modern rock music
and Celtic associations well before other artists did; and I make a
note to ask Barry about this. But first, we have some tea; we talk
about history; and we set the scene.

'In 1969–70,' Barry says in his gentle Northern accent, 'when we started planning the band, there had been a kind of lull for a few years – very little had happened in the music scene in the city. In the mid-'60s, say 1963–67, there had been a thriving group scene, a blues scene in Dublin. In Belfast at the time, Van Morrison and so on were doing the same thing, but then that just petered out. I suppose there was no critical mass in Dublin that would enable it to survive. Outside of the city, the showband scene was thriving – Dickie Rock, The Royal Showband and so on – and so beat music was regarded as an entirely urban scene. That meant that it really had nowhere else to go. It just withered on the vine and the showbands continued unhampered.

'There was the ballad boom, of course, from about 1966 to about 1970 – Johnny McEvoy and all the rest. That was pre-Planxty, broad ballads. And the ballads happened here in Ireland while pop happened elsewhere. So when The Horslips came along, there was Rory Gallagher and that was about it; Van Morrison had headed off to America. So we started up and Thin Lizzy started up at the same time.' He shrugs. 'And that was about it. I mean, the '70s in Ireland were dire, musically and economically: apart from us and Lizzy, nothing happened until 1977.'

'And what did you want to be?' I ask. 'What vision did you have?'

'Well, The Horslips came along as a semi-acoustic thing. We came out of a group called Tara Telephone who had been knocking about the city for a while. We were country boys who came to Dublin and worked in advertising: Eamonn Carr had played the bongo with Tara Telephone; Declan Sinnott and the poet Peter Fallon were members too; and we just amalgamated. We just felt our way along: I remember a night at the Pembroke Bar at the very beginning, when Phil Lynott was reading his poetry. I remember that I just observed, because I wasn't good enough to join in!' he laughs.

Barry then begins to talk about the syndrome: the effect I will hear many times in the weeks to come, the 'London Effect', in which bands left Dublin for England and – they hoped – for fame.

'Thin Lizzy then did a very classic thing,' he says. 'They took the classic route which everyone took at that time. They reached the top of the greasy pole in Ireland, and then they went to Britain and started again at the bottom of the next greasy pole. Decca released an album, did no promotion, and it was desperately difficult for them. There were so many bands at that time who just found it too difficult. I remember that there was one other band called Skid Row at the time, who could have made it: they were

Chilly Saturday at Merchant's Arch

ferociously talented and they played complicated music at 100 miles an hour, but bad management and lack of vision meant it didn't happen for them. And they weren't the only ones.'

I say: 'It sounds like it happened in the early '70s in Ireland as it happened in the mid-'80s. The same syndrome.'

'Well, music always comes around again,' Barry replies. 'It's always cyclical: the cycle of going to England and getting burnt and coming back; it has always happened in music. But we definitely didn't want to do that: we didn't want to have to uproot ourselves and start all over again in England. So we set up our own label, which we called Oats. We recorded in a stately home in Tipperary, and set about publicising ourselves, which we were good at, because we had worked in advertising. We knew the business. And,' he adds, 'we were uncluttered by questions of taste – our outfits were tacky, to put it mildly. We didn't have that anxiety, so it was easier for us.

'The Horslips were a glorious band – but we were a cul de sac too. What we did was really not exportable, so when we stopped, it stopped too – the genre that was called Celtic rock: I suppose that we created and were the best of the genre – for what that's worth! And it did well from 1972–1976, until people realised there was no money in it.'

This is my chance to theorise and so I leap in and ask, 'When you say it was a cul de sac, do you mean it was ahead of its time?'

He hesitates for a moment. 'Well,' he says at last. 'If we had had the good sense to be three really

Soaking Up the Rays at the Grand Canal

pretty girls and their brother, we would have done very well indeed – if you know what I mean?'

I laugh.

'Maybe we were ahead of our time,' he goes on dubiously. 'Our music just came out of left-field, and I suppose if you weren't Irish, then you would have found it pretty harsh. We were a rock band and we really belted it out. Really, I think we just overreached ourselves.'

I try again.

'Maybe The Corrs and so on simply had more cultural support. Ireland was different and ready to export itself more?'

'Well yes, but The Corrs offer more gentle music too; it's easier on the ear. We were never like that, so the response was always going to be different.'

That's true too; regretfully, I decide to stop theorising. Barry is clearly too much of a gentleman to tell me not to be silly, but I see that it's time to stop making too many parallels between The Horslips and The Corrs. Anyway, maybe there are none to be made.

'But we had a good time,' Barry goes on, 'and we stopped in time: ten years after we started in October 1980. And we shook hands and remained friends. And thank God,' he adds, 'we didn't do any reunion tours.'

We talk and drink tea for a while longer and the sun begins to shine through the long windows of the room. Barry seems to have thought a little more about The Horslips' legacy, because he suddenly says, 'There really was no musical carry-through from The Horslips. But there was a ... cultural carry-through, you might say.'

'How so?'

He explains.

'Our manager was a chap called Michael Deeney – a really good manager and a guy our own age. He was friends with Paul McGuinness, who now manages U2. In 1971, they started up a company called Headland Promotions and in September 1971, Headland ran a festival in Dublin. It was a very odd festival with Manfred Mann, and Georgie Fame – and we were on the bill, which was a great thing for us. Michael wanted to manage us and he had good ideas: for example he wanted to manage us out of Ireland. Headland subsequently was dissolved but Paul then used The Horslips template when he set up the U2 management company. The template was more or less the same: local roots, tight organisation, established in Dublin. You would use local people and train them up – Paul is a man of intelligence and probity and he took those ideas and built on them and it worked. And as you know, it has become the U2 trademark in the years since.'

It's true: U2's local roots and strong local organisation have always been one of the band's strongest cards.

'Because of that connection,' Barry goes on, 'in 1978, The Horslips were playing at Wembley and Paul brought a member of this band called The Hype to meet us. They had just renamed themselves U2: actually our designer Steve Averil had advised the name change. He also advised them to set their sights high, which was a great thing – although I doubt if they needed advising! So Paul asked us to show the band around Keystone Studios, and that was the band's first foray into recording. We messed about for hours and we started properly recording at 2am. Eventually, at about 7am we emerged blinking with three demos called' – he pauses – "Shadows And Tall Trees", "The Fool" and "Street Missions", none of which

Barry Devlin's Essential Dublin Discs

These choices are in no particular order. They are just five of the Irish albums I've enjoyed most over the years.

The Revenants, *Septober No Wonder* In fact, this was a mini album, but it made up in quality for what it lacked in quantity. Always liked the Revenants. Their drummer, Chris Heaney, was my nephew (and he was a really good, Bernard Purdie-style timekeeper), but they also wrote smart, catchy songs with a kind of wry sensibility and played them sparely and well.

Van Morrison, *Astral Weeks* – I first heard 'Madame George' in Luxembourg as the '60s turned to the '70s, drifting off to sleep, gradually getting more and more awake, finally sitting up in bed saying holy s**t what is this? Have been asking the same question on and off ever since. Just a great album.

Picture House, *Karmarama* – When I first heard Sunburst I knew immediately that these guys were the authentic heirs to Chris Bell and Alex Chilton in Big Star and the album confirmed it. Uplifting, funny, finely observed without being the least bit cynical. And that's just the drumming...

U2, *The Joshua Tree* – I love *All That You Can't Leave Behind* – and it's a remarkable thing that 26 years after U2 started they're still pushing the envelope – but I'm choosing Joshua Tree because it was the first time U2 absolutely got to the top of the mountain: lyrically, melodically and...um, have to say this, spiritually. They became great with this album and have pretty much stayed great since. Standouts are 'Outside It's America' and 'Where The Streets Have No Name' – well, I would say that, I did the video – but there isn't a bad track on the album.

The Undertones, *Best Of The Undertones* – Undertones. Album. It's an oxymoron, isn't it? This was the quintessential singles band, knowing, sly, sniggering. 'Teenage Kicks', 'My Perfect Cousin' and my favourite 'Jimmy Jimmy' really are the business, delivering perfect three-minute hits. Melodically and rhythmically they are as instantly plausible as The Ramones but lyrically they are far smarter. So it has to be a best of....

ever were released. We shook hands and I asked for a support slot when they made it big and that was that. We laughed and parted, but before I left, I said to Paul, "Mortgage the house and get a producer." Paul got Martin Hamnett as producer at that time.'

As we talk, I realise that Barry knows the band pretty well; and I make a mental note to do a little more research in future. He tells me a little later that he's working on a film script with Bono at the moment, to be called *The Virgin of Las Vegas*. He hopes for great things from it.

'Even then, U2 had "Great Band" written all over them. You could see the glue holding them together; they were extraordinary. If you ask me, they still are. But what always strikes me most is their lack of fear of the next album. Most bands are always afraid – I was always afraid! – but they are always looking forward, and they aren't afraid of hard work. Apart from the musical talent, they are prepared to stay as long as it takes to make something perfect. Sometimes they overcook, but hardly ever. I think their own personal low point was *Rattle And Hum* – they didn't like it at all – and for a lesser band, *Pop* might have marked the end of the road. But you know, this band just decided to learn from it and move on.

'Paul McGuinness is something of a good general: he's a good strategist and he had a good understanding that mistakes would be made, but he also always had a grand plan; something like 'The Triumph of the Will'. For example, while The Boomtown Rats rode the wave for a while, U2 distanced themselves from the New Romantic thing and punk and all the rest of it, and so have lasted longer. Being based here in Ireland helped that too: the physical distance protected them in a way that the Rats weren't protected. That's one good example of how they always played the game wisely well.'

We talk for a while about the impact the band had on the music scene in Ireland. In the '80s, Irish bands were being swept away to Britain as quickly as the record companies could sign them up. U2 became overwhelmingly dominant as the '80s progressed, particularly after the appearance of The Joshua Tree. They were a prodigious cultural force and the global interest in the band attracted

The Fashionable World: Main Street, Dalkey Village

attention to Irish music in general. Industry attention was focused on Ireland and Dublin in a way that was altogether new and Ireland and Dublin responded, seizing the moments as they came their way.

But a lot of new, young Irish bands simply weren't ready to be launched into a greater career – and yet they were launched anyway. Major labels signed up handfuls of new bands on the back of U2, and the weight of expectation and insistence on instant success proved in many cases to be crushing. Many were burned with their first album and returned to Ireland shattered by the whole experience.

'After The Unforgettable Fire,' Barry says, 'the world started looking for the new U2. It was like Liverpool and The Beatles: scouts would get off the plane in Dublin Airport and sign the first baggage handler they saw. You can count the bands: Light a Big Fire, Cactus World News, The Hothouse Flowers. There was this tremendous hype thing going on to grab the next U2 before someone else did.'

Thinking about this led me, as if by magic, to the Eurovision Song Contest.

The Eurovision Song Contest seems to dog Irish musical footsteps in the most peculiar manner. It is a contest, after all, that is the legendary last word in naff: the douze points and null points and 'Nicosia Calling' are the great beacons in the camp calendar. But in the late '80s and '90s, the Eurovision found a natural home in Ireland, which won the competition in 1988 and then for three years in a row in the mid-'90s. The Eurovision rules state that the winner of the contest must host it in the following year, which is a pretty good reason never to win it. But the Eurovision settled itself here comfortably, making itself at home, putting down roots and in the process nearly bankrupting RTE, the national broadcaster, which was obliged to fork out the money to stage it year after year. A strange and mortifying fact, and one calling for analysis too, if any author out there is brave enough to tackle the subject.

One of the many connections between Irish music and the Eurovision comes in the form of The Hothouse Flowers, the extrovert and colourful band chosen to provide the entertainment in the interval of the 1988 contest. The venue was **The Point Depot** on the city quays, vast, cavernous and largely used for mega-concerts, opera and musicals. The Flowers played 'Don't Go', which subsequently did well in the UK and Australia. They're a good example of a band tipped for superstardom on the back of the U2 phenomenon, and a good example too of superstardom that never really happened.

So I pipe up, 'I remember The Hothouse Flowers at the Eurovision. It was a bit too much, I think. It just didn't work.'

A brief silence, then Barry says, 'Yeah – actually, that was me. It was me who set that up.'

I blush in scarlet mortification. 'Oh.' I really must do more research. But Barry seems unfazed.

'No,' he says drily. 'It hasn't been all good. I was asked to advise on how Eurovision could be made more hip.

> **The Point Depot**
> East Link Bridge
> North Wall Quay
> Dublin (636 6777)
> The city's biggest music venue: vast and barn-like, it is used mainly for big-name concerts and other spectaculars.

We wanted it to be like The Tube, and instead the Eurovision probably ended up finishing The Hothouse Flowers. But you know, there were great moments too, and lots of these bands nearly made it. They were all over America at the time and U2 was touring continually at that stage too; they would always put those bands on as support. So there was this vast population of Irish bands, but they didn't work out. The bottom line is that the next U2 was U2 itself: they reinvented themselves. And today, they are right at the heart of Dublin: think about the landmark tower in Docklands, with their recording studio at the very top.'

We talk for a while as the morning wears on. The '70s, when The Horslips were touring, was so fundamentally different from today. Economically, culturally, and politically, everything has changed.

'When we would roll into an English town in the '70s, the IRA might have been there a fortnight before us; and what was going on in Northern Ireland coloured everything. In the '70s, it was a case of the Stockholm Syndrome: we were holding them hostage and they knew it. But today, everything has changed.'

This particular cultural moment, he says, has a lot to do with the Irish economic boom and also the Irish sense that Ireland isn't purely an economic adjunct to Britain anymore. Confidence began to develop in the course of the '90s: a lot of consolidation took place and people began reassessing matters. Now, today, the country is even more open.

'I'm not saying it's all roses,' Barry says, 'but there is more confidence and more mix, and that makes all the difference.'

It is a theme I will hear many times in the weeks to come.

IT'S NOT possible to talk about Irish music, its history, its profile, its cultural associations and significance, without talking about the English and British connection with Ireland. The histories of the two islands, Ireland and Britain, have been tangled together for so long and the consequences of this entanglement have been so profound, that neither can ever be viewed in isolation from the other. Certain threads are consistent, most prominently an English and then British colonial discourse that consistently attempted to achieve mastery in Ireland – imaginative mastery as well as political and economic control of the country. Nothing new there: colonial discourse has always and everywhere concerned itself with taking and keeping power, and with controlling culture as well as the economy. In the case of Ireland, however, this control was never fully achieved. While the country's economy was fully exploited by England for centuries, cultural and imaginative control was always more difficult to achieve.

Giraldus Cambrensis – Gerald of Wales (1146–1223) – was the first recorded British traveller to record the state of things in Ireland. He came over with the Normans in the 12th century and travelled the country for several years recording impressions that were undoubtedly propaganda, but were also a useful source of knowledge for modern historians too. His copious writings were plundered and used by later propagandists in the centuries that came after. Giraldus had much to say about the Irish:

'They are a wild and inhospitable people. They live on beasts only and live like beasts. [...] This people is a barbarous people, literally barbarous. Judged according to modern ideas, they are uncultivated, not only in the external appearance of their dress but also in their flowing hair and beards. All their habits are the habits of barbarians. Since conventions are formed from living together in society, and since they are so far removed in these distant parts from the ordinary world of men, as if they were in another world altogether and consequently cut off from well-behaved and law-abiding people, they know only of the barbarous habits in which they were born and brought up, and embrace them as another nature. Their natural qualities are excellent. But almost everything acquired is deplorable.'

Gosh.

Giraldus' comments are recognisable to any student of Irish history. They provide the well-spring of all the clichés of the Irish – as lazy, untrustworthy, dirty, the women whorish and the men feckless, the whole country rife with Popish superstition – that have come down through the years. Interestingly, however, Giraldus had words of praise – indeed, just about the only words of praise in the whole course of his writing – for Irish music:

'It is only in the case of musical instruments that I find any commendable diligence in the people. They seem to me to be incomparably more skilled in these than any other people I have seen.'

The movement is not, as in the British instruments to which we are accustomed, slow and easy but rather quick and lively, while at the same time the melody is sweet and pleasant ... they glide so subtly from one mode to another and the grace notes so freely sport with such abandon and bewitching charm around the steady tone of the heavier sound, that the perfection of their art seems to lie in their concealing it, as if it were the better for being hidden. An art revealed brings shame.'

This curious incoherence persisted as the years went by. Giraldus' writings concern themselves with itemising the wealth of the Irish countryside, the better to exploit it when the right time came – and later writers followed this scrupulous care in making similarly exhaustive economic inventories. Yet these same writers were simultaneously conscious of Ireland's store of cultural wealth and envious too, as if aware that cultural riches could not be accessed, exploited, and controlled in quite the same way.

Edmund Spenser (1552–1599), for example, is one of England's central poetic figures and author of *The Faerie Queene*, which remains one of the landmarks of Tudor literature. Yet this same author was one of the first voices in history to bluntly speak of the importance of civilising Ireland, to exploit its land for the common English good, and to civilise its people too, if necessary by exterminating them for their own good. After Spenser, the colonisers were always associated with tamed pastures and coppiced woodland, with nature abundant but tamed and channelled to the common good. By contrast, the Catholic Irish became explicitly connected in historical documents with wild places and darkness, forests and marshes. As Richard Stanihurst (1547–1618) grumbled, even their beasts were not to be tamed:

The Irish Cowes are so stubborne, as many tymes they will not be milked but by one woman, when, how and by whom they list ... and

the inhabitants were no less forward [obstinate] in their obedience
to the State, then their Beasts were to them.

Spenser and Stanihurst, like many others after them, understood
the importance of destroying the institutions that maintained a sense
of cultural cohesion. In the case of Ireland, these included the
manuscripts produced in the ancient monastic scriptoria and learned
houses. In Irish culture, literature and history were not regarded as
separate, but as aspects of the same body of knowledge, and so
historical facts were recorded alongside songs, sagas and myths to
create a potent corpus of collective lore called in Irish seanchas. This
is one example of the profound difference between the existing Irish
cultural traditions and the ideas imported with the colonisers, and
shows too why these same colonisers were anxious to destroy a
culture that they could scarcely understand.

And yet, and yet – this same Spenser set his famous poem
'Epithalamion' (1594) in a positively Arcadian Ireland, where music
ran through the land like streams:

Harke how the Minstrels 'gin to shrill aloud
Their merry Musik that resounds from far.
The Pipe, the tabor and the trembling Croud
That well agree withouten breach or iar.
But most of all the Damzels do delite
When they their tymbrels smyte
Thereunto doe Daunce and carrol sweet
That all the senses they do Ravish quite...

WHEN I leave Barry, I refuse his offer of a lift back to the DART and
instead walk down the hill to the main street of the village. On a
Tuesday morning, the village is quieter: the weekending daytrippers are
safely in the city and the shops are moving to a more normal rhythm.
On a whim, I walk to the end of the main street and round the point,
passing ever more expensive houses as I go. Eventually, I make my way
down to the beach at Killiney. On this chilly day, the steeply shelving
shingles and sand are more or less deserted. The hill rises steeply above
the beach and now and again a DART train rattles past. Castellated

turrets and high walls rise through the trees and it feels a world away from Dublin. Perhaps, I think with sudden surprise, perhaps I wouldn't like to live out here after all.

Trailing the Icons
(or: Where do Westlife Buy Their Shoes?)

THE FOLLOWING Saturday afternoon, Ann-Marie and I decide to experience – or rather Experience – the Rock 'n' Stroll Trail through the city centre. This Rock 'n' Stroll Trail is something we have been meaning to do for a long time, in fact, for years. We are driven more by anthropological curiosity rather than by sheer enthusiasm: we have heard of this feature of city life from several different sources and we are determined to finally have a look for ourselves.

The Rock 'n' Stroll guides the unwitting visitor through the city-centre streets, stopping off at a building here, a corner there, pointing out their associations with musical greatness. We're certain that there must be many of these associations; in a city like Dublin, indeed, they must be ten a penny, and we want to see how they are represented.

We meet at the Tourist Office on Suffolk Street, which is housed – radically – in an old church. The interior is something of a mess, I've always thought, but thankfully we don't have to go inside. Instead, we stand in the cold wind and look at the first stop of the Rock 'n' Stroll. A plaque is fixed to the old stone wall of the church: the plaque is made of...Perspex, we think, and looks like a vinyl record. 'The Rock 'n' Stroll Tour begins here', the sign says tersely. We look at it and then at each other.

'It looks tacky,' Ann-Marie says at last. It does. 'But at least it's supposed to be a vinyl record and not a CD.' At least it is, but it's scant comfort. We look at it and walk on to the second stop, outside the Duke pub on Duke Street a few steps away.

The second Perspex disc tells us that in this pub The Hothouse Flowers 'would exchange money made from busking for pints of Guinness'. It is badly phrased: we wonder what exactly it means.

Dublin's Rock 'n' Stroll Trail

'Dublin's Music Trail' is how the information booklet markets it. 'Take time and Rock 'n' Stroll Around Dublin,' it suggests cheerily. 'You never know who you might meet!' To this end, the tourist authorities pin a series of plastic vinyl-esque information discs to the side of buildings all over central Dublin and invite visitors to partake of the city's cultural riches. The

problem is that the Trail doesn't really do justice to Dublin's rich and varied music scene. Strike that: it doesn't do justice at all to Dublin's rich and varied music scene.

One issue is that the Trail doesn't even attempt to be comprehensive, instead directing unwary tourists towards businesses, pubs and restaurants who have sponsored the guide. So we find out that The Hothouse Flowers drank in the Duke pub, The Corrs played a gig at HMV, and the Boomtown Rats drank coffee in Bewley's… Smell a rat? You should.

Yes: the Rock 'n' Stroll Trail is a marketing exercise – no more and no less. And it's a crude one too, reaching its sorry nadir with the breathless knowledge that Ronan Keating worked as a shop assistant in Korky's shoe shop on Henry Street. ('Korky's: famous for it's [sic] collection of unusual and reliable footwear.') If you haven't yet thrown away your guide in despair, now you surely must.

Bleakest of all: U2's plastic disc commemorating early gigs at the Dandelion Market on St Stephen's Green is now fixed to the wall of TGI Friday. Second bleakest of all: the entry celebrating the Baggot Inn – which no longer exists. It was demolished last year – but it seems that nobody has told the Rock 'n' Stroll authorities. What a mess.

'It means that they would buy pints of Guinness here after they finished busking,' I say. 'But it seems designed to make you think – I dunno – that they were engaged in some sort of primitive barter system.'

I tell Ann-Marie about my conversation with Barry Devlin a few days before; about my clanging reference to The Hothouse Flowers on the Eurovision. She looks sympathetic.

'Oh dear.'

'I didn't know,' I say. 'I didn't bother doing any research.'

'Oh dear.'

I shake myself. 'Tell me about The Hothouse Flowers. You were a fan, weren't you?'

She nods. 'Oh yes. I was a big fan – even before the Eurovision. I remember seeing a gig at the Olympia and they were terrific. I saw them busking on Grafton Street, and I saw a big big gig later – 35,000 people.'

'Truly, a hardcore fan.'

'Well, they were cool. They were the first band in my time who merged folk with rock. I mean, The Horslips did too, but they were before my time and they were more Led Zeppelin-esque too. And the Flowers sang in Irish too: I remember Liam O'Maonlai singing 'Carrickfergus' half in English and half in Irish. We thought they were the coolest thing ever.'

Then they imploded: it didn't happen for them and they weren't taken seriously in the UK. Today, though, they're back and have recently been touring alongside Ricky Warwick.

'*People* was their first album,' says Ann-Marie. 'And then *Home*, which I really really loved. They were a very emotional band, and you get carried away with it when you're a teenager. "This is the saddest song I've ever heard"; and then "this is the happiest song I've ever heard". But what I really loved was that they used to sing all the time about Dublin: they were very placed and located in Dublin. There's a song on *Home* called "Christchurch Bells".'

She pauses. 'Have you met The Frames?'

'Oh yes,' I tell her. 'Well, one of them, anyway.'

'The Frames are the same – very placed in Dublin.'

A refuse lorry arrives and begins belching smoke onto us and we beat a hasty retreat. As we walk to the next nasty Perspex disc, our talk turns to U2 – about the Windmill Lane studios and the long graffiti-ed wall. Ann-Marie says she used to go there: 'I went there sometimes; there were always tourists there: Americans and Japanese tourists, and French girls letting off steam about how much they loved U2 and wanted to marry Adam.'

Anyway, it was part of Dublin life and now it's gone, otherwise it would almost certainly be part of the Rock 'n' Stroll tour too, boasting its very own Perspex disc.

On South Anne Street, we discover that the Perspex disc is attached to the wrong building, and our hearts sink even more. The Perspex disc is pinned next to a Thai restaurant: 'In the late 1970s, DJ Dave Fanning performed here at McGonagles, which was the main venue for all major punk and new wave bands.' At least the syntax is correct, even if the facts are wrong. I scratch my head and look around and Ann-Marie points bleakly down the road.

'This wasn't McGonagles. That was McGonagles.'

'That' is a hollow façade held up by iron girders; behind it is an empty building site.

'And before it was the Crystal Ballroom, where showbands played.'

Well, I think, at least Dave Fanning is mentioned. Today, he has been passed out by such DJs as Tom Dunne and Donal Dineen, but in his day Fanning was tremendously influential in the development of rock music in the city. He gave many bands their first breaks, playing their demo tapes and generally promoting their work. U2 is just one example and to this day, the band continues to send Fanning a first preview copy of a new album.

'When I was a teenager,' Ann-Marie says as we walk towards Grafton Street, 'you listened to Dave Fanning every night to find out what was going on. He played bands that weren't in the charts and Irish bands.'

Lately, he hasn't been so valiant: Fanning has been on the panel of Eurostar, which is selecting the Irish entry for the Eurovision Song Contest.

We are both feeling increasingly disillusioned, increasingly suspicious of the Rock 'n' Stroll tour, and it's freezing cold. As we

2

Dublin's Rock Icons

go in search of fresh Perspex discs, we look at the brochure. It lists shoe shops where Westlife would buy shoes; and pizza restaurants where Sinead O'Connor apparently worked as a waitress. It is terrible.

The Boomtown Rats are commemorated on Grafton Street and we both testify to a long admiration for their work. Ireland was always going to be too small for Bob Geldof, we agree, but songs like 'I Don't Like Mondays' stand the test of time. Chris de Burgh is commemorated outside a fast food joint and we pass on hastily, our eyes averted; Christy Moore's Perspex disc is supposed to be outside the Gaiety Theatre, but there is no sign of it.

'How come Chris de Burgh is there, but Christy Moore isn't?'

Christy Moore is cool too, we agree: he is cross-generational, happy to be political, and able to command attention whenever he plays. The reunion concerts for Planxty are now packing out the Vicar Street venue; Moore has just been awarded the inaugural Honour award of the Irish Recorded Music Association. We walk on.

As it turns out, the only Perspex disc which holds our attention for any length of time is the one commemorating Phil Lynott. It stands out amid the cheap, terribly naff advertising for shoe shops that is the Rock 'n' Stroll Trail. Lynott's disc is positioned on Merchant's Arch, where the pedestrian zone of Temple Bar gives way to the busy Liffey quays and the entrance to the Ha'penny bridge. We gaze at the disc for a while and then retreat from the traffic, back to the square behind where booksellers are plying their trade in the regular Saturday market.

Lynott's appearances on *Top Of The Pops* always made waves in Ireland. Not because of anything he did particularly, but simply because of who he was: a tremendously charismatic, tremendously cool black Irishman who made remarkable music. The loud rock music – 'The Boys Are Back In Town' – and the solo material he did with Mark Knopfler is equally impressive. His lyrics are like poetry; and he is iconic for all sorts of reasons, not simply because he died young.

'Black Pearl' should still be the theme to *Top of the Pops*, if you ask me,' Ann-Marie laughs. 'And it's cool again to like Thin Lizzy: did you know that one of the guys in The Darkness plays in a Thin Lizzy T-shirt in every single gig? I wish I had seen Lizzy live – just once.'

'His later stuff just doesn't fit into any kind of category and the videos are a real representation of how terrible Dublin was in those days. There were no jobs, no money, and everything was falling down. Temple Bar didn't exist in its present state: you came over the Ha-penny bridge and there was nothing very much on the other side. He managed to evoke all that. Of course Thin Lizzy was never an Irish band: it was only Irish because Phil Lynott was in it.'

It is just too cold to stand around, even to talk about Thin Lizzy, and so we walk across the Millennium Bridge and take refuge in Blooms Yard, a new courtyard created just off the quays. There is a new wine bar on the square and people are playing chess at the tables within. There is a deli, and a juice bar – all signifiers of a new Dublin far removed from the ruinous city of Thin Lizzy – but we make a beeline for the café selling proper Italian hot chocolate, and served with an accompanying espresso cup filled with chocolate Rice Krispies, and begin, slowly, to thaw out.

3

Music For Whistle And Guitar

The Trad Scene

WINTERS in Ireland tend to be gentle affairs. A good deal of rain falls, of course, but Dublin is noticeably less wet than other parts of the country. Even in the depths of winter, several weeks can go by without so much as a shower. It's a far cry from the west and northwest coasts

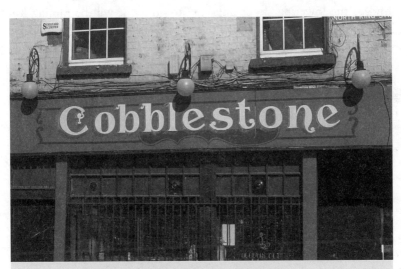

Classic Old Dublin: the Cobblestone Bar, Smithfield

of Ireland, where winters and summers alike can be positively drenching. The westerly winds that come off the Atlantic dump floods, cataracts of rain on these parts of the country. A theory, in fact, has long been doing the rounds: it posits that if the weather had been a little more kindly, there would be no Troubles in Northern Ireland. In other words, the floods of rain have put everyone in a bad mood for generations. It's a popular theory.

And so when I initially came to Dublin, I was startled by what I imagined was the city's Saharan climate. Clear, frosty day succeeded clear frosty day that first winter, and I remember hardly a day of rain. As it turned out, that particular winter was anomalous and was succeeded by a summer of drought. No year since has been quite so parched. But all the same, Dublin gives the lie to the idea that the Irish constantly have an umbrella at the ready. It really isn't like that at all.

With this in mind, then, picture a particularly grim January evening. It is six o'clock and the sun has long since set. It has been raining all day, not mild-mannered showers by any means, but instead heavy, drenching rain. It rained all the previous night too and, if the lowering sky is anything to go by, it will be raining for hours to come. It is the sort of night, in short, which should be ignored. Curtains should be pulled, fires and lamps lit and casseroles put to simmer in ovens. It is certainly not the sort of night to be splashing wretchedly along the Liffey boardwalk in the teeth of an icy wind.

And yet, here I am. I usually enjoy the experience of walking the Liffey boardwalk. It was an expensive but attractive Millennial addition to the city and it allows pedestrians to enjoy the river and the views well clear of the heavy traffic thundering along the quays. It hangs suspended over the water; gulls are usually to be found perched on its rails or wheeling overhead. On fine days, small wooden kiosks are opened up to sell coffee; and couples, tourists, lone walkers, stop and sit and close their eyes in the sunshine. It has allowed Dubliners to renew their acquaintance with Anna Livia, the goddess of the Liffey. For years, the choking traffic meant that the

Ha'penny Bridge and Liffey Boardwalk Under Winter Skies

river was essentially shut off from view and so the boardwalk has been greeted delightedly as a tremendous success. I hear a few days later that the boardwalk is going to be extended east, along Eden Quay towards the present site of the Abbey Theatre. And much of the appalling traffic will soon be removed from the city centre when the new Port Tunnel opens in the north of the city. Ambitiously conceived and vastly expensive, the tunnel will channel all heavy vehicles underground and down to the docks; the traffic-clotted quays will be able to breathe more freely as a result. It all sounds cheerful, almost visionary and certainly environmentally aware.

But the boardwalk isn't very pleasant tonight and nor is my mood. There is a hole, it seems, in the sole of my shoe, for it squelches as I walk and I feel my temper shortening with each step. I turn off the boardwalk in the end and, thankfully, cross the road and enter the Epicurean Food Hall, where I am meeting my friend Margaret Healy, who is a devotee of trad music. We are going to Hughes' pub, behind the Four Courts. We have never been there before, although it is famous as a traditional Irish music venue.

New Dublin: Smithfield Under Construction

The Food Hall is quiet at this time of night. A few of the variety of food stands are still open, so I order a pitta filled with chicken. It comes in a lime, coriander and yoghurt bath and is delicious. I slowly begin to dry out, to thaw; Margaret arrives, looking as bad-tempered as I did a few minutes before.

'What's that?' she asks without much ado. We have known each other too long to bother with polite greetings and niceties, especially when we're wet.

'Chicken.'

'Is it nice?'

'Mmm,' I grunt.

'Can I try some?'

'No.'

'Go on, let me try some.'

'No. Get your own.'

She gets her own.

Before we go to find Hughes, we decide we will stop off at **The Cobblestone**, which is after all the most famous of Dublin's music pubs. I am anxious to renew my acquaintance with it, in fact, now that I have heard that it may be demolished and rebuilt. Margaret hasn't heard this: she is appropriately scandalised. 'They can't do that!' she exclaims. But they can and they probably will.

The Cobblestone has the bad luck of being located in the middle of Smithfield, Dublin's latest 'renewal zone'. Temple Bar was the original cultural quarter and of course is still going strong – even if it is better known as a drinking and not a cultural quarter. But the mixed success of Temple Bar has led the city to try, try and try again, and Smithfield is the target this time round. The area is one of the city's oldest inner-city neighbourhoods, one of its most run-down and one of its most atmospheric. It has always been predominantly working class and although many of the old fittings are gone now, the markets are still going strong. At the heart of the district, Smithfield Square itself is undergoing dramatic changes and redevelopment.

When Margaret and I arrive in the square on this soaking and freezing night, there is hardly a soul to be seen. It occurs to me again that for a supposedly fashionable and trendy part of town, Smithfield is oddly bleak. The square, of course, is far from complete: new buildings line one side, but the others are still a mess of hoardings and cranes and half-completed apartment buildings. The great steel gas burners that are Smithfield's main signature, are only lit on Friday and Saturday nights and so tonight they march in a long dark line along the side of the cobbles. At Christmas, the plaza plays host to a Yule market and to a skating rink and concerts are sometimes held here in the summer. But there is nothing happening tonight, nothing at all; and it feels more like a heart of darkness.

The Cobblestone
77 North King Street
Smithfield, Dublin 7
(872 1799)
This pub's future was uncertain at time of writing – but ring and check, because the Cobblestone offers Dublin's best trad music.

3

The Trad Scene

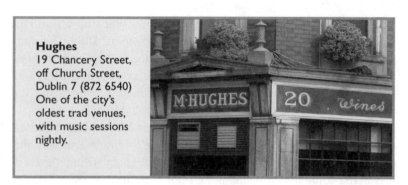

Hughes
19 Chancery Street,
off Church Street,
Dublin 7 (872 6540)
One of the city's
oldest trad venues,
with music sessions
nightly.

'I think the problem is that it's a square at all,' I say suddenly.

'What?' Margaret wipes the icy raindrops from her eyes.

'The square. I sometimes think that Ireland shouldn't really go in for squares and plazas. They look so awful in bad weather; and the weather is so often bad.'

She looks around absently.

'Come on: I need a drink.'

'Except if they had a roof, maybe,' I say. But I'm speaking to myself: Margaret has already vanished into the pub. I follow her out of the rain.

The Cobblestone is a classic Dublin pub: L-shaped and quite plain and unadorned, except for the usual quantities of polished, gleaming wood and mirrors. Its very plainness marks it out as the real thing: fake Irish bars tend to have all manner of knick-knacks; their mirrors are usually breathtakingly ornate affairs, with bevelled edges. The Cobblestone doesn't go in for bevelled anything – you can tell this at a glance.

Tonight, it is half-empty: the weather has kept people indoors.

'No music?' I murmur.

'Too early; too wet. We could hang around and have a drink, but I think it'll be hours yet. Maybe even eleven o'clock.'

We have a drink but nobody else comes in while we're there. After a while, we decide to go on to Hughes.

'That's the thing,' Margaret tells me as we edge our way once more into the rain. 'The Cobblestone does it properly: people come in and play music at a certain time. It isn't like the pubs in Temple Bar, where they kick off at six in the evening for the tourists. Up here, it begins later and the pace is more normal.'

I know what she means. In the tourist pubs of Temple Bar, sessions sometimes begin not even at six o'clock but at lunchtime. On Saturday afternoons, you can hear the fiddles playing as you pass by, which is all very well, but is hardly a normal state of affairs. I find myself wondering about this as we splash along: authenticity is something of a sacred cow in Dublin, but I hardly know what it means, if it exists – or if it should exist in the first place. Maybe the pubs dismissed as tourist traps are in fact as authentic as the Cobblestone.

TO BEGIN with, we can't find Hughes. The rain is falling harder than ever and we feel like extravagantly astray tourists. The problem is that the streets all around Smithfield and the Four Courts have an unpleasant edge and while Margaret says nothing, it is clear that we are thinking the same thought: we should really be at home; this is really not a good place to be; we must be mad. Eventually, after much wandering, splashing, and trailing around in the rain, and in embarrassed mortification, we go into a police station and ask for directions.

Hughes, when we eventually discover it, turns out to be a strange place. I feel a definite sense of relief, of course, to be out of the rain. And it's a cosy pub. But why all the plastic flowers? There are extravagant plastic bouquets of flowers sitting on the centre of each table and more are suspended in hanging baskets from the painted ceiling and in little round containers fastened high up on the walls. It looks like Laura Ashley, I think, and feel confused as I stand dripping rain.

'It looks like Laura Ashley,' I murmur. 'Doesn't it?'

She shrugs. 'Dunno. Don't ask me. I don't go to Laura Ashley.' We order drinks and sit down.

There is hardly anyone here either; and I begin to wonder if it is the end of the world. It is a rare thing to walk into one Dublin pub

Top Five Trad Pubs

Dublin may be packed with music pubs, but not all are worth your patronage: some are little more than jumped-up tourist traps and best avoided. As a general rule, steer clear of the pubs in Temple Bar: good music is to be had in Temple Bar, but you have to search amid a sea of cliché to find it. Instead, look elsewhere for your music: you won't have to look far.

Hughes (map: 17) and **The Cobblestone (map: 16)**, tucked away behind the Liffey at Smithfield, are wholly unreconstructed pubs – and are all the better for it. Both are old and more than a little worn, but such places attract the best practitioners of the art and the most knowledgeable audiences. In both places, sessions tend to begin late, as good Irish sessions usually do – usually around 10pm. The Cobblestone is a little more intimate, Hughes a little more ad hoc in its arrangements – but both pubs have considerable, if occasionally eccentric, charms.

O'Donoghue's (map: 7) on Merrion Row is another unreconstructed pub. It remains much the same as it was in the '60s in terms of atmosphere – and décor. O'Donoghue's is that rare thing: a veritable tourist mecca that is worth a visit. The tiny premises are packed throughout the day and music is to be had throughout the day too – most of it excellent. Take time to look at the photographs on the walls: this place sometimes seems as much museum as public house.

At **The Harcourt Hotel (map: 8)**, you can listen to music most nights of the week – and into the early hours too. Musicians tend to gravitate here when sessions are finishing elsewhere: just turn up and you can usually rely on an impromptu session.

Up at Christchurch, **Mother Redcaps (map: 12)** is a great rambling barn of a place and a famous venue in the city. It offers trad music

in the evening and find it more or less empty; it is even more strange to find two empty pubs in succession. And it is almost ten o'clock by now: surely somebody should be coming in.

But eventually, at around 10:30pm, Hughes begins to fill up. Some locals appear and take tables in the corners of the room; then a few men and women appear carrying instrument cases – mainly flutes and fiddles, I think – and set up shop at the back of the pub.

throughout the week, with jazz and blues on Fridays and Saturdays. The Sunday trad session is best known: come shortly after noon and you can listen to music all afternoon.

The Cobblestone, 77 North King Street, Smithfield, Dublin 7 (872 1799)
Hughes, 19 Chancery Street, off Church Street, Dublin 7 (872 6540)
Harcourt Hotel, 60–61 Harcourt Street, Dublin 2 (478 3667)
Mother Redcap's, 40–48 Back Lane, Christchurch, Dublin 8 (453 8306)
O'Donoghue's, 15 Merrion Row, Dublin 2 (660 7194)

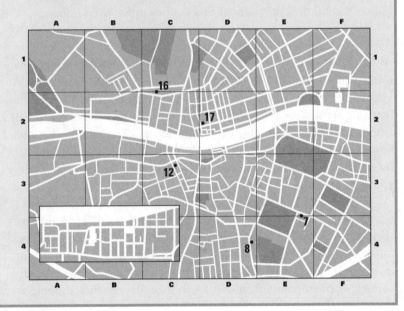

More appear and more and within ten or so minutes, there are a group of maybe 12 musicians gathered in a circle. They arrange themselves so that their backs are facing the rest of the room and polish their instruments and begin to tune up.

This is the usual way that sessions are arranged. Real sessions are played for the musicians' own pleasure first and foremost; they are not played for the audience, which is more or less ignored. Certainly tonight, as I sit at the table nearest the musicians, I sense that the audience is being studiously ignored. The players talk animatedly among themselves, then one or two fall silent as they begin to play; a few more join in, then a few more – although the entire circle never plays at the same time.

We listen quietly for a while. There are six men, six women: the men are predominantly older; the women are in their 20s and 30s. It's clear that most of them are learners, amateurs; the music seems thin and repetitive. And I see too that there are no other instruments: there are only fiddles and flutes. I turn towards Margaret, who knows a good deal more about this kind of music than I do.

'This is an amateur group,' she says, anticipating my question. 'I think it's local people, using the bar as a kind of focal point. See how the younger ones are all learners?' I nod. 'And see how there are two instruments being played?' I nod again. 'So it's just – not exactly impromptu – more that they gather and play and learn. It's good to listen to, but that really isn't the main purpose of it.' She takes a sip from her drink and says: 'Though it never is, not really. This kind of music is never really about playing to an audience. If people want to listen, then well and good, but this is all about people playing to amuse themselves.'

This is what my mother has always told me too. 'Imagine no television, no soaps, no radio – so what did people do? They amused themselves whatever way they could. Telling stories or playing music: it was either that or go mad. Imagine a winter night on a farm in rural Ireland, with the rain falling. Those people had to do something to stimulate themselves – so they played music. Simple as that.'

I think about this, as I watch the earnest, concentrated expressions on the faces of the players facing me. In a lull in the music, Margaret leans forward and asks the name of the reel which they have been playing. The musicians look startled but nobody answers, until one woman – 60-ish, silver of hair and a dead ringer for Carol Shields – raps out an answer. The music has begun again and I cannot hear her; Margaret sinks back into her seat again and rolls her eyes.

'Frosty pussy,' she says.

'The music sounds a bit thin,' I reply and she nods.

'Well, it does – or I suppose it does – they have only two instruments. But I think we're conditioned to think this. Do you know what I mean?'

I shake my head and she goes on thoughtfully.

'I mean: we have this idea that Irish trad music should always be – I don't know – wild and rollicking and loud with 50 different instruments all playing at the same time. But I always think that this is a new idea. People wouldn't always have had access to 50 different instruments, so the music they're playing tonight – just flute and fiddle – is as true or real as any other. Maybe more, because it's so simple in its forms, with just people playing for themselves. We need amateur players too. How else will new people come along?'

Cormac Breatnach

I THOUGHT about my night in Hughes a few days later, as I was walking through town. The rain was long gone and it was a cool, breezy day; the sky was overcast but no showers were threatening. I had just left **Queen of Tarts**, where I had had a slice of lemon sponge cake and a chat with its proud maker, Yvonne Fallon: she was delighted with herself. Now I walked down through the cobbled streets of Temple Bar in the direction of the Irish Film Institute.

At this time on a weekday afternoon, there was no music to be heard. Instead, the air was full of scents: spices wafted from a new Persian restaurant and from a curry house next to it; the smell of tomatoes and garlic swept across from a pizza restaurant. I cut through Meeting House Square, which was created in the early '90s during the initial reclamation of Temple Bar and which is hedged around by new

Queen of Tarts
4 Cork Hill, Dame Street
Dublin 2 (670 7499)
Tiny – but one of the best cafés and pastry shops in town, with everything home-made on the premises.

modern buildings: the Ark Theatre, Gallery of Photography, Gaiety School of Acting, and the Photographic Archive. It always feels like a sheltered, calm space: the wind tends not to slice through its heart and there is occasionally outdoor theatre, late-night film shows, with something colourful or pleasant going on. As I clattered over the smooth limestone flags, I remembered a night-time screening of *The Wizard of Oz* the previous summer: the audience wildly cheering the Good Witch of the South ('Only bad witches are ugly!'), booing and hissing at the Wicked Witch of the West.

But, as a result of my insatiable greed, I invariably associate the square with food. Two restaurants open onto opposite sides of the square and today as I passed, I glanced into Eden to see what was going on. Not much: it was the mid-afternoon lull; the heatlamps on their veranda were turned off. There were a few food stalls in the square itself: it was not as vibrant as the posh Saturday food market, but I still managed to buy some Irish cheese and a few olives. I had been here in the past in wet weather and it was fairly wretched, but now there are ambitious plans, just announced, to install a retractable roof over the square, à la Wimbledon, and so protect the food stalls, the cinema-going public, and the diners from the inclement Irish weather. Temple Bar really wasn't so bad, I thought as I headed off, because food always pads me against gloomy thoughts. And thus fortified against disaster, I made my way up into the **Irish Film Institute**.

The Irish Film Institute (IFI) was called the Irish Film Centre (IFC) until a few weeks ago and to me it always forcefully symbolises the successes and pleasures of Temple Bar. It is the area at its finest. It was the flagship project of the district when it was first planned, designed, and opened in the early 1990s, and today it is coping well with the passage of time. The complex was built – appropriately enough – on the

---

Irish Film Institute
6 Eustace Street
Temple Bar, Dublin 2
(679 3477)
Two art-house cinemas, plus bar, restaurant and bookshop – all grouped around a glazed atrium.

---

site of Dublin's former Quaker Meeting House and comprises two cinemas, plus bar, café, meeting rooms and a bookshop; the whole ensemble is gathered around a glazed atrium or plaza. The IFI had been in my mind a few days previously, in fact, when I had grumbled to myself – since nobody else was prepared to listen – about the dismal dampness of Smithfield Square. It was an unreasonable thought to think, of course – Smithfield is too large for a glazed roof, or any other kind of roof – but I thought it all the same. In hindsight, I suppose the hole in my shoe had added to my irritation. So the news of retractable roofs over Meeting House Square had cheered me up. I was meeting Cormac Breatnach here. Cormac had been recommended to me: I had wanted to meet someone 'innovative', I had thought vaguely, someone with a long background in Irish music, and someone influenced by other kinds of music too. And a friend had said: 'You should really speak to Cormac. He has made a few albums and you won't have heard anything like them before.'

I had never seen him before, of course, but I identified him easily enough: tall and slim with a bright, attractive face. We greeted each other and made our way upstairs to the long gallery of the café which overlooked the atrium below.

Up in the gallery, we both ordered mineral water. Christmas was still too close to be drinking anything else; nobody I had met in the last few days could stomach the idea of alcohol. So we sipped abstemiously and Cormac told me a little bit about his background.

'I think that my appreciation for music is based on my background: half-Irish, quarter-Spanish, quarter-German. I can't speak German, though, and although my mother was Basque, she brought us up on Castilian. I think she was influenced by the war in Spain and Germany: this probably influenced her decisions. The rules of the house were: Spanish and Irish, no English.'

I sat up at this. It rang a bell. I had just finished reading a new book, a memoir by the Irish writer Hugo Hamilton. In it, he describes his upbringing in Ireland after the war. His mother was German, his father Irish and Irish-speaking; English was banned in the house. It was a riveting read.

And so, after a moment, I said, 'Have you read Hugo Hamilton's book, *The Speckled People*?'

He smiled, nodded.

'I have.' He laughed. 'I found it very interesting. In fact, I can relate to a lot of it. Hugo is a friend of the family, you know, and I wanted to write to him and say, "You know, you wrote a damn good book."'

'It really was a damn good book. I've just finished it.'

'Could you relate to it?'

I shook my head. I couldn't relate to it, I said – not really, not to the specifics. But it still grabbed me. We spoke English in our house; it was all very simple, thank God. And I can't speak a word of Irish. It all sounded extremely stressful. Cormac laughed at this.

'Yes, it did. Well, it was. My mother came from Spain, came to Ireland in the '40s, from an utterly different culture, with war problems, and God knows what. The influence of our background ….' He tapered off, but began again after a moment.

'There are so many advantages to that kind of background. My musical influences, for example, were very eclectic. My parents had a collection of old records they picked up in the '50s: Bulgarian music, Spanish, Basque, and Irish. I was the youngest of six, so it was all The Beatles for me too. So many influences. And of course, politics always comes into it too.'

'Well – we don't have to talk about politics if you don't want to.'

He shook his head again. 'If you want to know the person, you have to know the whole person, I think.' He paused. 'And besides, when I was growing up, there was so much going on with student politics, socialist and Republican politics. It was all part of the deal; and all these ideas intersect and influence each other.'

I nodded agreement.

'I first got to play the tin whistle with a gardener-folklorist friend of the family. He would teach the local kids for free: bagpipes and flutes and whistles – he made the flutes himself – and he would take us out for trips. A great artist. And then, at the age of 11, I heard The Bothy Band when I was doing my homework. I

Wrap Up Warmly: Saturday Food Market, Temple Bar

was just blown away by it: a crystal-clear sound of traditional music, but with a modern influence behind it. Beautiful arrangements. I was – inspired. I borrowed money off my mother, bought a flute, then paid her back. Just a wooden flute – I suppose when I think about it, musicians would have been playing a similar instrument in the 1800s. I was hugely influenced by The Bothy Band, Paul Brady, Andy Irvine, The Chieftains, and Sean O'Riada – who of course changed the whole way we looked at traditional music.

'I was lucky enough to go to a co-ed school and at lunchtimes, instead of heading out to play football, the older lads would sit and play music. I was really into my whistle playing and so they picked me out and I would play with them. We entered school competitions and I felt great, hanging out with these older lads! Not just music competitions either: painting and drawing, all the arts, and poetry. And all through the medium of Irish – it was a bit like the Fleadh Ceoil. The most significant thing, though, was that it wasn't very traditional. Instead, it was open to all sorts of other influences.'

As Cormac talked, I was reminded again of the debates in Irish traditional music surrounding the notion of the authentic; the debates between the traditional musicians of Comhaltas Ceolteoiri Eireann and the less traditionally minded. It is a debate that has ebbed and flowed, now vigorously and now less so, for years. It is a debate entangled in notions of nationalism and national identity and politics; and I felt myself back away from discussing all this with a comparative stranger.

This is a debate that flows across all aspects of Irish music. Irish history, received notions of Irish history, the debates which splutter into life occasionally surrounding revisionist takes on history: all these serve as reminders of how all aspects of Irish culture remain highly politicised. As I sat in the bright, modern surroundings of the IFI café, I remembered one of the debates about The Wolfe Tones, who specialised in playing nationalist rebel songs and who were admired and vilified in equal measure in Ireland. This particular debate had sprung from the fact that one of these rebel songs had won a competition hosted by BBCi to find the record of the century. The BBC had been embarrassed, of course, but more interesting had been the reaction, a mixture of mortification and glee, in Ireland itself. One commentator had labelled The Wolfe Tones 'the musical wing of the IRA'; and when the band announced that it was disbanding last year, *Irish Times* columnist Fintan O'Toole wrote that it was a great day for Irish music. Then he said it again on television and was booed by the studio audience.

All this flashed through my mind as I listened to Cormac speak. There was a world of difference between a bunch of musicians playing in a pub, The Wolfe Tones' rebel songs and, say, Sean O'Riada introducing the harpsichord into Irish music while at the same time dismissing the American- and English-influenced ceili bands of the 1920s. But, in the midst of this muddle and confusion, one thread seemed to remain constant. This debate was all about authenticity. What was authentic and what was not?

I felt that I could hardly turn these dishevelled thoughts towards Cormac and have him tease them apart, right there and then. But as it turned out, I didn't have to ask him any questions. He too was obviously a mind reader, because he quite suddenly began to describe a lecture he had recently given at Glór, the new traditional music centre at Ennis in County Clare on Ireland's west coast. I listened, feeling both fascinated and oddly inhibited at the same time. It's difficult to discuss Irish politics with a stranger.

'It was a lecture,' he said, 'about the idea of tradition and change. I said to the audience, "Look, this debate – what is authentic, what is not – is 25 years too late." And, you know, it is too late. I regard myself as a musician, not as a 'traditional musician'. Like so many other people, I was open to all sorts of influences and that means that I've no hang-ups any more' – he pauses – 'although I once did. I've been open to all sorts of jazzy-bluesy influences and I think that once you realise that people around you aren't necessarily on the same wavelength, you have to decide whether to join them or keep on doing your own thing. And eventually I decided to do my own thing.'

I nodded. I understood that.

'So my formative years were about soaking up all sorts of great influences. I remember meeting Davy Spillane and he said, "Oh, there's a new group called Moving Hearts and I'm thinking about joining them. I've an offer to be in a film called *Traveller*. What do you think?" And I was going: Moving Hearts – mmm, dunno about the name, what are they about?'

Cormac laughed at the memory.

'And really, it turned out that they were one of the best groups we've ever had. And so progressive too, aligning themselves with all sorts of social issues.

'I suppose that my basic attitude is live and let live. For those who want to compose music, then great, and if you want to push the boundaries out, then great too. In that sense, I'm a bit different from the more traditionally minded artist, the Comhaltas musician, who learns locally or from generations of local influences. That's fine – great. But for those of us who cannot but be influenced by other influences, then – great too. We have to be allowed to do our own

3

The Trad Scene

Cormac Breatnach's Essential Dublin Discs

Many of the instrumentalists below compose their own melodies as well as dipping into the traditional well of Irish tunes. I am also taken with their arrangements skills. They have all recorded more than one album, but I've included a few favourites below.

Flook – English-based band featuring flutes/ whistles, bodhrán and guitar. They create music that is energetic and beautiful. I am particularly taken with the fine playing of Armagh flute player Brian Finnegan. Their album *Rubai* is well worth a listen.

Swap – Swedish fiddlers Ola backstrom and Carina Normansson join forces with British piano accordionist Karen Tweed and guitarist Ian Carr. The resulting eponymous album features truly inspirational music!

Karen Tweed and Timo Alakotila – Karen here joins up with Finnish piano player Timo. The pair is also joined by other talented musicians on the May Monday album.

Sonny Condell – Ex-Tír na nOg and Scullion guitarist and songwriter Condell is so talented that it is disappointing to learn that he has not yet been recognised internationally. He writes all his own material. Try the *Forever Frozen* album.

thing. Certainly, I align myself with the school of thought that says that artists should be allowed to inspire and subvert in all sorts of ways. As an artist, I think you have an obligation to do that.'

Cormac sat and thought for a second.

'But having said that, I don't think art can ever be used for propaganda purposes. Artists cannot ever be accused of propaganda, otherwise their art becomes meaningless, and any political organisation would use an artist if it could. It's essential to maintain independence of thought and action and to be seen to do that.'

Emer Maycock and Donal Siggins Members of the younger generation; Emer has toured widely with the Afro Celts. She composes her own material and plays a variety of instruments: cello, fiddle, flute, whistle and uileann pipes. Phew! Talented Donal Siggins ably accompanies her on guitar. Her debut album, *Merry Bits Of Timber*, and her latest, *Playground*, are both remarkable.

Susan McKeon New York-based Susan (from Dublin) has proven herself as one of the best female songwriters on the scene. I love her album *Prophecy*.

Slide Combining mainly flute/piano, fiddle, concertina and bouzouki, this band is extremely talented and so energetic that they have to be seen live to appreciate them fully.

Puck Fair Jazz flautist Brian Dunning (formerly of Portland Oregon, now living in County Kildare) smoothly blends jazz with Irish trad; he is probably the first flautist to have done so since the 1980s. Check out the album of the same name.

The Bothy Band No collection is complete without recordings of this trad band from the mid-1970s to the late 1980s. The Bothy Band were remarkable and profoundly influenced every musician that recorded afterwards. My favourite Bothy album is *After The Wind, Into The Sun*. If you like the music, then of course check out **Planxty** also! Have a listen to *The Woman I Loved So Well*.

Maighread Ni Dhomhnaill One of Ireland's finest singers – with Donegal connections. Listen to Idir an da Sholas, which was produced by Planxty's Donal Lunny.

At this, I mentioned my (granted: rather incoherent) ideas about The Wolfe Tones. Cormac thought again for a second and then said, 'I think it's wrong to turn around and say that The Wolfe Tones shouldn't be listened to, and don't have a constituency. That's wrong too. In my last album, *Music For Whistle And Guitar*, we play two rebel songs – our own version of two songs. One is a bluesy version of "The Foggy Dew", the 1916 song. And the other is "Down By The Glenside": "I met an old woman…" And then we go into a slow reel.' He raises his hands into the air. 'We're just giving it a new life, with new colours. I think people were afraid for years of going near those songs, for fear of being seen as aligned to the Provos or someone who supports violence. All that crap, all those stereotypes – like all you want to do is kill.'

'You're simply reimagining songs?'

He nods.

'Yes. Exactly. Absolutely. So why should The Wolfe Tones not do their stuff, sing their songs? Let them; they're entitled to. They don't try to do anything else. I have no hang-ups about that.

'But I'll tell you what I do have awful problems with: I have the most awful problems with censorship. I was in Denmark recently and came across a website called Freemuse (www.freemuse.org) who are funded by the Danish Foreign Ministry. What they do is deal with music censorship. Musicians are being tortured and killed all over the world for their music. We have a terrible history with censorship in Ireland. Philip Glass had a programme here a few years ago called *Songs Of The Dispossessed*, which interviewed some singers: Tom Waits played the banjo, and Christy Moore did an interview with Patsy O'Hara, the hunger striker from Derry. Because of this, the radio stations here banned it. Censorship has always been a big problem here in Ireland – official censorship is dangerous enough, but unofficial censorship is almost worse and it has always been a bad problem in Ireland. Any leanings at all, any evidence of thinking – absolutely unacceptable!!' He shakes his head in disbelief and we sit for a moment in silence. Then he looks up. 'Back to music?'

I laugh. 'Please.'

'IT HAS been a good musical life so far. I set up a band with a few friends and we called it Sea Shanty. Then I took time off on my own, bought a saxophone: I wanted to be the greatest traditional saxophone player in the world, learned the concertina, on to the fiddle for a year, then went back to the flute.

'And then, I came across Donal Lunny at a party.'

Donal Lunny is one of the most influential figures in Irish music. He has acted as musician, composer, record producer and general influence on Irish music for the last 30 years and has been a key member of that group of Irish musicians – Christy Moore, Paddy Glackin, the piper Liam O'Flynn and so many others – who have brought traditional music to enormous audiences outside Ireland. He mainly plays keyboards, guitar, bodhran, and personally developed the bouzouki to use in myriad ways. And his name had been in the papers once more over the last few weeks. So I listened more carefully as Cormac went on.

'At that time, The Celtic Orchestra was being put together – a great idea in terms of music. Five flutes, uilleann pipes, eight fiddles, percussion. We did a recording for the Pan-Celtic Festival in 1985 and then out of that came a band for the O'Riada Retrospective at the National Concert Hall – three nights in 1985.' He sips some of his mineral water. 'It didn't really work: there were too many musicians and half of them didn't turn up; we just didn't have the coherence.

'Anyway, after that, Lunny came to me looking for flute players. He said, "I'm looking for ideas for flute players. Any ideas?" And I said, "Me! Me! Me!"

'So in 1987, we spent three and a half weeks rehearsing 22 minutes of music for The Donal Lunny Band. I was flute player and we had Sean Og Potts on pipes, Manus Lunny on bouzouki, and Donal played the keyboards. It was brilliant and a record came out of it. Out of that too, we were invited onto *The Session* on RTE. Donal bumped into Elvis Costello on the street and he ended up joining us: we played some of his songs too – I remember there was one about Derek Bentley. The music was brilliant. Matt Molloy came on and meeting him was another dream of mine. I was afraid of dropping my flute.

'After that, I went back to work on my own for a while and then I formed Méristem; we made one recording. It was wonderful: I put down the flute and picked up a low whistle in the key of F. It was introduced by The Bothy Band and made by Brian Overton in England. And then I carried on and formed Deiseal.'

Trad Terminology

The language of Irish traditional music is peppered with phrases and references that the newcomer or outsider may not understand. Some words are borrowed from the Irish, a language that is notoriously difficult for the uninitiated to understand and to pronounce – but which is intrinsically related to traditional music in Ireland. But in spite of this linguistic opacity, Irish traditional music is known and recognised throughout the world in recent years – a sure sign that the music itself travels well, even if its vocabulary occasionally does not.

The essence of traditional music is its oral nature: the music passes, through a process of continual selection, from generation to generation. This process of continuity is intrinsic to the tradition – once an oral link is severed, for whatever reason, those stored collective memories are lost for ever – and this, of course, has happened throughout history.

For this reason, the work of archival institutions in storing, recording and collating is vital. But at the same time, the musical tradition reflected by that archive continues to evolve, to select, to continually change. In an age of modernity, this process of evolution means that the form is inevitably open to all manner of cultural influences – and we can see this process at work throughout the corpus of Irish traditional music today. This has led to a debate over the present and future form of Irish music and over what, if any, should be its limits. It is a debate echoed all over the world and against all kinds of contexts – and perhaps it is the case that since Irish traditional music has always absorbed other cultural influences, it can scarcely stop doing so today.

The labelling of forms of Irish music as Celtic is little more than a cunning ploy by the marketing folk – it doesn't really stand up to rigorous inspection. Ireland's Celtic past is a fact, for sure, but it is only one aspect of this particular island story – and the eddies of history have introduced so many other aspects that harking back to a pure Celtic past is a difficult and problematic notion. Irish traditional music has always taken its influences from the society and historical moment in which it existed – and so it is as much a cultural hybrid as the Irish population itself.

We can see this simply by glancing at the history of Irish traditional music. To take only one example, Irish music was deeply influenced by American economics in the early years of the 20th century, when Irish émigrés and Irish-Americans became involved in developing Irish music as a fully-fledged and marketable cultural industry. The result was to inject new life and energy into a struggling culture – but also to change that culture profoundly. The céilí band was wholly a creation of the 1920s – and today is a ubiquitous and precious component of traditional music.

Here are a few terms and Irish words that may need unpacking:

Sean-nós or 'old-style' singing is the oldest form of singing extant in Ireland today. For the most part, it takes the form of unaccompanied singing in Irish and its form and structure changes according to district and region. Sometimes, sean-nós is performed standing, sometimes sitting; sometimes the audience is silent and at other times it is encouraged to intervene and interject. What never changes, however, is the remarkable lyricism of the language and its emphasis upon articulation of emotion rather than upon actual narrative.

Sessions, now ever-present aspects of the Irish music scene, are comparatively recent innovations; they made their entrance in the mid-20th century. The vital component in any session is the circle of musicians itself. A session is by no means a concert: the musicians play and in the meantime the audience tends to go about its own important business of conversation and drinking. It is usually only in the tourist pubs that a crowd gathers with the specific intention of silently listening. That said, the format is fairly loose: applause may be brief or cursory, but is not exactly forbidden. Go with the local flow.

Uilleann Pipes are a version of the Scottish bagpipes and first appeared on the scene in the early 18th century. The pipes (pronounced *ill-un*) were always expensive and for this very good reason, their playing was never widespread. In recent years, however, the establishment in Dublin of Na Píobairí Uilleann, or Society of Pipers, has sparked wider interest in the instrument and its music.

The **Bodhrán** is an ancient instrument and today is an important part of the traditional music repertory. It's simply a drum, its playing surface stretched, tambourine-like, between a circular rim. It is ostensibly a simple instrument – easy to use and to understand at a basic level – and it lacks the more obvious complexities of uilleann pipes and accordions and concertinas and what have you. But although the bodhrán may not be complex in itself, it requires great skill to be played well. It relies so much on tone and rhythm and so can therefore sound horrendous – flat, monotonous, heavy, utterly lacking in charm – if played badly. Instead, the instrument requires considerable delicacy of technique. Thankfully, excellent bodhrán players are plentiful in Ireland!

3

The Trad Scene

He looked at me, presumably mind-reading again.

'Méristem is a Greek term: it means stem tissue which is capable of dividing and forming new growth. Deiseal is Irish: it translates as "following the progress of the sun".'

'Like flowers do'

He frowns.

'Flour?'

I explained.

'Oh – yes, exactly. I thought you said flour, singular.' We laughed; I was relieved to have made an intelligent contribution at last.

'Deiseal was a trio: low whistle, bouzouki and double bass. We did one recording called *The Long, Long Note*. It's a famous traditional tune, but I extended it and inserted an interpretive piece in the middle and added a section of another tune at the end. American sections too: it was pretty jazzy.'

I heard it was pretty innovative too, I told him; he looked pleased, but said nothing.

'Then we released a second album, *Sunshine Dance*. Deiseal Mark Two was pretty jazzy too. We were in America and met this jazz singer in France called Mirabelle de Nuit. She came down and started singing, and ended up writing a song for us which we recorded. It was great – spreading trad music all over the place. We did some touring: Scotland, the Azores, all sorts of influences and music all over the place.

'Then Deiseal finished in 1996; and I made *My Musical Journey* in 1998 – 20 musicians coming on and off, and I sing songs in Spanish and Irish. Now I live in Wicklow and my music is much quieter and more thoughtful – all guitar and whistle. I worked with Martin Dunlea, who teaches jazz in Ronan Guilfoyle's school of jazz.'

The sun had set while we talked: the glazed roof was now black and we wandered into a discussion on Germany: he had toured there, I had just come back.

'Great place, great venues. We went to Berlin: Stadthallen, all over the place. Compare that to Dublin.' He grimaces. 'We played in Passionkirche in Kreuzberg. Two Tibetan restaurants in one street. It was amazing.'

He looked at his watch and apologised: he would have to go. Then he said, 'You know, Irish music is in such a healthy position. There is nowhere in the world where Irish music hasn't reached: The Chieftains on the Great Wall of China, Dervish in China. And no matter what you think of Riverdance, they have really brought something around the world too. It really affects you when you see it abroad: I saw it

Georgian Onlookers: Merrion Square

in London and could hardly believe it. I did a bit of whistling on the main track, so I had some interest in it. Do you remember the first time?'

'At the Eurovision. God, I think everyone remembers that.'

I remembered it anyway. Everyone in Ireland knew that Irish dancing was going to be the featured entertainment in the Contest's interval; but nobody knew what to expect. We had been promised an extravaganza – and when they finished, the Point erupted into a roar and an applause that I had hardly ever heard before. Riverdance today is viewed in some quarters as a rival to Eurovision itself in the competition for the 'Ultimate in Naff', but I don't think anyone will forget the incredible stir caused by that first extraordinary show.

'I think that's what I'm mainly interested in,' I said. 'The images of Ireland that are projected; Riverdance projects such a powerful image of Ireland around the world.'

He nodded. 'Musicians are incredibly powerful emissaries: you have such enormous influence and you can have such an impact on

3

The Trad Scene

Planxty

The '70s in Ireland was the '60s everywhere else. It was a decade of diversification; of greater influence from abroad; of political change and greater freedom for women. People in Ireland started taking drugs; hippies set up communes on islands off the west coast. Planxty sprang from this context: it formed in 1972 and became a legend in the world of Irish music.

Planxty was an extraordinary and highly influential band. It took Irish tradition and fused it with Eastern European music, with socialist American music by Woody Guthrie and Bob Dylan, with the jigs and reels and the ballad boom that had happened in Dublin at the end of the Sixties. Planxty was an instrumental, acoustic band, with bouzouki, bodhran, mandolin, uilleann pipes and guitar; and the original lineup featured Christy Moore, Andy Irvine, Donal Lunny and Liam O'Flynn. Over the years, however, the band's composition has continually changed: other members have included Paul Brady, Bill Whelan (of Riverdance fame) and Matt Molloy of The Chieftains.

'Nowadays,' says Leagues O'Toole, the editor of *Foggy Notions*, and author of a book on the band, 'people listen to that kind of music again and can hardly believe that it was first being played a generation ago. Planxty had really picked up on new music then and they were doing then what some people are doing now with electronic music and so on.

'The purists didn't like it so much – some of them. But Planxty found that other traditionalists really gave them the seal of approval: they knew that Planxty would keep the music fresh while respecting it.'

And still respecting it: in the spring of 2004, the original Planxty reformed and played a series of sell-out concerts in County Clare and at Vicar Street in Dublin. The resulting album, *Planxty: Live At Vicar Street*, is now available.

Line-up:
Christy Moore: Lead vocals
Donal Lunny: Bouzouki
Andy Irvine: Mandolin and guitar
Liam O'Flynn: Uilleann pipes

3

The Trad Scene

people, depending on their mood. You have to be very careful, and very respectful. You have a duty.'

As he went, he said, 'Did I tell you? I got two free tickets for the Planxty reunion concert.'

At the Music Archive

IT MIGHT rain from time to time in Dublin, but it doesn't snow very much. In the course of this last winter, for example, it hasn't snowed once in the city, although there have been heavy falls in the mountains to the south. From most points in the city, you look up and see the great bank of mountains along the southern horizon. Not particularly high mountains, it's true – in fact, most other countries would call them hills – but impressive and atmospheric all the same. In true capital city fashion, Dubliners like to call them the Dublin Mountains. But on the maps, they are the Wicklow Mountains and they contain some of the last remaining great tracts of wilderness in Ireland. I have a friend who lives on a farm near Blessington, high up in the hills. Sometimes, when it is clear and calm and pleasant in Dublin, I ring her and discover that it has been snowing on Blessington all night, or blowing a ferocious gale. I met her just a few weeks ago and she told me that her greenhouse had collapsed in the wind the previous night.

'My red-hot poker seedlings are ruined.'

I was startled: I hadn't even remembered there being any wind the previous night.

'There probably wasn't any wind in Dublin,' she replied glumly.

You can be in the mountains within an hour of leaving the city centre. The great saddle in the hills due south of the city is called the Sally Gap: it is heavenly in late summer, when the heather blooms purple and mauve and the moorlands roll out on either side of the road for miles. The road descends at last into the valley of Glendalough, the old monastic refuge of St Kevin. The remains of the monastery and of its Round Tower can still be seen on the valley floor and the whole place feels as isolated and atmospheric as it must have done in the 6th

The Fag on the Crag: Oscar Wilde Memorial, Merrion Square

century. Even on summer weekends, with the daytrippers and tour coaches packing the place out, it is possible to walk into the woods and along the lakes and quickly leave the hordes behind. There are other magnificent destinations too, including the mansions, gardens and a waterfall at the Powerscourt estate; and the Palladian mansion at Russborough House. Russborough was once famous for its art collection – paintings by Goya and Velázquez, among others, were housed here – but the paintings eventually had to be moved for safekeeping to the National Gallery after a series of heists. The house itself, though, is as magnificent as ever – and just a short journey from the city. Dublin is fortunate to have such places on its doorstep.

I look up as I cross the road towards Merrion Square and see the mountains. It is a bitter day: the weather has become chilly once more in the last few days and the nights are freezing. It has been snowing up in the mountains. I think about Russborough today, closed and shuttered for the winter season, and fancifully imagine its grounds blanketed in snow. This thought makes me look to the left, to where the National Gallery sits grandly on the west side of the square.

Merrion Square is the distinguished and most intact of Dublin's great Georgian public spaces. Townhouses line three sides of the square, while the fourth side – the west side – is taken up by the buildings housing the Natural History Museum and the Irish parliament buildings, as well as the National Gallery itself.

Of all these public buildings, the **Natural History Museum** is probably my favourite. It is a relatively small museum: dinky is the word that comes to mind, although dinky does not, perhaps, do justice to its fine neo-classical lines. Inside, though, it is not dinky at all. Reconstructed dinosaurs occupy pride of place on the ground floor, but the rest of the building is a positive chamber of horrors, a charnel house of nightmarish Victorian obsessions. Things are pickled in vinegar, suspended in brine, animals and pieces of animals line the walls and shelves. Needless to say, all these horrors make it a brilliant place to spend a few hours with a child. Children love horrors, even if they pretend not to.

The **National Gallery** itself is just a few hundred metres away. It has become one of the city's top destinations in the last few years, as the result of its remarkable new Millennium Wing. As in galleries the

Natural History Museum
Merrion Street
Dublin 2 (677 7444)
Dublin's Natural History Museum is extraordinary, a veritable charnel house of horrors. Maintained as an example of the Victorian mania for collecting, preserving and archiving, it features a vast range of  stuffed mammals and reptiles and insects pickled in brine. Perfect for the children, of course, and for any adult who enjoys the ghastly side of life. Pride of place goes to the vast dinosaur skeleton suspended in the central hall.

world over, its cafés are one of the principal magnets, but you could spend most of the day wandering the lofty gallery spaces in the original building or the new galleries – cut through with unexpected windows, voids and holes which allow the sunlight to enter. It is a brilliant addition to the cityscape: I go there a good deal now, and not only for cups of coffee. The Beit Galleries house the refugees from all those incessant robberies at Russborough and I go there a good deal too.

For most people, though, the gardens at the centre of Merrion Square are the main draw. For gardenless apartment dwellers, the lawns and pristine flowerbeds of the gardens are one of Dublin's most beautiful places; and they are set off dramatically by the sight of the upper floors of the great townhouses that line the square. The lawns are dotted with memorials and busts: the latest is a tall, elongated bronze chair commemorating Dermot Morgan, comedian and creator of Father Ted; and he has been joined by a louche statue of Oscar Wilde in the northwest corner of the square, opposite his former family home.

On this bright, chilly day, I cross the gardens and go up the steps of one of the tall Georgian townhouses. I am on my way to the **Irish Traditional Music Archive**, which occupies the building's second floor. The Archive is a crucial element in Ireland's cultural mosaic: it was established in 1987 with the purpose of bringing together, for the first time, a comprehensive collection of traditional music-related materials, including recordings, videos, books and photographs. It has been successful too: its collection is now the largest in the world.

> **Irish Traditional Music Archive**
> 63 Merrion Square, Dublin 2 (661 9699)
> The Archive is situated on the second floor of a fine old Georgian townhouse overlooking the square. It is one of the most important archives of its kind in the world and includes an extensive library and sound archives. The Archive is open to the public from 10am–1pm and 2–5pm, Monday to Friday.

**National Gallery
of Ireland**
Merrion Square West
Dublin 2 (661 5133)
This has always been an impressive gallery, but the beautiful new Millennium Wing has drawn even more visitors.

3

The Trad Scene

As I march breathlessly up the stairs, I feel amazed – as I always do – at the idea that families could live in these massive houses, but they did. Merrion Square was long the city's most fashionable address, but few people live here now and the houses, for the most part, are given over to offices.

'I think there is a certain amount of retreat from a self-conscious idea of fusion and towards older forms,' Nicholas Carolan says. Nicholas is the director of the Archive and he is proposing a slightly different take on matters musical. I feel myself to be quite the expert on the area now and so I look at him dubiously.

'Really?'

'I think so. If you think about it, it makes some sense to say this. Remember the sheer amount of archival material now around: there is so much more; and this means that younger musicians are now as intimate with dead musicians as they are with contemporary music.' He smiles. 'If you know what I mean. And so, this has its impact on what they produce.'

Perhaps I'm not such an expert after all.

'There is a general impression that this sort of music belongs with professional musicians,' Nicholas goes on. 'People like The Afro-Celt Sound System, who have laudably attempted to take the norms of other ethnic music traditions and mix them with the Irish.

'But the most prominent traditional groups like Altan, who are self-consciously trying to ground their music in their own locality of Donegal, very consciously cleave to that. Or Danu sing in Irish: they tour and sing to audiences in a language that is obscure to those audiences; and Dervish sing in Irish as well as English. People seem to be standing their own ground, their own familiar turf, a little more. Traditional music has always been very locally-based in Ireland – we can see that in Dervish, for example, too.'

I remember my conversation with Cormac and ask, 'Was there resistance to that model?'

'Oh yes,' Nicholas says mildly. 'Certainly. After all, Irish music is an art form. There are always progressive and conservative trends in art – all art – and this is the way it is in Irish music too. But there has never been a time when Irish music hasn't innovated. Reels and hornpipes are part of the content of Irish music, but these are actually innovations from the end of the 18th century. Now they are regarded as core aspects of the tradition. Ceili bands are seen as very old-fashioned but they are creations of the early 20th century: they absorbed aspects of American and British popular music in the 1920s. The bass, the pianos – these are all new.' He shrugs. 'But some people will accept that it takes all kinds, while others are more dogmatic.'

He goes on, making it clear to me his take on these matters.

'The Archive has always interpreted Irish music in the widest possible way. We were always expansive in our attitudes; traditional music is a broad church and composed of many threads and traditions. Take, for example, *Moore's Melodies*: the words are written by a known poet, as Thomas Moore was, writing in a very literary and not in an oral tradition, but taking aspects of oral tradition – song melodies and arranging them for voice and piano in what was an alien musical idiom. But there is an element that derives from Irish oral tradition in all this, the connection is there and so we include it. If a brass band plays a traditional melody arranged for brass, we would include it. Crossover, fusion – we document it all and we don't judge. We simply record what is being done and make it available to the general public. That is our purpose.'

As the interview ends, Nicholas tells me: 'There is a sense that this music is rural-based, but that was simply because more people formerly lived in the country than in the cities. But at one point in the 20th century, more people lived in the cities, in Dublin. It isn't a necessity that this kind of music is based in a particular context; it's simply a condition of interaction that this kind of music appears. It has nothing essentially to do with rurality or urbanness or anything else. It's simply about living – people living their lives.'

The Oral Tradition

I LEAVE the Archive later that day, after a look around the collection and a chat with a few more members of its staff. I have a sense of the Archive as cool spectator of the eddies and currents of Ireland's music history, scooping up the evidence and making no judgements. I also have more of a sense of those currents and eddies: I know I should probably take a lesson from the Archive on how to be non-judgemental, but instead I walk away deciding how silly it is to be fighting for a purity of history and a purity of music, when it is self-evident that this music never was pure in the first place. Take *Moore's Melodies*.

I have been told that Thomas Moore is sometimes called Ireland's National Poet.

'Ireland's National Poet? Says who?'

Says a bundle of websites, apparently. And indeed, a quick search of the Web reveals a crop of websites originating from the Universities of Nagoya and New Mexico and making this very claim. I screw up my nose: I have seldom heard anyone in Ireland call Thomas Moore Ireland's National Poet. Maybe I have never been listening.

Not that Moore was not interesting and deeply significant: he was, both culturally and politically. *Moore's Melodies*, composed between 1807 and 1834, were translated into many European languages: they were the literary craze of the day, opening up as they did a unique oral culture to outside view. As Nicholas Carolan had shown me, the *Melodies* were an exercise in taking oral melodies and placing them into a written mould. Nothing wrong with that per se, of course, but the Melodies had a lasting effect on Ireland's oral musical culture and hence a lasting influence on the country's culture and history in general.

Memorial to Thomas Moore at JJ Smyth's Bar, Aungier Street

The germ of Moore's project came in 1792. In that year, the city of Belfast, with its large and independent-minded Presbyterian and Catholic populations, hosted a Harp Festival as a means of focusing attention on Ireland's older traditions and skills. Edward Bunting collected the proceedings of the festival in *A General Collection of the Ancient Irish Music* (1794). But Bunting could not understand the basic structure of the music and therefore the first translation had taken place in his book even before Moore got his hands on it. Moore then added further translations, although he was keenly and defensively aware of the issues involved:

'Had I not ventured on these very allowable liberties, many of the songs now most known and popular would have been still sleeping...'

Ireland, like any country, was a mongrel country: endlessly shaped and formed and altered by the chance effects of history. I hurry home through an Arctic gale; my nose is turning redder and redder and by the time I am safely home, I feel like an ice cube.

THE 18TH century has always been regarded as Dublin's heyday. It was in these years that the Georgian squares and terraces and monumental buildings that we see today were constructed. The exquisite Four Courts and Custom House were designed by James Gandon and raised on the city quays, and Trinity College embarked on the greatest building spree in its history, creating the austere quadrangles that today lure the tourists. It was in these years that Merrion and Fitzwilliam Squares were formed on the southern side of the city, and Mountjoy Square, Gardiner Street and Henrietta Street on the slopes north of the Liffey, becoming the most fashionable quarters of Dublin in which to maintain one's townhouse. The exquisite new Parliament House was opened opposite Trinity in 1731.

Dublin has exerted a dramatic influence on the rest of Ireland for centuries, of course, but in the 18th century, its architectural energy was more than matched by its political and cultural vigour. In the years leading up to the 1798 Rebellion, Ireland seemed to be moving towards a consciousness of national unity, quite independent from its connection to Britain. The Irish parliament, sitting in its new home on College Green and composed solely of members of the Anglo-Irish Ascendancy, began to exert its political autonomy, demanding a level playing field for the Irish economy, and a greater degree of economic and political freedom. It was a brief historical moment, but heady too. Reading the texts and documents of the time, it is easy to sense the electricity and vigour of a time when Jonathan Swift was preaching at St Patrick's Cathedral, and Trinity was turning out graduates of the stature of Burke, Congreve and Goldsmith. In these years, Dublin, as a centre of economic and literary activity, was second only to London in its vigour.

But this period did not last. In 1796, a French invasion was botched and two years later, Wolfe Tone's United Irishmen uprising – in which Thomas Moore himself was suspected of playing a part – was crushed. The Act of Union in 1801 created a United Kingdom of Great Britain and Ireland, and the country's brief moment of autonomy was finished. But the political and cultural impulses of the 18th century left a permanent mark on Irish cultural life. For one thing, it established Dublin once and for all as the centre of the country's cultural life. In particular, the city's publishing industry became well established; and this in turn impacted profoundly on Irish music. *Moore's Melodies* was only one example – and although it was the most famous, it was by no means the first – of the written word intervening in what had always been an oral-based culture. Dublin was always important as a place which controlled the publication and dissemination of the printed word, as a place where ballad sheets were printed, as a place to which performers from all corners of the land migrated and met and influenced each other, and in that sense, the city itself profoundly influenced the oral tradition.

'YOU CANNOT talk about Dublin music without talking about Zozimus.' It has been growing steadily colder for several days. The snow on the mountains looks thicker, heavier than ever, and the winds slicing down into Dublin from the north are bitter. The weather reports have been forecasting doom: blizzards and Arctic winds and wind chill galore. On the radio this very morning, I have listened to a Canadian meteorologist advising people on how to cope with adverse winter conditions. 'Carry a candle in the car,' he says. 'It'll help to warm you up.' Then another contributor is interviewed. 'It really feels like we can't cope even with the idea of cold weather in this country,' she chides, 'much less cold weather itself. We all need to wise up.' Underneath the heap of my duvet, I agree.

I have a date for lunch, which means that I eventually have to struggle from underneath the duvet and get ready. Later, I struggle up through the bitter wind and buy flowers from the flowerseller on Baggot Street; she looks frozen to the ground. I wait for 30 minutes for the bus and when I emerge at the other end, it feels colder than ever: I am in the southern suburbs of the city; the foothills of the mountains are closer; the wind coming off the snow is icy. I am relieved to ring the doorbell and be ushered into the warm house.

I first met Aidan and Joyce O'Hara a few years ago, when I was researching a radio programme about the cultural connections between Ireland and Newfoundland. Joyce is Canadian and Aidan had lived in Newfoundland for several years in the 1970s, teaching and researching and working in media – and doing a good deal to resurrect the memory of the once-close ties between Ireland and Newfoundland. I knew that the oldest Irish diaspora community in the world was to be found in Newfoundland and had long wanted to go and see what remained of it at the end of the 20th century. So when the chance came to go, I jumped at it. Aidan enlightened me about Newfoundland then; and I hoped he would be able to do the same about aspects of Irish music today. But first, he tells me about Zozimus.

'His real name was Michael Moran. He is tied in with the whole thing about ballad writing, which is how many hacks made their money – by ballad writing. Goldsmith and the like.'

I am scandalised. 'Was Goldsmith a hack?' After all, Goldsmith was a Trinity graduate.

'Of course he was a hack,' Aidan replies bracingly. 'Hacks were paid for writing up these ballad sheets – paid a certain amount – and of course they would sell by the thousand. They were hugely popular. These hacks would write about an event, a robbery or a fire, in the traditional ballad sense. They were a means of communication: they enriched the lives of ordinary, illiterate people; they enriched their lives. Ballads added a love interest, romance, excitement.'

'Soap opera, then,' I murmur. '*Dynasty* or *Dallas* of the 18th century.'

'Exactly.'

I like the sound of that.

'And Michael Moran, Zozimus, was the most famous of them. He used to declaim these ballads on Essex Bridge.

> Ye sons and daughters of Erin, attend,
> Gather round poor Zozimus, yer friend;
> Listen, boys, until yez hear
> My charming song so dear.

I think about newly tarted-up Essex Bridge, its new 'bridge furniture', its plans to establish a permanent book market. I like the connections.

'Go on,' I say. 'So why was he called Zozimus?' I think vaguely: it sounds Persian or something. Not a Dublin name anyway.

He tells me. Michael Moran was a celebrated – in some quarters, at any rate – Dublin balladeer. Like Homer, he was blind and earned

3

The Trad Scene

his living by standing in public places in Dublin, reciting ballads for the entertainment of the populace. His store of knowledge became prodigious as he aged, until, as Yeats put it, 'he carried the whole of the Middle Ages under his frieze coat'. He earned the nickname Zozimus from one of his favourite religious stories: that of St Mary of Egypt, in which a certain Bishop Zozimus interceded to help a lonely woman fasting in the desert.

'Egyptian, then – not Persian,' I say. Well, I was nearly right.

But in the best traditions of public entertainers, Zozimus was a good deal more interested in poking fun at his contemporaries – especially Dublin's political class.

'You can see how influential these ballads were,' Aidan says and I nod agreement. He goes on, 'The history of song – it's all about ordinary working people: all about the history of ordinary people living and loving and getting on with things, and contributing to the world of entertainment in the process. It crosses the boundaries we are all conditioned to accept: the Irish have contributed to English entertainment but the English have contributed to Irish song too. People don't discriminate in their acceptance of culture in that sense: they apply their own aesthetic and they are non-judgemental.

'Nationalism and all the rest of it – ordinary people didn't have the time to get into all that. Life was too difficult to allow the time. Ordinary people, Catholics and Presbyterians, understood that they were being made to suffer by the establishment but this understanding was at a personal level, not at some over-arching national level. And besides, you really can't compartmentalise culture.' He looks at me. 'You're from Derry. Well, the best example is "Danny Boy" – "The Derry Air" or "The Londonderry Air", collected by Elizabeth Ross in the early 1800s. Many people tried to put words to "The Derry Air", but in the end it was a Somerset lawyer, Fred Weatherly, who actually attached the words. So in a way, it's as much an English song as an Irish one.' He shrugs. 'That's always the way with popular culture: it is shared and crossed and mixed by people; carried around by people as they move around the world; and then adapted to local circumstances.'

You only have to think of conceptions of Irishness – the way in which the Irish were perceived as they emigrated and spread around the world. Everywhere they went, they made waves, and stirred emotions: everything from hatred and fear and loathing through to indulgent tolerance. In the past, propaganda coarsened ideas of Irishness, and the Irish were represented as positively feral, certainly less than human. As we talk, I remember once more how Edmund Spenser, author of *The Faerie Queene*, proposed the extermination of the Irish, so that their land could be taken over and worked efficiently.

'Well, if you take Britain and Europe,' Aidan says, 'part of the alleviation of the image of the Irish on this side of the Atlantic came with Thomas Moore. His *Melodies* really helped to soften the image; and later, the stage Irishman helped to soften the image too, even if it was a stereotype. Then sports and music helped even more. By degrees, the image changed, but entertaining was absolutely crucial.

'And take America: the Irish in North America eventually got into the singing and entertainment business in a big way. You should read *Gangs Of New York*: it really puts the whole business of the theatre scene and the music scene into context. By getting involved in this business, the Irish managed to normalise relationships with their Protestant, Yankee neighbours, who had been so afraid of them. The Irish suffered terribly from negative stereotyping and suffered worse because they were poor, noisy and numerous across the Eastern states, Catholic and good at properly agitating about various issues. They frightened the life out of their neighbours. Singing and entertainment managed to smooth that away – to a certain extent at any rate. Popular culture again, you see? It was tremendously energetic in America and it made an enormous contribution to popular culture there. Think of Harrigan and Harte, for example, they were huge entertainers. Or think of George Cohan: Jimmy Cagney filmed his life in *Yankee Doodle Dandy*. And Irish – all of them.'

Later, when I come home and when I have warmed up again, I type in a Google search for Zozimus. The connection is slow, but a

Talamh an Eisc:
The Irish in Newfoundland

WHEN I visited Newfoundland in 1999, I was startled by the Irish presence in everyday life on the island. Before I arrived, I had been told that I would hear people speaking in Waterford accents who had never been to Waterford (or Ireland, come to that) in their lives. I had felt a fair degree of scepticism about this. But I arrived in St John's and took my first stroll down through the steep streets of the city to the waterfront – and I found that it was true: Irish accents were clear and ubiquitous. Later, I discovered that a kind of common knowledge of Irish culture, history and politics was also widespread among the people with whom I spoke.

The Irish diaspora in Newfoundland is among the oldest in the world – but in Ireland itself, there is little knowledge of this corner of North America and little knowledge of the fact that emigrants began sailing from Ireland to Talamh an Eisc (The Land of the Fish) as early as the 1600s, firstly to work on the fishery and later to settle for good. The Irish brought their culture with them, with the result that the traditional music scene in St John's is both heavily influenced by Irish trad music and is the most famously vigorous scene in North America. Irish music is played in the line of rowdy Irish bars on George Street, which runs close to the harbour in downtown St John's, and played also in the Ship Inn further up the steep hill.

This Irish music is usually played at the expense of the indigenous Newfoundland folk music – a variant of music that is strikingly like the Irish and yet unalike, containing notes of Irish, Scots, Breton and English. The local folk music, in other words, still carries the trace of the people who had come over to work for hundreds of years on Newfoundland's once brimming fishery. The fiddles, flutes and uilleann pipes were similar to Irish instruments, although there were curious variations here too: the three-row accordion, for example, was slightly different. But for all these quirks and branches, the dominant note was always firmly Irish.

I discovered, however, that knowledge of Ireland in Newfoundland was certainly not reciprocated in Ireland itself. I remembered very clearly a rancorous conversation in a Dublin bar the week before I left for Newfoundland. A direct flight from Heathrow to St John's, I told my friends, was much less than five hours: that was how close that part of North America was to Europe. Wasn't that surprising?

'Nonsense,' someone rasped across the table. She was thankfully not a friend, nor did she become one after that conversation. "I work in a travel agent: and I know for a fact that it takes at least twelve hours to fly to Newfoundland.'

'No,' I told her, coolly enough at this point in the story. 'It really doesn't. Maybe you should look at a map.' In hindsight, of course, I ought to have held my tongue – especially when it became clear that she was thinking of New Zealand; and that even on this point she was wrong.

IRISH MUSIC had survived in such intact form in Newfoundland as a result of geographical and historical conditions.

'In Newfoundland,' Aidan O'Hara had told me, 'the emigrant experience was always different. Life was absolutely marginal at all times. It was all about survival stuff. Newfoundland music was preserved as a result of extreme isolation – isolation from the world outside and also within Newfoundland itself. The island has always suffered from tremendous isolation, throughout its history. Nobody ever emigrated there after about 1800: instead, Newfoundlanders did what everyone else did: they left and went to the United States. And so the result is that traditional music there has remained the same: dominated by Irish influence, but with a touch of others too.'

'But you know,' he went on, 'it may have been characterised by isolation, but in other ways, the Newfoundland experience was not so very different from other Irish migrations. It was simply a continuity of the seasonal migration that characterised Irish labour movements. Instead of picking potatoes or harvesting corn in England and Scotland, they harvested fish in Newfoundland – a short hop across the Atlantic, which is after all at its most narrow between Ireland and Newfoundland. Dublin port would have seen these migrants passing through all the time.

'These workers were a feature of rural Ireland – they passed through the villages with their spades or their sickles, heading off to Britain. And this went on for hundreds of years. And of course it was a two-way thing: they brought songs and music back with them, for what else could they do in the long winter nights? And that's where songs entered the Irish experience. Ordinary people did what ordinary people always do: they mixed and mingled, whether they were Irish or English or whatever; and the English language was creeping slowly in too.

'For Newfoundland, the songs helped to stave off the tedium. They lifted the heart in those appalling Newfoundland winters; and took their minds off their hard and tedious jobs.' He shrugged. 'It's just people again – the experience of people's lives.'

3

The Trad Scene

link eventually comes up. It is for the Zozimus Experience. I grimace and read:

'The Zozimus Experience,' the website squeals at me, 'is perhaps the most unique and innovative Dublin tour and is street entertainment with a capital E. The tour has been described as being "wacky, highly original, a nutcracker of entertainment".'

I make a mental note to avoid it, and go to bed.

3

The Trad Scene

4

Spielsprecht

Dublin On Stage

O'CONNELL Street is the city's main thoroughfare. It's imperially wide, stately and impressive – or at any rate it was stately and impressive until the '60s, which was when the rot set in. Fast food joints and cheap shops colonised the street. The shoppers dived into the side streets or took themselves south to Grafton Street a little more often and the IRA got in on the act by blowing up Nelson's Pillar,

which, in spite of its imperial associations, had provided a focal point for the entire area. Before long, O'Connell Street became a strip which people would actively avoid, especially at night. It became a shell and a byword for how a whole district of a city could fall from grace with alarming speed.

Today, O'Connell Street is undergoing something of a painful renaissance. The politicians and planners

The Gate Theatre, Cavendish Row

decreed that it must be so – shamed, perhaps, by the appalling state of Dublin's main street; and embarrassed by the blasts of negative publicity. For those with an interest in such things, the turning point came when the city council moved heaven and earth to stop a sex shop opening at a prime site directly opposite the GPO. The council failed – you can't stop the market, no way – but the fact that they tried at all was instructive.

Today, the street has been ploughed up: the drug-dealing public toilets have been sealed, the footpaths widened and the road narrowed, traffic diverted and a plaza laid in front of the GPO's stately portico. The Millennium Spire, tall and silver-gleaming and controversial, has been erected close to where Nelson once stood, and so the street has a focal point once more, even if it is mildly controversial in its bulk and design. The new LUAS trams will criss-cross the street from the summer of 2004; and new silver birches are being planted to replace the gnarled and 'pollution-unfriendly' lime trees lately removed by the authorities. O'Connell Street, it seems, is looking up.

It should not prove too difficult a job to turn this street around. Its main institutions remain, miraculously, in place in spite of the neglect of years. Dubliners still meet 'under the clock' at Eason's booksellers; and sneak up to catch an afternoon show at the Savoy cinema. They still go to the Gresham Hotel for a drink or afternoon tea; and they still plunge into a refurbished Clery's department store to buy wedding gifts. They still go to the GPO to buy their stamps and take in the atmosphere of this massive building, which is hallowed as a result of its central role in the 1916 Easter Rising. O'Connell Street, still imposingly wide and well proportioned, can easily be made to be graceful and buzzing again.

Much is said of Dublin's north–south divide: the Northside is poor and the Southside is wealthy, so the saying goes, and the Liffey might as well be as wide as the Atlantic. Behind most clichés, there is a grain of truth and so it is in this case, but it is also true that behind this cliché, there is a good deal of complexity. It is significant, for example, that much of the city's cultural life, as well as its main shopping area, continues to cluster around O'Connell Street. The **Gate Theatre** anchors the north end of the street as it has done for decades, and the famous **Abbey Theatre** still lurks in its unimposing site just east of the boulevard.

These two theatres have famous histories. The former is associated with the city's well-heeled and cultured set, with an air of sophistication, and with European sensibilities. The latter – celebrating its centenary in 2004 – is inextricably associated with WB Yeats and Augusta Gregory, and the assertion of Ireland cultural autonomy with passionate audiences and riots in the aisles. But there is more to Dublin theatre than the old stories and associations. Both theatres, and others in the city too, have long brought music onto their stages in various shapes and guises and forms, and to various kinds of welcome.

I have been to very many productions in Dublin in which music played an integral part. Some of these productions worked and others did not, but all were stimulating. Brian Friel's *Performances*, which premiered at the Gate in the autumn of 2003, is an example of a play which perhaps pushed its musical element to extremes, and which perhaps did not work. *Performances*, which dramatised an aspect of the life of Janáček, featured a string quartet which appeared on stage to play out the final 30 minutes. The effect was startling. I'm not ashamed to say that I hardly knew what to think, though it was comforting to gather afterwards that most of the audience felt much that same way. That Friel should choose such a device was perhaps not surprising though, given the persistent implication in his drama. This is outlined even more explicitly at the conclusion of *Dancing at Lughnasa* (1990), which has recently been revived at the Gate, that is, that music can communicate and express emotions in a way that language can never manage.

Gate Theatre
1 Cavendish Row
Parnell Square
Dublin 1 (874 4045)
Dublin's most elegant theatre features an intimate and democratic auditorium; a cosmopolitan range of European and American drama is supplemented by new Irish writing.

4

Dublin On Stage

Abbey Theatre
26, Lower Abbey Street
Dublin I (878 7222)
The most famous of the
Dublin stages, still offering a
combination of Irish and
European classics and new
writing on its two stages.

abbeyonehundred
What will **you** see?

In *Juno And The Paycock* (1924), Sean O'Casey makes use of the
Dublin tradition of the 'noble call' as part of a communal sing-song:
a song that was judged a success was greeted as a 'noble call'

Juno and Mary stand up and, choosing a suitable position, sing simply
'Home to the Mountains'. They bow to company and return to their
places.

Boyle (*emotionally, at the end of song*): 'Lull...me...to...rest!'
Joxer (*clapping his hands*): 'Bravo, bravo! Darlin' girulls, darlin' girulls!'
Mrs Madigan: 'Juno, I never seen you in better form.'
Bentham: 'Very nicely rendered indeed.'
Mrs Madigan: 'A noble call, a noble call!'
Mrs Boyle: 'What about yourself, Mrs Madigan?'

After some coaxing, Mrs Madigan rises and in a quavering voice
sings.

Mrs Madigan: 'If I were a blackbird I'd whistle and sing;
An' follow the ship that my thrue love was in;
An' on the top riggin', I'd there build me nest,
An' at night I would sleep on me Willie's white breast!'

Becoming husky, amid applause, she sits down.

'Ah me voice is too husky now, Juno; though I remember the time
when Maisie Madigan could sing like a nightingale at matin' time. I

remember as well as I remember yesterday, at a party ... singin'
"You'll Remember Me" with the top notes quiverin' in a dead hush
of petrified attention, folleyed be a clappin' o' hans that shuk the
tumblers on the table, an' capped by Jimeson, the barber, sayin' that
it was the best rendherin' of "You'll Remember Me" he ever heard
in his natural!'

O'Casey's *The Plough And The Stars* (1926) provoked the famous
riots at the Abbey, but other drama has been received more warmly.
Billy Roche's *Cavalcaders*, for example, which played at the Abbey in
the 1990s and which has been much revived since, revolves around
the lives of members of a barbershop quartet, around the idea that
history is doomed always to repeat itself. Dion Boucicault's *The
Shaughraun* is being revived at the Abbey this summer as part of the
theatre's centenary celebrations.

Other shows exploited music in Dublin's past. Handel wrote his
Messiah in Dublin and premiered it in Temple Bar in 1742 to a
thrilled citizenry; it is still sung each Easter on the same spot. The
Irish novelist John Banville wrote a play a few summers ago called
Dublin 1742 based on these events and it was staged at the Ark
Theatre, the city's 'cultural space for children'. The Ark lies in the
heart of Temple Bar, backing onto Meeting House Square. It is a
curious building – if you're a grown-up. Everything is tailor-made for
children, so that the stairs are more shallow, the door handles are
lower and the urinals closer to the ground than people generally
expect. The effect is to walk, Gulliver-like, into a world in miniature
and, of course, to make one reassess the effect upon children of living
in a planet of giants. It is a brilliant building and a hub of creative
energy.

The fact that Banville was writing such a play had made me
curious in itself, for the austerity of novels like *Copernicus* have
never suggested to me a pronounced interest in the world of children.
But there it was: the old judgement thing kicking in again and finding
itself flawed again. In fact, *Dublin 1742* was a brilliant creation, an
extravagant comic melodrama, inviting the audience to imagine a

4

Dublin On Stage

series of scenes in the city in the year 1742. Georg Friedrich Handel is frantically organising the final rehearsals for *Messiah*; he spars and spats with Thomas Arne, composer of *Rule Britannia*, who incongruously enough lived in Dublin at the same time. Around them swirl other characters who added to the tumult of Enlightenment Dublin: the philosopher Bishop Berkeley, the diarist and gossip Laetitia Pilkington, singer Susanna Cibber and actress Peg Woffington. Vibrant and colourful, the play took figures out of history, dressed them sumptuously and set them loose among an audience who might not be expected to be especially receptive to a tale of 18th-century sacred music. It was warmly praised.

This thread of democracy found its most famous expression, perhaps, on the stage of the old Theatre Royal on Hawkins Street, near the Liffey on the south side of the river. The theatre is gone now and has been replaced by a particularly drab office building, but in its day it played host to a particularly successful strain of musical theatre and vaudeville, championed in particular by Maureen Potter and Jimmy O'Dea. O'Dea died in the '60s, but Potter continued working until comparatively recently. She died in April 2004; and she, O'Dea and the Theatre Royal itself have all earned a place in the musical history of the city.

Musical theatre in the city has also been profoundly influenced by the American and, in particular, by the European tradition.

Susannah de Wrixon

I HAVE arranged to meet Susannah de Wrixon in front of Bewley's Oriental Café on Grafton Street. Something of a Dublin landmark, Bewley's has been a fixture of the city for generations, selling coffees, cakes and its own range of teas to a greedy populace. For years, it was one of the very few places in the city where you could buy your coffee beans and have them ground for you there and then – a note of European chic appreciated in the days when Ireland was a good deal less cosmopolitan than it is today. As for Grafton Street, it remains the city's posh shopping street, but has lost much of its distinctive nature.

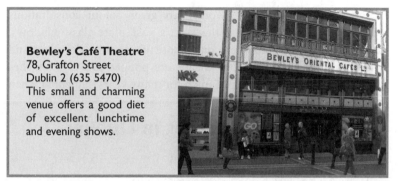

Bewley's Café Theatre
78, Grafton Street
Dublin 2 (635 5470)
This small and charming venue offers a good diet of excellent lunchtime and evening shows.

Long and narrow, it is positively thronged each weekend, and the buskers stationed every few metres compete to attract the attention of purposeful shoppers. But the shops strung out along the length of the street are mainly chain stores today – multiples, as they are called in the business. The local shops, for the most part, vanished long ago, and the new shops gaze at each other across a variety of red pedestrian brick that is reminiscent of a bleak English suburban shopping precinct. The red brick, to my mind, is most definitely a mistake.

When I first came to Dublin in 1990, Switzers department store still faced Brown Thomas across Grafton Street. Brown Thomas was posh and atmospheric: a warren of small rooms which led off each other and which seemed designed to confuse the shopper. There was none of the stark lighting and streamlined effects that characterise department stores today. Switzers was quite posh too, but a little larger and a touch more democratic. I hardly ever went into either of them, to tell the truth. They were not happy hunting grounds for a student on a budget, but I well remember going with a friend to the John Rocha room in Brown Thomas: she was trying on an expensive coat and I was there to give it the thumbs-up. This was all a long time ago, before individual lines of Rocha candles and throws and thumb-printed crystal wine glasses had ever been dreamed of.

Today, Switzers is long gone. Brown Thomas has moved across the road into its former premises and updated them, adding those hard white lights and sleek escalators and more perfume counters than are possible to count. Women are given colour consultations and facials right up against the store's vast plate-glass windows. Today, it is possible to press one's nose up against the glass and watch in perfect safety as blackheads are popped just a few inches away. A friend, who lived in Munich for many years, lamented when

Theatre and Cabaret in Dublin: Some of the Best

Dublin is a famously theatrical city: the tales of the riots at the Abbey are the stuff of legend, although the scene has calmed down a little since then. The streets of the city are by no means groaning with theatres, but you can generally rely on a handful of excellent shows playing at any one time.

The Abbey (map: 39) (26 Lower Abbey Street; 878 7222) is the country's National Theatre. The shabby '60s building on Abbey Street is presently the focus of some debate: it is obvious that the theatre badly needs new premises but not quite so clear where those premises will be situated. Rebuilding on the existing cramped site has now, apparently, been ruled out; relocating to a more generous space on O'Connell Street is a possibility; a brand-new Docklands site is also possible, though unlikely. It looks as though the Abbey will stay where it is for the next few years at any rate, showcasing a combination of classic productions and original Irish writing on its two stages.

The Gate (map: 40) (1 Cavendish Row, Parnell Square; 874 4045) is generally considered more sophisticated and cosmopolitan than the rival Abbey. The theatre occupies gracious and elegant premises at the north end of O'Connell Street: the auditorium is intimate and democratic, the bar charming and round-windowed; the theatre itself is about to embark on rebuilding work which will result in less cramped backstage areas. The Gate tends to offer productions that are a little more populist but also highly polished – though from time to time it gambles on new Irish writing.

The Project (map: 34) (39 East Essex Street, Temple Bar; 679 6622) is located in the heart of Temple Bar. The building was completely rebuilt recently and Project productions are decidedly less mainstream than those on offer at either the Abbey or the Gate. Avant-garde pieces find a natural home in the two performance spaces and the programmes mix music, cabaret, theatre, the visual arts and dance.

he saw this: 'In Germany, the treatment rooms are upstairs and out of sight. They're not in the shop windows!' Indeed.

Meanwhile, Marks and Spencer has colonised the old Brown Thomas premises; and now the two stores eyeball each other across Grafton Street. It was a move much lamented at the time. Ireland and

Bewley's Café Theatre (map: 37) (78 Grafton Street; 677 6761) occupies a small space on the third floor of Bewley's Oriental Café on Grafton Street. A small corner stage and a serious mixed bag here: occasional cabaret nights are mingled with all manner of innovative and original theatre; and the Lunchtime Theatre slots (1:10pm–2pm Mon–Sat; prices vary and include soup and sandwich) are usually well worth a look.

The Cobalt Café (map: 72) (16 North Great George's St; 873 0313) offers occasional cabaret nights and quite right too, as this elegant café occupies a former Victorian performance space on lovely North Great George's Street. The café itself is elegant and doubles as an art gallery.

Other venues worth a look include **The Ark Children's Cultural Centre (map: 35)** (11A Eustace Street, Temple Bar; 670 7788); and the **Samuel Beckett Theatre (map: 36)** in Trinity College (608 2266), which offers a broad range of theatrical work.

4

Dublin On Stage

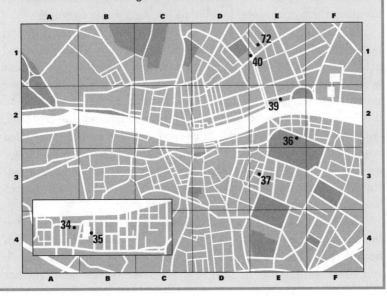

Dublin were losing all their individuality and their distinctiveness, it was claimed in the letters pages of the *Irish Times*; soon we would all be wearing the usual mass-produced underwear and life would never be the same again. Today, a decade on, we probably are all wearing much the same underwear; the food is better in Ireland, and the cosmopolitan influence is more pronounced, but life hasn't stopped.

All these changes should make people thankful for Bewley's, which has remained in its place as the city has changed all around it. And indeed, it is still busy, though maybe less busy than it was years ago, before a host of predatory competitors came snapping at its heels. Lately, Starbucks have announced plans to open up 30 cafés across Ireland, and so times are set to get even tougher for Bewley's. Their cafés are less atmospheric today too, ever since they removed the board games and free newspapers a few years ago in order to stop people coming in at two, buying cups of tea and then sitting until six playing chess. The cafés also feel a little larger, so all that business of wandering upstairs and downstairs looking for a table is just a notch more stressful than it used to be. The coffee grinders were taken away and so the aromas were lost. This was clearly a mistake, so the company is installing them once more, in a bid to lure back fickle customers.

As you can see, I don't much like Bewley's – much-loved institution and all that it is. And so, when Susannah appears out of the crowd and greets me, I suggest we get the hell away from its busy entrance. 'Let's go to Powerscourt, shall we?' She agrees, with a touch of relief, and we turn off Grafton Street's ugly red pavement and up the narrow alley to the Powerscourt Townhouse Centre: lofty and high and glazed of roof, with three floors of cafés and shops surrounding a central space filled with light and air. Powerscourt is probably a little too fashionable for its own good, but you can listen and talk with relative ease, without shouting, and you don't have to carry a tray around for months looking for a table; both of these things are good.

Last time I saw Susannah, I had just caught her poisoning a dog by slipping slug pellets into its food; she had looked well pleased with herself. It was becoming fairly clear to me that she was a psychopath and I was waiting for the men in white coats to come and take her away, to make the world a safer place. And so, as we settle ourselves at a table overlooking the atrium, I ask her how she is.

'Oh, I'm fine,' she says sleekly. 'Very well indeed. You saw me kill the dog?'

I nod. 'How is filming coming along?'

'Completed it last night.' She takes a sip of mango juice. 'I was taken away in an ambulance.'

'Good.'

'Yeah. Inevitable, really.'

'Mmm.'

For the last few months, Susannah has been guesting as a lunatic nightclub singer in *Fair City*, RTE's soap opera set in the fictional Dublin suburb of Carrickstown. In the slow unfolding of the plot, it hasn't been made immediately clear that she is a lunatic, of course, but now it's beginning to be alarmingly apparent that all is not well; I have the sense that she is enjoying every moment of it.

I know her better as a singer. I have been to see several of her shows and remember her *Tribute to Peggy Lee* concert with particular fondness. Naturally, Susannah has a great voice but she also has the ability to bring a sense of intimacy to the audience and into the venue, and as a result, the whole package has considerable charm. I have just been to see her Christmas show at the new

Pavilion Theatre beside the harbour at Dun Laoghaire: it was a light, sparkling and sexy show, and came complete with her Trio Con Brio of piano, bass and drums. Not a corpse of a poisoned dog in sight.

'How did you get into singing in the first place?' I ask her. I know she is a professionally trained actor.

'Well,' she says in her light Cork tones and considers. 'I sort

de Wrixon Con Brio

4

Dublin On Stage

of fell into it. In fact, I never considered myself a singer; and most of the time, frankly, I still don't. I consider myself an actor. But at one point I wasn't getting enough work as an actor and I started hanging around with musicians and got interested in their music. I started singing a few songs at Velure in the Gaiety and then I did a few shows with Camille O'Sullivan, and it was all rolling along nicely.'

She takes another sip of juice.

'Then Ella Fitzgerald died and we put together a show about her. And then I joined The Nualas. Did you know The Nualas?'

'Oh yes.' Everyone in Dublin knew The Nualas before they finally dissolved a few years ago. They were a group of three female singers and stand-up comedians, all clad in heavy wig, horn-framed glasses and heavily rural Irish accents. I saw one of their last shows in the now-defunct HQ venue on Middle Abbey Street and remember laughing all the way through their routine.

Susannah laughs as we talk about them.

'I was with The Nualas for a year and that was constant work, brilliant work, my voice got really trained up. Then I got a job with the Abbey and then I did my own cabaret show at Bewley's – *Café Cabaret* – Waits and Gershwin and material from *Cabaret* – a real mix of stuff.'

'Bewley's is a great venue,' I agree, with more than a touch of hypocrisy; and drink some more coffee.

I must be a dreadful hypocrite, in fact. After all, I steered us away from its front door not ten minutes before. But then, there is more to Bewley's than heavy trays being carried up and down stairs.

On the third floor of the large and ornate Bewley's building on Grafton Street is one of the city's most charming institutions. The Bewley's Theatre Café is a small room, with a smaller stage in one corner, and it is used for lunchtime and evening theatre. I have been to many lunchtime shows there in the past: for a few euro, you can get soup and a sandwich and a play beginning at 1:10pm sharp, ending just before two. Monologues, comedies and more powerful material – all slotted into a lunch hour.

For the evening shows, the heavy velvet curtains are pulled, the candles are lit on the small round tables, wine is served and longer shows are staged. It was courtesy of Bewley's, in fact, that I first came across Susannah a few years ago – at the very *Café Cabaret* show she has just mentioned. I remember it was a beautifully balmy summer night – comparatively rare in Dublin – and the packed little room rapidly became so hot that the windows had to be opened behind the heavy curtains to allow air to drift in from Grafton Street. It was a splendid, elegant, stylish show.

''Then Peggy Lee died,' Susannah goes on, 'and I loved her music; and so I put together a show. That's still my favourite show – all carefully put together, all scored. In that sense, I think I probably feel more related to jazz than anything else.'

'I remember the Peggy Lee show,' I say suddenly. 'It's probably the wrong word to use, but it felt educational.'

'Educational!' Susannah laughs. 'God.'

'You know what I mean, though,' I say hastily. 'I came away knowing far, far more about Peggy Lee than I'd done before.'

She looks pleased. 'Yes, I do know. Peggy has always been my most successful show; the most in demand.'

In that show, Susannah had spiked her songs with a running commentary, with descriptions of various episodes of Lee's life: the travails, the triumphs, and the migrations. She had kept it very light and charming and never heavy with description or analysis, and yet the effect was penetrating. I left Bewley's with the kind of insight into Lee's life and music that I never could otherwise have gained.

'Dillie Keane – you know Dillie Keane?'

'Yeah – *Fascinating Aida*.'

'*Fascinating Aida* – right. She says that cabaret is the art of putting stories together in song.'

Well, that was the Lee show, I think, for sure.

'It must be intimate, regardless of the size of the venue,' Susannah goes on, 'and in that sense I am certainly a cabaret singer, because I like my shows to be always intimate.

'But cabaret has odd connotations in Dublin. It's either all-singing, Irish dancers shows in Jury's Hotel; or the real Weill and Brel and Piaf and Dietrich, that's the real cabaret. And in that respect, I don't do that – not the fishnets and bowler hats. In that sense, I'm a jazz singer, or a bit of a mix.'

I shudder a little at the thought of the big hotel cabarets that Dublin goes in for, and immediately hate myself for my snobbish attitudes. But no, cabaret is an art like any other art; it has its hard, tough and political side too. So maybe more than most, it doesn't bear diluting in hotel function rooms. I say, to take my mind off my spiky thoughts, 'Which jazz musicians have you worked with?'

'Well, Ronan Guilfoyle, of course – he's a heavyweight. Are you planning to meet him?'

'I am,' I nod and go on: 'So – do you think your influences have been mainly American? I mean, Peggy Lee and Minnelli and all.'

She considers. 'Yes. In the sense that there is an old-style glamour about my shows – conventional classical, '40s oldies. I love the old movies, and at the moment I'm working on a lunchtime piece by Dorothy Parker.'

Susannah pauses.

'The cabaret scene in Dublin really struggles,' she says at last. 'It's not like Paris, Berlin, or New York. There are no venues and there is no tradition. It's a fight even to get the space and the publicity – every time.'

So why, I ask, does she think cabaret has such shallow roots? She shrugs.

'We didn't have the writers. In New York, there is a tradition of musicals going back generations – lots of writers and lots of interest. In Paris and Germany, there was the war and Weimar and trauma, but we had a different history – not necessarily less traumatic, just different. So we have to borrow from other cultures. Of course, sometimes, people say that this isn't right, but I definitely think we have the right to borrow and interpret.

'We had the folk songs, of course, and the storytelling, all the richness of oral culture that was then adapted and written down – all of that amazing stuff. Those are our dominant traditions, but we have to borrow cabaret. We never had the experiences that other countries had, but people hear the songs all the time and recognise them instantly, even,' she laughs, 'if it's only from ads. So they are part of our culture now. I remember the people who came to Peggy Lee were amazed at how many of them they already knew without realising it.

'I think that maybe it's the same with classical music in Dublin. The traditions aren't there; it's supported and a few people are passionate about it, but it has never become a mainstream art form. But you know: people love it! They bother to come and then they love it.'

Camille O'Sullivan

SUSANNAH has mentioned Camille O'Sullivan several times in the course of our conversation and I decided I must meet her. I had gone to several of her shows over the years, although not for several years, but I was still conscious of her career as a singer. Not only were her posters all over town several times a year, but she had performed in the Dublin Fringe Festival a few months ago to sell-out crowds and had been the subject of several admiring profiles in the papers. I had a sense that her career was on a cusp.

Actually meeting Camille, however, proved to be inordinately difficult. I rang and left message after message; I emailed her website and managed to get hold of her personal email and tried that too, but all to no avail. Then, when I had given up hope, she called me. She was sorry, she said, she was trying to get her new tour sorted out and it was difficult and time-consuming; she had no manager of her own; she had to do everything herself. Could I meet her next Thursday morning? Then this was postponed too; she had to go to Cork. How about next Monday at 9am sharp?

'Are you sure this suits?' I said, feeling slightly giddy.

'It suits me,' her voice came down the line apologetically. 'I'm really very sorry to have messed you around. It definitely suits.'

That Monday morning at 9am was freezing cold. Another icy front had moved down from the north and more snow had fallen in the mountains overnight. I arrived in the hotel lobby just before nine and made myself presentable, urging my nose to lose its redness before anyone else came into sight. Hailstones pinged off the windows of the building. Outside, the road was full of cars and the footpaths of pedestrians all hurrying to work, but inside there was nobody else about. I sat down and waited, gagging for a cup of coffee.

We had arranged to meet in a hotel on Camden Street, in the south inner city. The area has been renamed the Village Quarter in recent years – a marketing ploy, of course, if ever there was one. It is a coherent district of town in its own right: family butchers still survive here for example, alongside flower sellers and a fruit market, and these now jostle with new delicatessens and Scandinavian furniture shops for attention. Whelan's is hereabouts too and next door is its new sister venue the Village – smooth and cool and upmarket. They, and others like them, keep the strip active after the olive- and tapenade-sellers have shut up shop for the night. It surely needs no renaming strategies to remain coherent and attractive. So I thought anyway, as I sat and watched the hailstones bouncing off bowed heads outside.

Camille appeared shortly after 9am. She was smartly dressed, chic in a long coat and patterned scarf that she unwound and unwound for several minutes. Someone appeared at last to take our order, presumably attracted by the bustle and energy. I ordered coffee thankfully and we both subsided into deep armchairs and began to thaw out.

'I saw you a few days ago.' I have suddenly realised this.

'You did? Where?'

'In the Library Bar at the Central Hotel. I was chatting to someone and you were being interviewed by someone. I thought I recognised you: I was spying on you.'

'Oh yes – were you there? I was being interviewed by the *Sunday Times*.' She laughed. 'There was an article about me in it yesterday.' She grimaced. 'It was good actually, a nice piece, but I'm never sure how these things are going to turn out. The whole publicity thing is always difficult, I think: I find it difficult to gauge, and read it. I can never remember what I said, and it always takes me a day to go and look at it.'

The coffee arrives at last and we both fall on it like wolves. I ask her, a little absentmindedly as I stir my cup, about her background and influences.

'Well, both my parents came from outside Ireland.'

This was no surprise: she looked and dressed and carried herself in a way that signified un-Irish influences in her background.

'My mother is French – which I suppose is why I love Jacques Brel – and my father is an O'Sullivan reared in England. We, my sister and I, were born in London and were brought back to Ireland when we were young. We were brought up in a small place outside Cork. I suppose our upbringing was pretty bohemian: TV was thrown out and we relied on each other for entertainment; we kept ourselves busy. We were trained in ballet and piano so we learned about movement – ' she glanced up from her coffee cup, 'and you know, that is absolutely vital for this kind of work. You have to be aware of your body, and of movement when you are singing other people's songs. If you're a singer-songwriter it's different: it's your own work, you possess it, you can do what you like, but I have to be responsible for other people's words, other people's work. So I'm glad I had those classes and that grounding.

'My parents had a huge collection of music: The Beatles, Deep Purple, Tchaikovsky, Gershwin. Madly eclectic, and we fiddled with the record player all the time, setting out to perform this music in the living room. So I never learned to like or hate certain kinds of music: rock or classical or pop. Nothing like that; that filter never really kicked in for me. So when it comes to cabaret, I'm always anxious about the kind of cabaret I do. I see it as a much larger thing to which you can add

Camille O'Sullivan: The Dark Angel

all kinds of threads and ingredients. It's not simply a 1920s or 1930s phenomenon: it's something to which you can introduce other elements.

'The first time I sang was at school. I sang in *Anything Goes*, and it was amazing. It was Gershwin, and I'd heard Ella Fitzgerald sing it. It seemed to open up something in me and I seemed to have a knack for it. I had never thought about being an actor or singer, so at that point, I did nothing very much about it. Instead, I went off and trained as an architect for six years in Dublin. But I acted in lots of student plays, and worked with Susannah de Wrixon on lots of plays, and it all went from there.'

She took a sip of coffee.

'In those early days, it was all about discovering Dublin and having the city opening up for me. You know how that is?'

I nodded. I remember this too: coming to a city that I hardly knew a thing about and setting out to explore it a little. I remembered walking down to Temple Bar just as the plans were swinging into reality to turn it into a cultural quarter, and feeling perplexed and startled at the run-down nature of the whole district, so close as it was to the city centre. In those days, not so long ago, so many areas of Dublin possessed the kind of slightly seedy and ruinous air that only years of disadvantage can bring. So I nodded. Yes, I said, I understood.

'I remember passing the old Project Theatre in Temple Bar: Agnes Bernelle was singing and I just wandered in. She was just practising at the time, rehearsing, and it was amazing. It was only when I was at the Da Club later that I realised the impact she had had on me.

'The Da Club was an amazing place. There was nowhere else to go at that time: it stayed open until two in the morning and that was amazing for Ireland.'

I laughed. In those days – that recurring phrase once more – the only place you could go late at night was the vomit strip on Leeson Street. On this long, sloping Georgian street which ran south from St Stephen's Green, you could visit any number of basement bars and there buy bottles of sweet plonk at vastly inflated prices. You could only buy bottles of cheap plonk; there was nothing else for sale. And amazingly, lots of people did – chiefly businessmen buying the plonk for girls half their age. When the nightclubs closed, at 3am or so, which was very, very late for Dublin, you would turn for home along Leeson Street across pavements covered with broken bottles and vomit. It was charming.

So, when the Da Club came along, it was truly a breath of fresh air. Not that it was an especially pleasant or sparkling venue: it certainly wasn't. But it possessed a certain atmosphere and provided a critical space that Dublin had sadly lacked. For those reasons, its memory is cherished in the minds of many people in the city.

'I'm sad that it's gone,' Camille said. 'I did a show about Cole Porter and people walked out because it was a show devised around Porter's sexuality; it was shocking for some people. *Curse of a Bad Tune*, it was called. I had to kiss another woman in front of my parents and I was young enough at the time. But I realised then that these songs were too nice: there was a whole different aspect to them!

'Then I did *Jacques Brel is Alive and Well...* – my mother had always discussed these songs with us, so I felt I knew all about them. I did the show for a month, then went to Berlin to work as an architect –' she paused. 'And that trip: it was like it was meant to be. It was 1994 and so Berlin was being ploughed up all around us and stitched back together again; and the whole artistic scene was in a ferment. People always turn to the arts when everything is changing and in flux. They need it more and more, and so art always responds. Berlin was really like a circus then: nights out wouldn't begin until 11pm and would go on all night. I remember a place on the east side of the city filled with half an aeroplane and a sculpture garden, which showed films upstairs. And I was thinking: Dublin?'

'We're not in Kansas any more?'

She laughed. 'Something like that. And German people don't care. They're not like the Irish: they simply don't care about the idea of pleasing you. Irish performers – and I'm as bad as anyone else – are accustomed to the idea of pleasing the audience. But German performers don't care so much and if the audience shouts *Scheisse*. Well, it isn't going to hurt the performer, and at least there's a reaction.'

4

Dublin On Stage

Agnes Bernelle

ANY serious discussion about cabaret in Dublin must make mention of Agnes Bernelle. She was the Rosetta Stone of the city's cabaret scene: it can't be understood or decoded without reference to her. And the more one does refer to her, the more conscious one is of the extraordinary twists of history that brought her to the Dublin scene in the first place.

Agnes was the Berlin-born daughter of a Hungarian Jewish father and a German mother. She left Germany before the outbreak of war to go to school in England and in the end she never went back: her father joined her there for his own safety and her mother, who worked in the Berlin theatre scene, left the city and Germany in the very nick of time – escaping from a restaurant and the SS, rushing to the railway station and fleeing the country for England before she could be arrested and imprisoned or worse. Agnes lived for years in England, helping the Allied war effort and establishing herself as an actress and singer in the austere post-war years. Her one-woman show, *Savagery and Delight*, which was based on the work of Weill and Brecht, toured the world before Agnes moved to her husband's Irish estate at Castle Leslie in County Monaghan, northwest of Dublin. The house is probably best known in these times as the spot where Paul McCartney got hitched; but the estate and family were long-established in the area and had a long history which predates even the McCartney era.

Agnes had already lived a life which was full by any standards, but in 1969 her marriage failed and she moved to Dublin for the second phase of her

As Camille talked about Berlin, I remembered Cormac Breatnach's glowing praise of Berlin: the magnificent venues, the quality of the response, the general wealth and rich texture of the city's artistic scene, and the sense of hunger for this in Dublin and impatience at the fact that cultural expectations here are – not lower, but certainly different. That, of course, was why the Da Club had the impact that it had: because it expected certain standards from its audience as well as from its performers.

In the years since, other venues have come on stream in Dublin. I first went to see Camille sing at the Cobalt Café on North Great career – as a singer and actor on the Dublin stage. It was at this time that she became something of a model for Irish actors hungry for a blast of the cosmopolitan, the new and the different. Agnes obliged, bringing *Mitteleuropa* to a Dublin that was still more than a little provincial and stirring up an often stagnant theatrical scene in the process. She introduced to the city the aesthetic and darkening atmosphere of real cabaret – the music of Berlin and Munich and Weimar Germany.

'I worked with Agnes,' Susannah de Wrixon says. 'I worked on her last show – *Merlin* at the Beckett Centre in Trinity College. It was about King Arthur and I remember that she played a witch who looked into the future. She was an amazing woman – fifteen years before she died, she was given a month to live. They wanted to remove one of her lungs and she refused.

'She was extraordinary in performance – really amazing. She was imperial, in a way – she had that whole German background, that confidence and cosmopolitan aesthetic – and she was a gentlewoman. It wasn't her singing voice that was amazing – it was her whole persona: she could hold an audience like no-one else I have ever seen. Her shows were amazing – so intimate – and she had people like Marc Almond and Tom Waits and Dillie Keane write songs for her.

'She didn't emote at all when she sang it. She was very cold and it worked brilliantly – it's the way it should be. It's so full-on that you really can't emote any more. Ought not to, I should say.

'But she really inspired everyone. Agnes inspired us all.'

4

Dublin On Stage

George's Street on the city's northside. This street is a good example of what can be achieved in Dublin if the will and finances are there. The long sloping row of Georgian townhouses are a classic example of their kind, but had been allowed to rot gradually for years, until in the 1980s, when they were in danger of being condemned and pulled down.

Dublin has always had a difficulty with its Georgian heritage. For many years and especially since independence in 1921, the city's unrivalled stock of Georgian buildings has frequently been neglected or even demolished altogether. The best–worst example of this careless attitude came in the 1960s, when the Electricity

Supply Board decided to bulldoze a whole terrace of townhouses to build a brutal headquarters for itself, close to Merrion Square. At that time, this row of houses formed a section of the longest Georgian terrace in the world, but this cut no ice with the apparatchiks, and in the face of protest, the demolition went ahead. This was the worst, but certainly not the only, example of cultural vandalism in Dublin.

As for North Great George's Street: the whole road has now been restored and become subject to a conservation order. The protection afforded to this street is more the rule than the exception today, but Dublin nonetheless remains careless and ambiguous in its attitudes towards its colonial past.

The Cobalt Café occupies the ground floor of one of North Great George's Street's elegant houses. It is fairly elegant itself and more of a cross between a salon and an art gallery than a regular café. Its beautiful interior space was a music venue in the 19th century too, so there is an agreeable circularity about the fact that it hosts regular concerts and cabaret again today.

Camille said: 'I went back to Berlin a few years ago on a Goethe-Institut grant. I went to the Spiegeltent and it was magical: dark night, and trees lit up with fairy lights. Again, like a circus, or a David Lynch movie: the tent was lined with bevelled mirrors and red velvet. There is such a variety of cabaret in Germany, you know: we

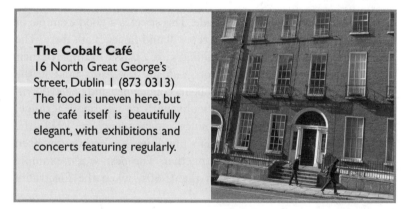

The Cobalt Café
16 North Great George's Street, Dublin 1 (873 0313)
The food is uneven here, but the café itself is beautifully elegant, with exhibitions and concerts featuring regularly.

4

Dublin On Stage

were watching Cora Frost, who is a punk cabaret performer. She was brilliant, fantastic and the audience was all shapes and sizes and ages. Germany and France have such a long tradition of cabaret, whereas the Irish cabaret scene is supposed to be something like Blackpool. That's why the title cabaret sometimes annoys me, because it can mean really anything at all; it signifies so many things to so many people.

'I had been getting into Kurt Weill and had been going to see Agnes in the Da Club and was just blown away. In cabaret, the words are so important. The words are difficult to listen to in the German, because it's so tough and my German friends would say: "I can't listen to this!" but I was fascinated by it.

'I started doing shows in Andrews Lane Theatre and at the Velure Club at the Gaiety Theatre and then did the Brel show in the Da Club; The Nualas were going on at the same time; and all sorts of activity was going on. I think we were lucky to have the Da Club: The Sugar Club and Cobalt Café are great but just not edgy enough! People need to be relaxed with a little drink in unusual surroundings.' She paused again. 'You heard about the Spiegeltent show last year, didn't you?'

I nodded.

'Well,' said Camille, 'that's what I mean. That's why the late shows at the Spiegeltent were so brilliant. You had the music, but you also had these incredible surroundings.' She shakes her head. 'It was magical.

'But back in 1995 and thereabouts, all that was in the future. There weren't so many people doing cabaret of that sort. Agnes Bernelle was the real article. Have you read her autobiography, *The Fun Palace*? When you do, you wonder how it can be all real. People had a notion that singers had to be always young and always pretty, but she held a room transfixed without even moving – she only had to flick her eyes.'

Camille sat forward a little in her seat.

'And honestly, it just clicked with me then. Agnes sang amazingly – but not well. What she did was sing-speak – *Spielsprecht*, they call it – and when she did that, people believed it much more because it was coming from the heart. I found it all very emotional and moving: you could believe that she had really lived that life and had those experiences. She had, up to a point. She would have hung out and met Dietrich and so on, and what was amazing was that she was in Ireland of all places! Elvis Costello and Marc Almond and so on, she was so held in such high respect, but it's only now that people are realising what they had here in Dublin.

'I got to talking to her one night at the Da Club and she was smoking away. It was a mad scene: a Nuala was changing in a corner of this tiny room as we spoke. She just said, "You know, darling, good singing destroys the song: you need to sing and you need to act too." That was all. That was all she needed to tell me.'

As she talked, the theme from *The X Files* comes on in the background. I glanced up; Camille looked around, shook her head.

'But there are some things I would never do. I've sung in restaurants and café bars and so on, and it was soul-destroying: people eating as you sing and ignoring you. It was like performing at a feis and your mother sitting in the front row with her arms folded and ignoring you – really soul-destroying. I would never do it again. There are some things I'm happy to do and some songs I'll happily sing, but you always need to be sustained in some way. The Ella Fitzgerald show, for example, it was good stuff, but I did it for over a year and there was no sustenance left in it for me; I couldn't have done it for much longer. I realised that I needed songs that were more dramatic and angsty.' She leaned back again and said drily: 'Or so I thought, anyway. I've since realised or learned that it's good to relax and enjoy the songs and not perform too much.'

Someone was obviously deciding to try out a full record collection somewhere, because *The X Files* faded and 'Nimrod' from *The Enigma Variations* took their place. We paused and ordered more coffee.

HAILSTONES have been falling on and off for several days, but I have tickets for Camille's show *The Dark Angel* in Whelan's. The *Sunday Times* profile has certainly done no harm. People tell me the gig is more or less sold out. I should make sure I'm there early. I wrap up and go out, my feet crunching on the now-frozen hail. I walk along the canal: the swans are beached on the banks, their heads well tucked under wing; the copper statue of Patrick Kavanagh by the water's edge is silent, as frozen to his bench as the hailstones are to the ground.

I arrive at Whelan's early, but the queue is already going around the building. I join the end of it and stand freezing. A couple slips in just behind me: they are 30-odd and the woman is silent, but her companion is roaring drunk and still carrying a half-full glass of lager. He hardly seems to know what he is queuing to see.

'What kind of line is this? Why don't they provide heatlamps on a night like this?' he laughs raucously and his voice carries embarrassingly; he is Canadian or American. Everyone, including his companions, studiously ignores him. The crowd of people, I notice, are all shapes and sizes: older men and women are waiting patiently. They carry an air of never having been to a gig in Whelan's in their lives.

'This line is so long! This wait is so long!' He takes a swig of beer, but he is right there. The doors ought to have opened at 8pm; it is now 8:20pm and the queue is not moving. Irish concerts, gigs, planes, trains, automobiles, and everything really – they never run to time. I feel a little sympathy for the drunk. My feet are frozen.

But at last the queue moves and before long I am shuffling into Whelan's, startled as I always am at the relatively modest size of the place. There's room for about 400 here – no more. The balcony is already full; the few seats are already occupied. I station myself at the back, where I have a reasonable view of the little stage, get a drink, and wait.

Camille and her band appear on stage at nine o'clock or so. She is clad in a short, tight, black jacket and black trousers and she begins to sing. She doesn't move so much as a muscle: she stands dead still and unmoving on the stage, and allows the words and the slice underneath them to do the work. This continues for two songs, three songs and the crowd is rapt immediately. She is singing in German.

Camille's Favourite Cabaret Numbers

Possibly one of my favourite songs to sing is Jacques Brel's 'Marieke', which is essentially an homage to his Belgian roots. When Brel left Belgium for France, many people in Belgium felt he had abandoned them and had been taken on board as the New French Singer. I like it because it's so emotional and moving and it means so much to different people: some people feel it is a war song, for example, to their lost loved one. But it originally was an homage to Brel's own Flanders land and it's sung in Flemish and English. 'Marieke' is a great song if you're approaching Brel for the first time: it has delicacy but shows a real power behind his work also.

I love Nick Cave – I always have, from way back then. My favourite is 'People Ain't No Good'. This was one he wrote in the mid-90s and it shows how he can write a love song in the most subtle way – no sentimentality but still getting to the core of how sad something can be. He does fantastic things with piano, bass and drums and his voice itself – he just speaks it. His music, Waits' music: they are the contemporary version of Brel's songs; Cave and Waits simply do it in a modern and more simple idiom. That whole Cave album, *The Boatman's Call*, in fact, is a big favourite of mine. And I love Tom Waits too. *The Black Rider* is my favourite album, and of course his albums are like stories in themselves, so I wouldn't single out specific tracks.

Then there's Leonard Cohen. I always loved Cohen: both his own work and the interpretations people have done of his music – and I feel pretty obsessed by his music these days! I recently got hold of *Songs Of Love And Hate* and 'Avalanche' and 'Joan Of Arc' are my current top numbers. He is very wordy and it takes time for his music to stick with you – but then it really does stick.

Going back in time again to Germany, Hollander and Weill…I suppose 'Surabaya Johnny' is my favourite Weill number – but there are lots of others too! And Hollander: he is known for the songs he wrote for Dietrich, but I love 'Liar, Liar' – which I sing in *The Dark Angel*. It was written just before the Weimar cabarets were closed down and was a vision of how Germany could have been – and it has incredible resonances for audiences today too.

As the night goes on, I understand how uncompromising this show is. She has called it *The Dark Angel* and it is indeed black and bleak in its energy, but it is gripping. A Dublin audience is unused to an artist who makes not the slightest effort to curry favour. Even when she switches her costume, even when the lights change to reveal her face caked in thick, dark make-up, even when she begins screaming that she is 'a Vamp!', and the crowd laugh – even then, she holds herself in a lofty manner and her eyes are kept above the crowd at all times. *Scheisse*, she seems to say. If you don't like it, then tough. If you don't like it, then go to hell. Go home.

From my perch at the back, I see once more the sheer variety of the crowd. Men in suits have just come from work, 20-somethings are on a night out, women in their 50s and men in their 60s look like they would prefer a seat, and I would too, but everyone has been caught by the woman on the stage. There are two German women standing on either side of me; and we have been talking in English and in my pidgin German. Camille sings a few bars of 'Lili Marlene' and then switches at once into a heartbreaking rendition of Nick Cave's 'People Ain't No Good'.

> 'Seasons came, Seasons went
> The winter stripped the blossoms bare
> A different tree now lines the streets
> Shaking its fists in the air
> The winter slammed us like a fist
> The windows rattling in the gales
> To which she drew the curtains
> Made out of her wedding veils
> People they ain't no good
> People they ain't no good
> People they ain't no good at all.'

One of my new German friends turns to me and says, 'Her German, you know, is not perfect.' Then she shrugs, and speaks louder as the music suddenly increases in volume too. 'But it makes no difference. She will still be a star.' Her companion nods. Camille sings 'Mack The

4

Dublin On Stage

Knife' brutally; and ends with Hollander's 'Liar, Liar', the song of Germany's degradation. There is no compromise here.

'SOME people say, "Oh, you're doing too much dark stuff", but I think even the darkest music has an edge of euphoria to it. It isn't pitch-black; there is an edge of madness.' Camille sat back in the deep armchair, swinging her foot.

'Nowadays, cabaret in Dublin consists of performers working alone. In the past, Agnes was on her own and we were a group. I performed at Club Absinthe, a sort of club cabaret, at Andrews Lane and we were all – performers, audience – off our heads all the time on the green stuff. It was brilliant, you know, and very courageous. The organisers really looked after the performers too, which is so rare. I wish there was a venue like that now: a living room for the city. I don't mean anywhere pretty or clean, I mean a German thing for movies and music and dancing. I wish someone had the balls to do that now. Everything is so branded nowadays. If they really want the arts opened up, they should have a building like a church that's open all the time, where you can just walk in with a book.

'I went away for a year and decided that I really wanted to do this, so I came back and had my first couple of gigs in the Cobalt Café. I was very excited: collecting the music about Germany, and then about France, and getting into the swing of it again. I used comedy again, with the fishnets and so on; I was just finding my way.

'Now it's different. I realise I can still use the odd prop if I want, but I also realise that I can do less in general – less is more in this whole game. I realise I don't have to move on stage and then the impact is greater. I did a free gig in Bewley's and the organiser said, "Look, you're too dramatic; you need to do less." I was in shock: it was the Irish thing of wanting to please, wanting things to be a certain way.

'I find it easier to reach an emotional fluency when I sing in French or German, and so it's important. The audience need not necessarily understand the language; they can still connect personally, because it's about their own response. I have always imagined that I should feel it myself, but I see now that this isn't so important in performance. I still have to sing-speak and that's all.

'The music changes too. Sometimes you can sing a song for ten years and it's only after that length of time that it comes into focus – and then it shifts out of focus again; it comes and it goes. The performance has changed too: I guested with Damien Rice at Vicar Street and with other people and felt my way onto a bigger stage. I still feel unplaced. People say, "Why don't you write your own songs?" But I'm an actor too: I can speak-sing other people's words; musicians play Tchaikovsky, actors speak Shakespeare, I sing Weill. Weill hated the word cabaret; he called it *Art Speak*. He wanted the stories to be at the same level as the song.

'The Nazis wrote volumes of books about songs and instruments that were banned. In creating *The Dark Angel*, I looked at the songs of that period. "Liar, Liar" looks at Germany as it could have been. They were social songs of the period and that's what I'm interested in now. The cabaret world existed in its own right, to poke fun at the bourgeois world – and it worked. But the other songs – "Falling In Love Again" – they tend to dominate now; they have reached into the popular consciousness. When you hear the original music, though, the ones about burning the Reichstag down, it makes you realise the world of cabaret that was out there, and the variety of writers. Most of them died there; they didn't survive.' She stopped for a moment and then exclaimed: 'And then there is the French stuff, which is so emotional: it's all very schizophrenic!'

I asked her about the future. After all, I thought, there were surely only limited opportunities to be stretched and challenged in a scene as small as Dublin. She shrugged again, frowned, and spoke slowly.

'Well, in fact I do see tremendous scope. I have always loved Bowie, for example, and now I see that Bowie wrote songs like "My Death" from Brel. And Nick Cave and PJ Harvey doing Kurt Weill tracks. I was singing those pieces in the acoustic and they take them and make them contemporary and give them new power.

'I suppose what I'd like is to take my work, shake it up and make it more contemporary. I'm getting a little tired of the cabaret mantle, and also cabaret is getting a little crowded in a small city, a small scene.' She is quite frank, quite blunt. 'There are more performers now and not really enough room for everyone; I don't want to be simply laying a foundation for other people.

'I want to do different things and *The Dark Angel* is part of that. This show, about Weimar, is more experimental; people see the show and realise that that music is still relevant now. You know,' and again she leaned forward, and became more intent, 'it can be just as much about the present war, as it was about the looming catastrophe in the 1930s. People expressed themselves in a certain way in Weimar and then that was stopped. When people hear that music now, they realise that not very much has changed. So you can take the songs out of that context and put it into ours and it still makes sense; it's still about the darker human condition. Certainly *The Dark Angel* isn't a happy show and that makes me a little fearful, but cabaret in Germany has always looked at the darker side and I'd like to push things a little. I'm not so interested in pleasing people. When you think about Cave and Waits: they are storytellers; they probe plays and texts and turn them to music. So I want to hit on the head this idea of the woman on the stage, dressing up and singing. These are men's songs.

'The Spiegeltent was the best venue I have ever performed in. There were three shows: *The Dark Angel*, *Murder Ballads* and the Brel show, and I managed to meet Cave when he was in town. You meet your hero, and it was great to see him, and then you go to the Spiegeltent and the audience is really up for a brilliant night, in this brilliant venue. I wish there was a Spiegeltent permanently in Dublin. Then again, I would love to leave Ireland and go touring with the original Spiegeltent: I've actually written to them to suggest it. There's so much I could do.'

She looked at her watch.

'I really have to go. I have to go to the bank and then I have to rehearse for the Whelan's show.' She smiled, and added serenely: 'I'll be interested to hear what you think of it.'

She went.

4

Dublin On Stage

5

Christchurch Dublin Referential

Sacred And Church Music

PICK UP the *Irish Times* on any given day, leaf idly through its pages and the chances are that your eye will light up on an article about immigration. One of the great debating points in the country today is the place of migrants in Irish society: how many ought to be allowed in, how best to 'absorb' those that are allowed in, and on the wilder and most unsavoury fringes of the argument, whether any should be allowed in at all.

5

Sacred And Church Music

Dublin at Rest: St Francis Xavier Church, Gardiner Street

Twenty years ago, the problem facing Ireland was how to generate jobs for its young people, and how to stop the annual haemorrhage of citizens to Europe and America. At least, this was a pressing issue for families across the land; governments tended to look at emigration as a crucial safety valve which kept a desperate problem from becoming unmanageable. Even ten years ago, the idea of widespread immigration into Ireland would have been seen as utterly fanciful. But in the 1990s, a cursed editor or speechwriter dreamt up the notion of a Celtic Tiger, bounding across Ireland and generating jobs and inward investment with a benign swish of its striped tale. And, so the myth goes, the country has never looked back.

It's certainly true that Ireland has undergone remarkable social and economic changes in the last ten years. New roads and railways and general infrastructure have changed the face of the land and thousands of new jobs have checked the blight of emigration. On the other hand, Ireland remains a desperately unequal society, and you only have to spend five minutes in Dublin to see that fact for yourself.

Nor has Ireland coped particularly well with the corollary of this partial prosperity – immigration. The number of newcomers into the country remains modest in comparison to other European countries, but because this society was comparatively homogeneous for so long, a transition into a genuinely multi-ethnic society was probably always going to be painful; the growing pains loud and anguished. And so it has proved to be.

The idea that the Irish are somehow intrinsically racist – a notion floated occasionally by commentators – is of course nonsense. An entire nation of people can never share a single characteristic, whether it is racism or charm or musical ability, or anything else. And so, if you hear any of the old clichés about all the Irish having a great voice or a gift for the gab, you can instantly dismiss this out of hand as the mad foamings of the tourist industry. But Ireland is certainly having difficulty with its present changes.

This is a sprawling debate and one that will run and run, not least because of the oddities that continue to crop up. For every racist attack, there is a Chinese New Year celebrated with gusto. On the one hand, some of the fringe arguments you see in the media are positively shocking, but on the other, they truly are on the fringe. So this may be a country in a state of flux, but it is very far from being a closed or a tightly regulated one. Again, this can be seen on the streets of Dublin every day, as Ireland opens up and becomes slowly and painfully more cosmopolitan.

The Dublin Gospel Choir

IT IS a wet, dark morning – one of the very worst kinds of morning that Dublin can conjure up. The buses hiss slowly through pools of water lying on the roads and the golf umbrellas compete gleefully to stab pedestrians in the eye. In short, it is the sort of morning that makes me gasp with amazement that anyone would willingly choose to live here. The bus arrives late: it is packed with similarly sodden people and it inches its way through the early morning jams, through the city centre and across the Liffey. At the top of O'Connell Street I get out and splash my way balefully to the top of Gardiner Street.

In the 18th century, this street boasted Dublin's grandest terraces: long sloping perspectives with uninterrupted views of Custom House on the edge of the river. But as the city's centre of gravity shifted south of the Liffey, the great townhouses fell out of favour and by the early 20th century were little more than slums. And worse was to come: most of the properties on the west side of Gardiner Street were demolished and unspeakable apartment blocks – 'mock' Georgian in their lines and plastic windows, with multi-storey car parks below – were built in their place. On the east side, the houses remain: for the most part, they are now bed and breakfasts and backpackers' lodgings. At the top of Gardiner Street is Mountjoy Square. Some of the houses here have been refurbished and repaired, but this once-gracious square too still bears the scars of neglect and vandalism. Nearby is St Francis Xavier Church and close by, the SFX Theatre that is named after the church. I saw *Hamlet* there a few nights previous. Opposite the church's imposing neo-classical portico is my

5

Sacred And Church Music

destination: a large Georgian house. I knock, am admitted, and stand dripping in the hall.

'Cup of tea?' Kevin Kelly says, coming down the stairs.

'Yes, please.' My trousers are sticking to the backs of my legs.

'You look like you could do with one.'

'I HAD to choose whether to be a tyrant with the choir or to have some fun,' Kevin says and leans back in his chair. He is confident, tall, dark and, I think, about 26 or 27 years old. 'I chose the latter and so people have felt from the start that everyone had a certain amount of ownership of the choir. It took a while to settle down: we were all new and the choir was brand-new, so there was a certain lack of confidence.'

The Gardiner Street Gospel Choir is one of the most visible manifestations of the new Ireland. Only a few years old but well established, it has rapidly built up a reputation as a quirky, sexy and young outfit and has been blasted with a good deal of publicity as a result. It's clear enough that the media are hungry for other news about the Catholic Church that doesn't revolve around child sex-abuse scandals and falling numbers of the faithful at Mass; the Gospel Choir fits the bill nicely. But to see it as simply a manifestation of breezy media interest is probably to miss the point. The choir feels to me more like a happy combination of style and substance. And it is affiliated with Sli Eile, a youth group with a strong tradition and strong principles of social justice, which adds an even greater sense of substance to an already purposeful outfit.

'We started off with 8; now we're at 40 and have had to close the membership. We have a waiting list of 100, and loads of media exposure on RTE radio and television and in the *Irish Times*.' Kevin sounds by no means complacent – rather delighted by the interest from both media and potential choristers. 'People in Dublin knew that Gardiner Street church was quite conservative, so they were interested by this development for that reason too.' He pushed the fig rolls towards me in the basement kitchen of the house; behind me, the rain falls louder than ever.

'And what about the choir's genesis? Where did it all begin?' I ask through a mouthful of biscuit.

'Well,' Kevin says, 'I suppose it was my own faith journey. When I was in college, I still played the organ here at Gardiner Street, but I lost a lot of my faith in God. I eventually turned it around and then when I looked around me in the church, I was the only person below the age of 50.'

I can imagine this: for all its imposing grandeur, **St Francis Xavier** stands in the middle of one of the city's most deprived neighbourhoods. Behind the bed and breakfast joints and backpacker hostels of Gardiner Street lie whole neighbourhoods which have been ravaged by drugs, unemployment and official neglect; I can see that local people were probably not bashing down the doors of the church to get inside to pray.

'I wanted to do something about that. So I approached one of the Jesuits in the church and asked him what he thought about the idea of establishing a gospel choir. I knew he wasn't a bit sure if it would work, but he didn't want to stamp on my idea either; so he said yes and I went away and thought about it and decided to go for it.' He smiles ruefully. 'He told me afterwards that he was quite sure it would never work!

'Here's how I decided. I sat down with a Bible and said, "Look, God, if you want me to do this, then give me a sign." So I opened the Bible and it opened at Psalms and I saw Psalm 108:

"I will sing, O Lord, I will sing praises to the nations; awake O harp and lyre, I will awake the dawn; I will sing praises to the nations." Something like that.'

I say, 'So you thought: "Oh God, I have to do it now."'

He laughs. 'More or less. I ran off and started making calls to everyone. I asked everyone:

> **St Francis Xavier Church**
> Gardiner Street
> (836 3411)
> The Dublin Gospel Choir sings here every Sunday at 7:30pm.

people in the street, in shops, in the local area, and about 20 people said they'd come along to the first rehearsal. About 8 people turned up...and then it gradually built up. I was lucky: I had a real community of people to draw on. It began in May 2000 and it eventually took off.'

The conversation meanders away for a while. We start talking about music – what he likes, what I like. Then he says, 'I had always liked music like Radiohead and all the rest of it, but you know, it always seemed to me that it has a negative "O woe is me" side to it, you know? One day, I had picked up a gospel CD in a shop somewhere in town, and it was just so different, so uplifting, so –' and Kevin lifts his arms and waves them about – "Hallelujah!" in its tone, drum and brass and all the rest of it. The other stuff tended to get me down and leave me angsty. Of course, sometimes it's cathartic, but sometimes you're stuck in a cycle too. You have to get a balance.

'So I began listening to gospel a little more...and more and more: Beverley Crawford, Kirk Franklin, and Mary Mary. Even *The Preacher's Wife* and *Sister Act*...'

'*Sister Act*?'

'Yeah.'

'Maggie Smith,' I say appreciatively. *Sister Act* was on television a few nights ago. Kevin looks puzzled.

'Maggie Smith?'

'Yeah, she plays the Mother Superior,' I tell him, feeling fairly superior myself. My grasp on popular culture is as firm as ever. There is a silence and then Kevin says, 'No: I mean the film *Sister Act* – with Whoopi Goldberg.'

'That's right,' I say and this time think fondly about Whoopi Goldberg's star turn in *Star Trek: The Next Generation*. 'Maggie Smith plays the Mother Superior.' I pause, then: 'You mightn't recognise her, with the habit and all.'

'Oh. No – obviously not.' He says nothing for a moment. Perhaps he is reassessing the film in his mind; perhaps he thinks I'm a liar. 'Anyway,' he goes on, 'it's so difficult to get gospel music written down: it's mainly oral – learnt orally – except for music that has appeared in films and so on. So it was a real mountain of work. I arranged four songs to begin with. I was scouting around all the time, looking for appropriate songs, songs with a spiritual dimension.'

'And what did you come up with?'

'Well, we started with Sting, "Let Your Soul Be Your Pilot", then "Lean On Me" by Bill Withers. A gospel choir sings on Sting's original song; but Withers' song is only loosely gospel. But what I realised was that so many songs have spiritual lyrics. Then the third song we did was really obscure: "My Help" by a gospel musician in America; nobody over here would know it. And at the end we did Whitney Houston, "My Love Is Your Love".'

'Oh!' I say and feel startled. A memory of an '80s Whitney Houston album I once owned forces its way into my mind. Whitney was wearing a white vest and was apparently dancing. I repress the memory with a little difficulty and much more shame. 'Oh yes.'

'Well, it's explicitly faith-based, I think, but pretty loose too. Pap really –'

'Pap,' I agree. 'Yes.'

'But that's what we started off with. Then we finished with "I Can See Clearly Now The Rain Has Gone". Of course we changed it.'

He breaks into a rendition in a fine, confident tenor.

'Lord, look all around there's nothing but blue skies
Lord, look straight ahead nothing but blue skies...'

Then he looks at me and grins. 'See?'

I smile, and nod.

'Then,' he goes on, 'on the second Sunday, we sang a Van Morrison number: "Whenever God Shines His Light". There are two faith-based songs on his *Greatest Hits* – did you know that?'

'No,' I say and suddenly *Sister Act* seems a long time ago.

'Yeah,' he goes on. 'That and "Full-Force Gale", which he sings with Cliff Richard.'

I think: Oh God. I don't say it aloud, but I might as well have done, because Kevin says hastily, 'No, I'm not a fan of Cliff either, but he makes a good job of that. When I read the lyrics though, I

Top Venues for Choral and Sacred Music in Dublin

There is no shortage of excellent choral and sacred music in the city. The three cathedrals act as centres of excellence: all three boast exquisite choirs and these main venues are supplemented by additional activity across the city.

St Patrick's (map: 10) is the older of the two Anglican cathedrals; and it and **Christchurch (map: 9)** both feature Sunday sung Eucharist and Evensong, as well as a steady diet of special concerts for Christmas, Easter and other festivals. St Patrick's offers a sung Sunday service at 11:15 and Evensong at 5:45pm from Monday to Friday (3:15pm on Sunday). offers a sung Sunday service at 11am and Evensong at 3:30pm.

The Palestrina Choir sings at **St Mary's Pro-Cathedral (map: 20)** each Sunday at 11am, as part of the Latin Mass. The Dublin Gospel Choir sings each Sunday at **St Francis Xavier Church (map: 23)**, Gardiner Street, at 7:30pm; and elegant **St Ann's Church (map: 15)** at 18 Dawson Street holds regular lunchtime recitals.

St Patrick's Cathedral, Patrick's Close (475 4817)

Cathedral, Christchurch Place (677 8099)

St Mary's Pro-Cathedral, Cathedral Street (874 5441)

St Francis Xavier Church, Gardiner Street (836 3411)

St Ann's Church, 18 Dawson Street (676 7727)

could hardly believe it. Of course,' he adds, 'we always go for music that'll suit the band. We have a brilliant ten-person band. Brilliant sound, so that's a real blessing. Bass, bongo, all sorts.

'The choir is pretty mixed: we draw a membership with all sorts of people. We're affiliated to the Jesuits and to Sli Eile and are interested in social justice – that's a basic thing. But we take the membership of the choir strictly on the membership list and who's top of it. So the people are all sorts: well-off, working class, emigrants, one from Nigeria and one from Burundi, all sorts really, a cross-section, which isn't a bad thing.'

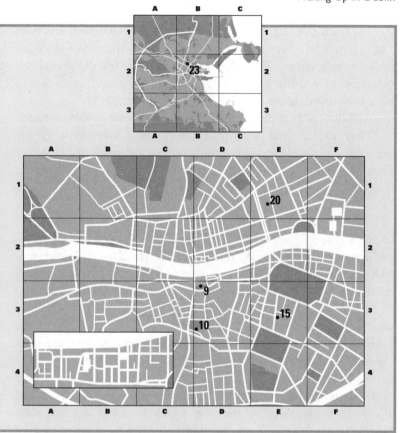

'And you sing as well as conduct?'

'I do. If you asked me to talk to a huge crowd, I'd be afraid, but I love singing and conducting in front of a big crowd. And I suppose it's also explicitly spiritual: singing and conducting to God.'

'Why is the media so interested?' I ask. 'Why do you think it has become so popular?'

'I think there are several sides. The first is that this needed to happen to the Church in Dublin. It was meant to happen: people needed to get involved. When people are moving away from faith, it's interesting that this should come along.

'But from a critical point of view: it's quirky, different, and new. The Church has been so criticised in Ireland that the media are probably relieved to pick up on lighter stuff too. It's also an explicit reflection of a more cosmopolitan Ireland. A gospel choir would have been unthinkable in Ireland 20 or 10 years ago.'

'And how did the older generation react? To the gospel element?'

'They didn't react against it,' he smiles, 'like some people expected. They were crying out for people to get involved – Gardiner Street was dying and this is literally an answer to prayer. So they are delighted.'

I KNEW that the Gospel Mass took place at 7:30pm on Sunday nights and I also knew I had to be there early. 'Be there ten minutes before Mass begins, if you want to get a seat.' This was such an unusual instruction to receive that I took heed of it; and was there punctually.

St Francis Xavier may be externally imposing, but inside it is positively monumental, and an expression of the authority of the Catholic Church in Ireland at the height of its power. Its lavish neo-classical decoration would not be to everyone's taste – but with its lofty dome and gilded ceiling it is certainly impressive. I had only ever been in the church during the daytime and when it was empty; and it had always been impressed on me how a church of this size and scale absolutely must be full of worshippers. Otherwise, it would be desolate. Certainly it was designed with the intention of being always full; and it must have been a wretched business for priest and congregation to watch attendance at Mass slide away year by year until the church and its parish were both dying on their feet. So I could see what Kevin meant when he called the Gospel Mass an answer to prayer.

When the Gospel Choir was first formed, the congregation had dwindled so much that Kevin and the organisers felt obliged to rope off the pews at the back of the church: by doing this, the congregation would feel obliged to sit close to altar and choir. When I arrived, I reflected that there was certainly no need to rope off any pews any longer: the church was quite crowded, and by the time Mass began, it was absolutely full.

A leaflet had been handed to me as I came in. 'Welcome to the gig at God's Gaff!' it said on the front, while on the back was the mock-up of the 'This Page Cannot be Displayed' page from Internet Explorer. Friends had sent it to me already by email, but I read it again as the church slowly filled around me.

'These Weapons of Mass Destruction cannot be displayed.

The weapons you are looking for are currently unavailable. The country might be experiencing technical difficulties or you may need to adjust your weapons inspectors' mandate. Please try the following...'

The organisers wore their affiliations on their sleeve anyway, I thought, and sat back in satisfaction.

The choir appeared at the altar and warmed us up with Sting. Its members were nearly all white and even though I knew that this would be the case, it was still surprising to me to watch them belting out the gospel music, and swaying to gospel rhythms. I thought that it all seemed distinctly, exuberantly, and profoundly un-Irish – and I was surprised at the depth of my cultural conditioning – for why should people not be exuberant at Mass? No reason, of course, except that they never were. Then again, I was clearly not the only one to feel a little out of place. Some of the congregation were singing, but others seemed happy merely to listen, which is the usual way in Irish Catholic churches. It is virtually impossible to get congregations to sing out – for whatever reason. I asked people about this in the days to come and they came up with all manner of theories: it was just an Irish Catholic thing; Irish people are pathologically self-conscious; it was all due to their/our potty training – the list went on.

By the time the choir had got to 'Something Inside So Strong', I had thawed a little; I even joined in, thinly and reedily at first, then with a little more confidence. At the altar, Kevin alternated between conducting his choir and conducting the congregation: he would turn around from time to time and exhort the people, with authoritative

5

Sacred And Church Music

gesticulations, to sing up. After the sermon, we were all given out little pieces of paper and pens and asked to write down three things that would help make our lives better. Again, my inhibitions got the better of me: I wrote nothing. And by the time the choir finished the Mass with a blast of Van Morrison, and I had left the church for the freezing night outside, I had realised with a series of little jolts that I was a good deal more inhibited than I had ever suspected...

'THE IDEA of authenticity: there isn't really such a thing and that's why gospel music is as relevant here as in, say, Chicago.'

The packet of fig rolls is nearly empty and Kevin and I are chewing the fat about the place of gospel music in Ireland. Some people have been surprised at the whole enterprise, he tells me and shrugs.

'Some people laugh at the idea of gospel music in Ireland, and say it isn't authentic, but it's as relevant here as in Chicago or Memphis. John Cusack came from Chicago, you know, and gave a sermon here. Of course, it's not on the same scale as it would be in south Chicago, but it works well here too. Music responds to local conditions. You can listen to jazz as well here and respond to it here as well as sitting in New York.

'What does authentic mean anyway?' I say.

'Doesn't mean anything.' He nods.

'And what about getting the congregation to sing? How has it worked?'

'I like to think they sing more than they do in other churches. Correction: they do sing more and we make it so they feel comfortable about it. We devised a section of the Mass where the soloist sings and the congregation is expected to respond. And they do more or less respond – more people sing than don't. But we have a transient section of the congregation too each week – people who are just curious and who won't necessarily join in. And we do things like introducing the Mass, to get people more relaxed.'

'And the whole self-conscious thing?'

'Well, I agree: Irish people are very self-conscious – very conscious of the people beside them and more lacking in self-confidence. By and large, it comes with practice – even in the choir. At the beginning, people in the choir didn't want to sing solos, but now there are some Sundays where I don't sing at all! Which of course,' he says with a note of regret, 'is the way it should be.'

The Palestrina Choir

THE PREVIOUS night, I had stayed at Dublin's most über-posh hotel. The Packenham Suite at the Merrion Hotel was the size of a football field and had everything a wealthy person could require. The platters of strawberries and pastries laid out in my suite as welcoming gifts were satisfactory; and so too was the swim and sauna in the marble pool; dinner in the Cellar restaurant; and hot chocolate served in a silver pot by a besuited servant. My bed was vast – I couldn't see from one side to the other.

Not that I am a wealthy person, of course. I was reviewing the hotel for a guidebook. But I certainly felt wealthy, if only for the night.

This dripping luxury made me want to live there for ever and ever – as people do: the hotel lets its penthouse by the year to anyone who is interested and rich enough. And certainly the thought of leaving made me quail. But leave I did: out of the heavy doors and down the steps and onto Merrion Square. It was a heartbreaking moment, especially as the chilly January day did not exactly welcome me. I squared my shoulders and screwed my courage to the sticking place, and headed off in the direction of the river and of the Pro-Cathedral, to talk about the Palestrina, the city's most famous choir. There is a long and vigorous tradition of sacred music in the city and I wanted to listen to some of its prime exponents for myself.

It is one of the many curiosities of Dublin's history that while the city has no Catholic cathedral, it possesses two Protestant ones within a few hundred yards of one another, both founded close on a thousand years ago. **Christchurch** sits on its high ground above the

5

Sacred And Church Music

Liffey, its chunky square tower and flying buttresses visible from across the city. Christchurch was the principal church within the medieval walled city; it has traditionally been the wealthier of the two churches and possessed of a greater degree of social prestige. St Patrick's is older: originally it lay outside the city walls and lower down on the hill, at first sight seems less impressive. In fact, it is a much more grand and interesting structure and has the more interesting historical associations too: Jonathan Swift preached here as Dean between 1713 and 1745, for example, and his tomb lies near the church entrance.

I remember his notions on how to ease the calamitous situation of Ireland's poverty-stricken peasants. In *A Modest Proposal* (1729), he sought to draw attention to the fact that English attentions to Ireland were bleeding the country dry, by proposing a cull of the children of the poor. Eat them, he said, thus in a stroke they would be put out of their misery, and at the same time, their parents would be assured of a good healthy meal. Everyone would be happy:

'I have been assured by a very knowing American of my Acquaintance in London, that a young healthy Child, well nursed, at a Year old, is a most delicious, nourishing and wholesome Food, whether Stewed, Roasted, Baked or Boiled; and I make no doubt, that it will equally serve in a Fricasie or Ragout (...) A Child will make two Dishes at an entertainment for friends; and when the Family dines alone, the fore or aft Quarter will make a reasonable

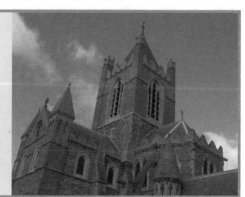

Christchurch Cathedral
Christchurch Place (677 8099)
Christchurch bells ring each Sunday from 10am; the choir sings each Sunday at 11am service.

5

Sacred And Church Music

Dish; and seasoned with a little Pepper or Salt, will be good boiled on the fourth day, especially in Winter.'

'Here he lies,' the inscription on Swift's tomb reads, 'where savage indignation can no longer lacerate his heart.' And since he was something of a savage lacerator himself, the inscription is nicely fitting.

Dublin's Catholic **Pro-Cathedral**, by contrast, lies tucked away off O'Connell Street. Pro-Cathedral is an abbreviation of Provisional Cathedral, implying that the main or permanent cathedral has not yet been built. Tiring of years of trying to tug either or St Patrick's back from the Anglicans, the Catholic Church in Ireland spent most of the 20th century drawing up elaborate plans to desecrate Merrion Square's architectural harmony by constructing a vast cathedral in the park in its centre. The new church, appropriately enough, would have faced government buildings, and so the new Irish state's reputation as a theocracy in all but name would have been well and truly sealed. That the plan never came to fruition is remarkable, although it is probably more remarkable that it was ever contemplated in the first place. Finally, in the 1970s, the plans were abandoned and instead, the park was leased, as a park, to the city.

On the morning I arrived at the Pro-Cathedral, the church doors were open and there was a scattering of people in the pews. I was early for my appointment in the presbytery next door, so I wandered around the building. As it happens, St Mary's Pro-Cathedral is an

5

Sacred And Church Music

St Mary's Pro-Cathedral
Cathedral Street
(874 5441)
The city's principal Catholic Church. The Palestrina Choir sings each Sunday at 11am.

impressive church in its own right, albeit built on an unimpressive site. Designed in Greek classical style and consecrated in 1825, it is decorated internally with mosaic, and a splendid central dome combines with high windows to flood the space with clear light. The tabernacle, set in the wall behind the altar, is made of crystallised ginger – well, it isn't really but it certainly looks as though it is – and close beside it is the memorial to John Charles McQuaid, the Archbishop of Dublin for some four decades from 1940. McQuaid wielded enormous power in the Irish Church and State in the 20th century: his relationship with the government was close and intricate – not to say deeply unhealthy – and in any study of Ireland's stifling and claustrophobic post-Independence history, McQuaid's name looms large.

I studied the inscription –

'By the Intercession of his Patroness Mary the Mother of God
May his Divine Master Grant him the Reward
Of a Life of Devoted Service to the Church.'

– and moved on.

As I left, a tough-looking little boy came pushing up the stone steps, brushing past the people entering and leaving. Everyone instinctively held their bags more tightly, and checked their pockets. I watched as the boy made the rounds of the cathedral, as worshippers kneeling in the pews grabbed their bags and coats; around me, the people tutted and sighed.

A little later, Pat O'Donoghue showed me into the presbytery's dining room. It was hushed and the heavy wallpaper and thick carpets seemed to soak up sound like sponges. Pat is the Director of Music in the Diocese of Dublin.

'The Palestrina Choir was established in 1903,' he told me. 'You know the name of Edward Martyn?'

I nod. Martyn was one of the prime movers behind the foundation of the Irish Literary Theatre, which became the Abbey. I hadn't known his association with the Pro-Cathedral.

'Martyn had a great interest in music and the liturgy: he had travelled widely in Europe and wanted the same standards applied in Ireland. He was part of the Cecilian movement who felt things had slipped and was looking back to an earlier period, to plainchant and sacred choral music. It was a back-to-basics movement, you might call it, as they understood basics.

'Martyn heard a choir in Clarendon Street in the city and he essentially poached them and established them as the cathedral choir.'

'Which must have gone down well.'

'Indeed,' he replied drily. 'His funding of the choir stipulated that its membership should consist of men and boys and that all of its music should predate 1600. Some of his ideas have been changed through the years, but the choir still consists only of men and boys. At the moment we have 26 boys and 14 men, which is more or less an optimum number.'

Martyn, I discover later, was zealous in his plans for the new choir. He had no doubt about the reasons why the quality of music in Dublin's churches was so generally appalling:

> i. the laziness of our Catholic musicians; ii. the want of knowledge and taste on the part of the clergy; and iii. the unpardonable laxity which, among a large Catholic population, permits such an unecclesiastic and unaesthetic custom to prevail as the singing of women in choir.

Martyn's bracing comments provoked a good measure of controversy at the time. But today, membership of the choir remains restricted to men and boys only.

'The membership of the choir is drawn from all over the city,' said Pat. 'It's a heavy responsibility – a great deal of time is involved. And unfortunately, there are very, very few boys from the inner city. We try, and last year we recruited one boy with a stunning voice. But he is the only one, which is a great pity.'

Pat went on to outline just how heavy a responsibility it actually was for the boys in the choir. Two hours on a Wednesday, three or four on a Friday and then Sunday Mass.

'I see.'

5

Sacred And Church Music

Pat nodded. 'And with traffic the way it is now, it really is very difficult indeed.'

The choir, he went on, now has a broad repertoire.

'A good deal of plainchant and Renaissance music, and a classic Mass once a month, Mozart or Haydn, with a classic Mass at Christmas and Easter, and Fauré or Duruflé in November. In the centenary year, we commissioned contemporary pieces from local composers. And of course they undertake tours in Ireland and occasionally abroad. We're planning a trip to Vienna, Bratislava and Krakow later in the year – if we can get the sponsorship. It could be a very exciting trip.'

What about ecumenical traditions, I asked. Are there such customs?

'Oh yes. We sing with the Church of Ireland choirs too. We're planning an ecumenical St Patrick's Day celebration: we will go to St Patrick's for Evensong and our coadjutor Archbishop will preach there.'

He paused and then said, 'But you know, in a sense, the choir is only one mass on a Sunday. It is prestigious to have a choir of that calibre in the diocese, of course it is, but there is a good deal of other music going on in the cathedral too, which we can never neglect.

'It is hard work. You have to do a lot of work in encouraging other people; there are continual efforts being undertaken to get people involved in music. I think melodic music, accessible music helps; and I think that Irish music helps too: I think that what is Irish in us is stirred by our own music and people do respond to that, whether by clapping or moving to music in a way that they wouldn't normally do. So on big occasions, the choir comes in and out and helps without grandstanding. You have to use it wisely.

'And you have to reach out as much as possible. At the moment, we're working on a multicultural celebration of St Patrick's Day up in City Hall."

'Oh yes?'

'We're bringing together Congolese, Filipinos, Ugandans, Nigerians, Irish and Brazilians – all together, all doing something and all coming together at the end, so that we're not all broken down into our little sets. We want to embrace as many people as we can; and I have many threads for which I'm responsible and which I have to keep an eye on at all times. And we've designed a card too, a tasteful and spiritual St Patrick's card, which feeds into the sense that this is a genuine festival, not some Paddywhackery. And so people coming to Dublin will see this aspect of the festival too and come along. That's the plan.'

Later, I went to the Latin Mass at which the Palestrina traditionally sings. I had never heard the Mass sung in Latin before and went with my mind full of pre-Vatican II services in which a remote priest would stand with his back to the congregation. But the church was full and the morning bright: the sun shone through the high windows, across the floor of the church and onto the twinkling crystallised ginger of the tabernacle. The choir sang in the gallery, first in English and then Latin, and the sound rose into the domed roof. The effect was spectacular.

The Christchurch Bells

ON A calm, frosty evening, I arrive at Queen of Tarts. The sun is setting and the café is winding down for the evening. The lights of City Hall glisten opposite: the chandeliers of its great atrium are fully lit and from the street I can see the beautiful vaulted ceiling. The building was opened after expensive restoration only a few years ago and as I look, I reflect that Pat O'Donoghue was wise in his decision-making: his multi-ethnic St Patrick's celebration can hardly be anything but a success in such a space. I go in, order coffee, but no cakes, and read the paper quietly until Leslie Taylor arrives.

Leslie is the Ringing Master at ; and I was introduced to him by the Queens of Tarts: both he and I are regulars in the café. I was intrigued when they suggested I meet him: I knew a little about the great bells of the cathedral but not very much. The Hothouse Flowers had their song 'Christchurch Bells', of course, but maybe that was less than relevant. All I was really conscious of was the place

Foodie Dublin

If, like me, you are an intrinsically greedy person, 'engaging' with a newly cosmopolitan Dublin tends to mean one thing: shopping for food, cooking food, devouring food like a maniac. Browsing through the vastly greater choice of new food on offer and then lugging it home in large shopping bags – these are the new pleasures of Dublin life. Ten years ago, even five years ago, the choice for consumers was still pretty limited: even good delis were still fairly difficult to come by,

Delicacies at the Queen of Tarts

except in well-heeled south Dublin suburbs. Middle-eastern and African food shops were non-existent. If you wanted a certain spice – tough luck. Well, it ain't like that today.

In the last few years, a genuine foodie culture has grown up in Dublin. Ireland, of course, always produced exceptional food – not surprising in a country where agriculture remains the economic driving force. But in the city today, you can stop off at specialist Irish cheesemongers to buy all your heart's desire, before heading to any number of little Italian delis to stock up on olives, salami and olive oils. Up on Thomas Street, amid the clattering of the street markets selling pyramids of cheap toilet rolls, a shop has opened selling Bosnian food; while the Russians have grocery stores amid the fruit markets of Moore Street. You can check out the stalls at the open-air food market in Meeting House Square. Or, if you're like me, you can round off a satisfying Saturday morning of hunting and gathering in the Middle Eastern shops along the Grand Canal at Portobello.

I still feel mildly perplexed each time I go to Spiceland. The familiar confines of a Spar are behind me as I survey the boxes and boxes of vegetables utterly unfamiliar to me. I see papery red onions and bursting, purple-veined garlic; I see glossily tight-skinned baby aubergines, handfuls of dusty string beans. There are little cucumbers sold whole, rather than monstrous half-cucumbers cut in half, encased in plastic and sold in the supermarkets; and there are chilli peppers in shades of green and scarlet and vanilla. But I also see great pale green globes that might be melons but clearly aren't; and other pale green things too – long and bulbous and rigid that I wouldn't have a clue how to cook. Ought they to be cooked at all? I made a mistake here a few weeks ago: I bought long, pointed shiny red peppers to bring home and roast. I thought they would be the same as, and much cheaper than, the chastely wrapped 'extra sweet' peppers that Marks and Spencer sells in its gleaming food halls. I discovered my mistake when my eyes began to water, my tongue to scar and my nose to run.

Inside the shop, the list of oddities goes on. The *Guardian* a few weeks ago featured a page of recipes involving pomegranate juice and syrup, which I carefully cut out, knowing that pomegranates regularly crop up in boxes outside Spiceland. Inside, there are little bottles of pomegranate molasses and they glint at me invitingly. My hand hovers: should I snatch and carry the bottle home? Or should I drift on towards the feta, filled with disdain? Once more, I haven't a clue: after all, in Lebanon, pomegranate molasses might be a local version of the ultimate junk. It might be their equivalent of a chicken burger or a bottle of Coca-Cola. I glance at the bottles of rosewater with the same feelings of confusion; then I sigh and walk on. It wouldn't do to be unfashionable, after all. Instead I play it safe and buy some haloumi cheese. I decide that what I really need is a personal shopper.

Spiceland is a chaotic sort of place: you help yourself (or stand in silent confusion). East, just up the road, is a little more designer-ish. It has a few tables, if you fancy a coffee; and on sunny days, a few more are placed under the crimson awnings outside – more in hope than expectation, since the buses belch past just a few feet away. I can shop for groceries here or just put together a platter of hummus and dolmades, or flatbread stuffed with felafel, and fancy myself in a souk in Damascus. It's a pleasant fancy, until I go outside again and the chilly, damp air slaps me in the face, pulls me up short and teaches me to keep my feet on the ground and my imaginings in check. The Irish weather is a great leveller.

Spiceland
4 South Richmond Street (475 0422); East, 22A S. Richmond Street (475 7066)

the bells held in the life of the city, and their significance at New Year in particular. On New Year's Eve, crowds gather in the street before the cathedral and at midnight, the church releases its thunder. It has long been a sacred tradition of the city, though exactly how long, nobody seems to know. And as for the art of campanology – well, I realised I knew precisely nothing about that.

Leslie comes in and greets me. He orders coffee too and Kugelhopf, and we talk. I feel a little conscious of my extreme ignorance: I hardly even know what questions to ask, and so I decide to begin with a few simple ones. How, for instance, did he come to the bells?

'I came to them from childhood,' he says. 'What drew me to them was the feeling of history and the sense of place – their sense of presence in the history of Dublin. Do you know what I mean?'

I do, I say: the sense that they have always been there, stitched into the life of the city. He smiles.

'Yes. Exactly. For all of the ringers, I think, it is a strange instrument, and unique too. It is so much public music: we ring for the city; the music is thrown out into the city, thrown out to everyone as they go past. It provides an atmosphere for the city.' He finishes off his Kugelhopf and then says, 'I like to think of it as a signature or musical background. It is quite romantic, you know, you could really wax lyrical about it. I think that it enters people's souls.' He sits back, perhaps a little embarrassed of speaking so passionately about the bells, but there is no need for any embarrassment. I know exactly what he means.

'And how long has the New Year tradition been going?' I ask, hoping for a clear answer on this point at last.

'Well, New Year we're not sure about,' he says, disappointing me, 'but certainly as long as I've been around – and I think at least a hundred years. People expect us to ring at New Year and there would be outrage if we didn't.

'The bells have been ringing since the Middle Ages, when the cathedral was founded and the bells mounted. The great bell at always struck the curfew and rang the Angelus too. After the Reformation, there was no more Angelus, of course, but the bells kept both a civil and sacred relevance by both striking the hours and ringing for prayer.

'The Corporation for a long time paid for the upkeep of the bells, which shows their civic importance. In 1670, an agreement was reached that the Corporation would assist in the increase of the number of bells. So six new bells were cast and the Society of Ringers was formed – which is us – and they had both a civic and a religious importance.

'There was the odd political upheaval that the society was dragged into. In 1688, the Lord Mayor took it into his head that the birth of the new Prince of Wales hadn't been celebrated cheerily enough by the bellringers; and he sent guards up to the cathedral and blamed the religious authorities. He didn't realise we were a secular body; he put the verger into the stocks!'

'1688: well, that was a bit of a fraught time,' I say, thinking about the Williamite Wars and the Siege of Derry and all the rest of it.

'Well, quite, fraught everywhere and at too.'

'And so you began...' I say absentmindedly and glance at the cakes ranged behind the counter. I should have ordered one.

'I began when I was 13. I'm 52 now and I've been Ringing Master for 15 years or so. So a lifetime, you might say.'

 has 19 bells – the greatest number of any church, anywhere. I am startled when Leslie tells me this: I had no idea that the cathedral held any world record at all.

'Oh yes,' he says, looking pleased. 'Since the Millennium, we have had the greatest number of bells in the world. The Millennium Committee gave us a grant, the cathedral covered the rest and we had five additional bells cast, which brought us up to 19.' His smile broadens. 'So we can be obnoxiously Texan in our attitudes – for the moment anyway. The cathedral in Perth, Western Australia, has 18 and so we can't exactly rest on our laurels.

'The sheer number of bells means we can make certain music. When we ring 19, it produces a noise: we add semitones to produce a noise that some people say is like the wail of a banshee. It certainly sounds strange and a little chilling. Some of the ringers love it, some ringers loathe it; it's certainly unusual.

'But it's difficult to ring all 19 at once. Usually, we ring 16 on special occasions. It's a difficult art in general – not easy at all. We used to ring 12 bells in the morning, 8 in the afternoon for Evensong, but now we ring more and more when we can.' I can see what he means about being Texan in his attitude: there must be a great temptation to be the greatest and loudest; and I admire his sense of style.

'Ringing is an entirely mathematical art,' Leslie goes on. 'All ringers must be good enough, but of course this means we must always ring to the lowest common denominator. The rhythm is static: we have no different length of note and we have a set speed. That's the way it must be. Each row of notes – or sounds – changes each time, so there is a multitude of variations. One mistake and the whole row fails. You understand?'

I think so, I say; I have blenched slightly at the sudden leap into the mathematical, which has never been my favourite topic of conversation. A memory lurches unbidden into my mind: of my claiming in a maths class long ago that 16 times 5 is 60; of my maths teacher rushing down the aisle and standing over my desk and screaming at me. My concentration once more snaps and I grasp in distraction at the loose threads of the conversation.

'The composition of the music is based upon a mathematic criteria,' Leslie continues inexorably, 'not a musical criteria. There is a concept of truthfulness about it, in fact: a particular number of changes is wrong. There's no room for flexibility.'

Then he suddenly relents and says, 'All it means is this: look.'

He pulls out a diary. I peep at it. On the cover it says Bellringers' Diary.

'Have a look.' I open the book and see pages and pages of long rows of numbers, with oscillating lines running through them.

'Oh,' I say.

'All it means is this: the rows of numbers stand for a row of bells rung in a different order – that's all it means.'

'So – there is a – a canon of ringing?'

'Yes,' he says and I smile with relief and the maths class begins to diminish in my mind. 'An enormous one. The representation in the diary is just the tip of the iceberg – the canon grows all the time. One of our own ringers has actually just composed an addition – of course, it has to be tested rigorously before it can be used. You see,

A Bluffer's Guide to Bellringing

The bells are heavy – that's the first fact to remember. They range from a quarter of a tonne to two and a quarter tonnes in weight. The music composed since around 1650 has developed to accommodate this fact, this situation.

The second fact to remember is that each bell is equipped with a complete wheel, and for every sounding heard, the bell has been swung full-circle. This means, first of all, that the music is performed to a constant beat and the notes are heard in varying orders in swift succession because of course the individual ringers cannot hold a bell steady and unstruck for longer than a few seconds before striking again. This is the music of the changes, since the art as performed in and elsewhere has been composed mathematically.

Bellringing has its own language and some of its terms have entered common usage.

Ringing the changes: Varying the order in which the bells are struck according to a pattern known to all the participants.

Method-ringing: Method is the equivalent of tune in other music. It is a series of predictable changes rung rhythmically.

Grandsire, **Plain Bob**, and **Stedman Principle**: Three examples from an enormous range of 'methods' in the repertoire of change-ringers.

A ring of bells: This is the collective term for a set of bells equipped to ring full-circle. Cathedral, with 19 bells, has the greatest number for such ringing in the world.

A peal: This has a limited meaning for ringers. It means the ringing of non-repeating 5040 changes, and can take as long as four and a half hours.

5

Sacred And Church Music

it has to be true, mathematically perfect. So we studied it and rang it and tested it and when it was confirmed, the composer named it "Christchurch Dublin Referential". We notice the uniqueness of it, but I'm not sure a layperson would exactly notice.

'As you can imagine,' Leslie goes on calmly, 'the number of changes that are possible in bellringing is not quite infinitesimal but is almost infinitesimal – certainly it's prodigiously long.'

'It's like trying to fill an enormous space?' I say. 'I suppose it must be like this – and the canon as it exists now only fills a small part of it. Would that be right?'

'Yes – exactly. And we can only ring so much – over a certain amount is simply an impossibility. So much rides on one ringer. It's not unlike an orchestra in that sense: one mistake can cause disaster, although equally a mistake can be retrieved. There is a human element to the whole thing, so mistakes are inevitable.'

'So what kind of a tradition does have? I mean, are you quite a traditional order?'

'Yes, we are,' Leslie says firmly. ' is very regimented and strict in its attitudes. Other bells, other churches, are more loose – the carillon bells in America, for example, and also at the cathedral in Cobh, near Cork – they ring melodies. And these have their place. But we never ring tunes – I suppose in that sense we are more scientific. We're certainly on the traditional wing. We inherited these traditions and we take pleasure in the uniqueness of them.

'I put together a group from scratch; most are novices but after three years, it's all coming together well. It's a huge task and difficult too, but hugely satisfying. It's extraordinary to see people develop and blossom in their skills. They begin with faltering steps but they blossom and develop an amazing sense of rhythm; and that's satisfying too. There's no question of a plateau: we sometimes pat ourselves on the back but we also have so much to do to be better and to challenge our brains, to strive to be perfect.' He laughs. 'It's like a straitjacket, I suppose, but a wholly satisfactory one.

'It's my ambition that we reach a standard, a level of performance quality that to the cognoscenti will be perfect. Of course, it's a closed and strange world. The layperson should demand a perfection and clarity of rhythm, but they will always hear human intervention and hurly-burly. I suppose people like that: they want to know there are people up there and not computers. I think, though, that in bellringing, perfection is a desirable quality, something to really strive for. What we want to do now is to reach out to the city in a more obvious way. We want to put on a concert series this coming summer on Friday evenings; and have people gather in the amphitheatre and listen.'

I nod, thinking of the fine, broad amphitheatre built into the hill below the cathedral. 'I think that would be brilliant. I think people would certainly come to listen.' I pause and then say: 'Can I ask you one more thing?'

He nods.

'Well, a friend told me that he came to the service of remembrance at after the Omagh bombing.'

Leslie nods again.

'He said that the bells were muffled; he said it was the most fitting thing he had ever heard; and very emotional too.'

After a pause, Leslie says: 'Well, it is a powerful thing. We muffle the bells by tying leather attachments to the tongues and so the bells seem to echo; it's called "half-muffling". It's what we do for respect.' He stops again and then says, 'For what it's worth, it's never planned or practised. It's always well intentioned and we take the decision always depending on the circumstances. But I'm glad to hear that your friend thought it fitting. Very glad indeed.'

LESLIE invited me up to see the bellringers at work, or at play; and I take him up on his offer on the following Sunday morning. The news is full of yet more cold frontal systems on the way and it is certainly freezing as I walk through the quiet Sunday streets and up the hill towards Christchurch. But the sky is high and blue and full of frost, and the old stone and flying buttresses glint in the sunlight.

I am early and hang around at the foot of the bell tower; there is nobody around except for a pair of tense-looking tourists. I greet them with a smile and a 'lovely morning' – I am full of the lovely morning – but they make no response other than to look yet more tense. Perhaps they fear I am an early-bird terrorist; and so I leave them to their fears and wander in the church grounds until it is time to meet Leslie. The crocuses are pushing up through the soil.

Leslie eventually appears and he lets me into the building through a narrow door cut into the stone at the foot of the bell tower. Stone steps spiral upwards and I close the door behind me and follow him, rapidly becoming giddy as I go higher. Narrow windows are cut into the walls and I notice with admiration that there are empty wine glasses carefully balanced on many of the sills.

At length, we reach the top of the steps, squeeze through another door and along an outside gallery on the roof of the south transept of the cathedral. I have hardly time to look around. I have never seen the city from this height or this angle, so I scan the view, before following Leslie through yet another door and up an even more narrow flight of steps.

'Mind your head.'

I mind my head and we emerge into the room below the bells. It is large and square and high-ceilinged; many bell ropes hand from the roof, encased in lengths of red material and blue. There are even more bottles of wine stacked on the sills of the high windows. Leslie catches my covert glance.

'I like to encourage a relaxed atmosphere,' he beams; and I realise I must reassess my notion of the ringers as somehow austere and remote. They are clearly party animals.

After a few minutes, the ringers begin to arrive in ones and twos. There is certainly no sense of punctuality; the bells begin to be rung at 10am sharp, but there are still people emerging through the doorway 30 minutes later. They begin with a few test rings and then, when a quorum of ringers are gathered, they begin in earnest. I expect the noise of the ringing bells to be deafening, but the heavy timbered roof dulls the sound. A few 'rows' are rung – I have the vocabulary now – and then more rows and more, each longer and more ambitious than the one before. And I can see how the romance can be infectious: the sound is floating into homes across the city. Then I imagine a guest staying in Jury's Hotel directly across the road and suffering from an acute hangover: presumably such a guest would find the noise less than romantic.

The ringers are jovial and relaxed, while at the same time utterly concentrated. Leslie keeps an eye and an ear out and once or twice I hear the sequence breaking down. In spite of Leslie's comments on perfection, I find this human touch endearing.

When the ringing is over, Leslie takes me up into the bell room, at the very top of the church towers. Through the long, narrow windows, the views across Dublin are yet more spectacular. I can see the mountains in the distance streaked with snow; the Sugarloaf Mountain away to the southeast; the spire of St Patrick's nearer at hand; and roofs and spires into the horizon.

'And here are the bells.'

I look: all 19 of them, covered in dust and finely balanced, some small and some enormous, all crowded together on a framework of timbers and struts.

'These are new bells,' Leslie says and points. 'And these ones,' and he points at the rows of older ones, 'these are the ones that Jonathan Swift would have heard, and Wolfe Tone. The very same bells.' He smiles and I feel a prickle run down my spine.

'That's quite a thought,' I say.

'The very same ones.'

5

Sacred And Church Music

6

Dazed By The Haze

Classical, Contemporary And Jazz Music

THIS IS where it breaks down.

Dublin's music scene is not divided into neat genres – no music scene is. Instead, the energy flows and overflows from one musical form into another, changing each profoundly and irreversibly – and

No Engineers Here: Dublin's National Concert Hall, Earlsfort Terrace

for the better. This happens in Dublin, as in all other cities: as culture changes and adapts, so too does music. Traditional music picks up elements and threads of ethnic music, of jazz, of classical; and these threads fuse to form something wholly new. This is reality. And so, while it is convenient and straightforward to speak of this genre of music or that one, it does not do justice to the complexity of the music scene in this city. It is like a dust ball, gathering more matter as it floats along.

The Classical Scene

THE NATIONAL Concert Hall sits on Earlsfort Terrace, on the south-eastern corner of St Stephen's Green. Large and grey and formidably Edwardian, it is the most imposing building in the area, and possesses perhaps the best site of any of Dublin's great public buildings. Inside, the hall offers generous public spaces: a wide, lofty atrium, the inevitable café, the John Field recital hall tucked in behind and then the main auditorium itself, which, with its galleries and organ pipes and modern lines grafted onto a neo-classical original, is moderately impressive.

The Concert Hall shares the building rather uncomfortably and certainly incongruously with University College Dublin's engineering department. The building was UCD's city site for many years until the university shifted into its unpleasant '60s campus in the southern suburbs of the city. With the greater part of the building vacant, the Concert Hall moved in during the 1980s and has, in the meantime, carved out an influential place for itself in Dublin's classical music scene. But perhaps the fact that it is in the building at all, or that the main auditorium is a converted university hall, or that it must

National Concert Hall
Earlsfort Terrace, Dublin 2
(475 1572)
The city-centre's main classical venue offers a large auditorium and a smaller recital space. A mixed bag of musical tastes, but classical continues to dominate.

Classical, Contemporary And Jazz Music

6

share its space with a crowd of student engineers, all say a good deal about Dublin's attitude to classical music and ostensibly 'highbrow' entertainment.

After all, there is no purpose-built concert hall in the centre of the city; and alone among western European capital cities, Dublin possesses no opera house either. In truth, there is no great demand for one and no strong tradition of either opera or classical music. The classical music scene in the city is energetic and talented and skilled, but small in relation to the size of Dublin. And so, while the cachet of classical music means it can command more government, financial and institutional support than other kinds of music, it nonetheless remains more than a little marginal; and the opera scene is even smaller and positively struggling.

And as for the Concert Hall itself: it has been involved in a long-running debate about its situation, its position in the city. Should it remain on the site and address the building's manifest problems? Or should it move elsewhere and commission a brand-new hall – what is always called a 'state-of-the-art' hall? In this sense, the National Concert Hall is in the same predicament as the Abbey Theatre, which has also been agonising for some years about its inadequate and decaying present building and engaged in a kind of marathon public consultation exercise over its future. The Abbey could remain on its dismal present site on Abbey Street; or perhaps move to a new and larger space on O'Connell Street; or move out of the city altogether into Dublin's developing Docklands. the *Sunday Times* recently reported that the Abbey remaining on its present, constricted site had been ruled out, but the whole debate has been running for some years now and is nowhere near resolution.

The Concert Hall debate has also featured a move to a Docklands site, but it is clear enough that the institution would much prefer to remain right where it is, in its spectacular present space. But its problems are pressing too. High on this list is the lack of backstage space and the fact that the smaller John Field Room cannot be used when the main auditorium is hosting a concert: neither space can be adequately sound-proofed. As I mull over these problems with friends in the music worlds, their wishes are ringingly expressed: clear out the UCD engineers and give us the whole hall.

In the meantime, the Concert Hall has been involved in a long-running, unpleasant and distinctly surreal debate with the Real Tennis Association of Ireland over the use of a former Real Tennis court in a gymnasium on the Earlsfort Terrace site. The hall wished to convert the court into its new recital hall; the Real Tennis Association wished them to begone; and the result was a case now making its way through the High Court. Prince Edward is a fan of Real Tennis and he got involved in the spat, writing a letter in

The Top Venues for Classical and Contemporary Music

National Concert Hall (map: 5)
Earlsfort Terrace, Dublin 2 (475 1572)
The NCH is the main city-centre classical music venue, offering a large auditorium and smaller recital space. A mixed bag of musical tastes, though classical continues to dominate.

Helix (map: 24)
Dublin City University, Collins Avenue, Glasnevin, Dublin 9 (700 7000)
The brand-new and still shiny Helix offers three excellent concert halls under one roof in the city's northern suburbs – and a steady diet of excellent classical and contemporary music (and much, much more).

Hugh Lane Municipal Gallery of Modern Art (map: 57)
Parnell Square, Dublin 1 (874 1903)
This excellent gallery, housed in beautiful Charlemont House, is home to the long-running Sundays at Noon series. Come here at, er, any Sunday at noon, for top-class classical and contemporary music.

National Gallery of Ireland (map: 50)
Merrion Square West, Dublin 2 (661 5133)
Contemporary ensembles give regular concerts here, in the sleek modern surroundings of the gallery's new Millennium Wing.

support of the association and possibly winning it few friends as a consequence. As it happens, the court case may well be a redundant one, as the signs are that UCD will indeed move its engineers out to the suburbs – if the price is right – and the Concert Hall take over the entire landmark building.

On the morning I walk along Leeson Street and up to the Concert Hall, the sun is shining and the beginning of a spring mildness is in the air, and so I swerve at the last minute and make my way to the back of the great building and into the Iveagh Gardens. Dublin is deeply, densely urban and its city centre is small and crowded – and

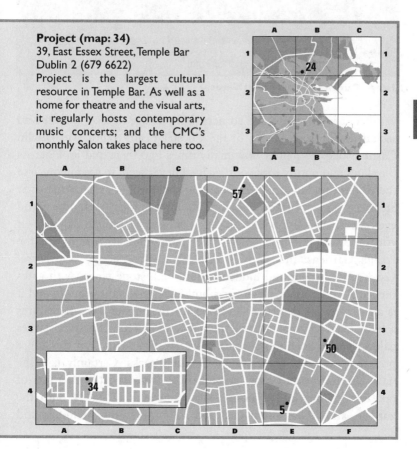

Project (map: 34)
39, East Essex Street, Temple Bar
Dublin 2 (679 6622)
Project is the largest cultural resource in Temple Bar. As well as a home for theatre and the visual arts, it regularly hosts contemporary music concerts; and the CMC's monthly Salon takes place here too.

6

Classical, Contemporary And Jazz Music

Iveagh Gardens: Dublin's Secret Garden

yet there are still areas and corners that manage to seem remote and secluded. The roof garden of the Chester Beatty Library in Dublin Castle is one: no matter how many times I go there and look across the slates and untidy roofs of the city, I never seem to see anyone else there. The tiny Huguenot Cemetery at the north-eastern corner of St Stephen's Green, tucked in behind its high railings, is another. And even Meeting House Square in the very heart of Temple Bar can – if you pick your moment – feel quiet and secluded. And as for the Iveagh Gardens: this park is Dublin's own version of the Secret Garden. It is silent and hidden behind high stone walls, with gates tucked away around corners and buildings hedging it around, and it is almost always deserted – even on warm summer days. It features a baby maze, a rosarium, a long sunken lawn and classical statues galore, not to mention a roaring waterfall, and it is in this sense probably the most successful of Dublin's parks. Certainly it is the most charming and I often come here to walk or sit with a cup of takeaway coffee and a book. The Concert Hall backs onto the gardens and it has often occurred to me that the buildings and gardens could surely be further integrated – rather than existing in separate universes as is presently the case. But then again, in my non-civic-minded moments, I have reflected that the gardens would then no longer be my own private space – and that would never do.

On this mild day, I walk over to the waterfall and glance balefully at a pair of tourists who have managed to scale the walls and get in here before me. One of them says, 'This place is open to the public, right?'

I smile with practised insincerity. 'Oh yes. For sure.'

'Only the thing is, doesn't seem like it is, y'know?'

It really doesn't seem like it is, y'know. But instead of saying anything else, I smile glassily, and retreat before they can engage me further. If I stay much longer, I'll be late for my appointment anyway. So I slip through the narrow door in the wall, into the grounds of the Concert Hall and into the large atrium. *Eine Kleine Nachtmusik* is being played over booming, blasting speakers: surely the volume is too loud? I resist the temptation to cover my ears and call out my business to the receptionist.

The Concert Hall has always had something of an image problem – for me, at any rate. While it offers a steady diet of good classical music – the National Symphony Orchestra of Ireland (NSOI) is resident here – it also offers all manner of other, wildly eclectic fare and the result can be pretty disconcerting to the visitor mildly looking for information. On this visit, for example, I have already seen a poster offering 'A Tribute to Brendan Kennelly'. Kennelly is an Irish poet and wit, and while such an evening will certainly get the bums on seats, it's a good example of the odd profile the hall offers to the world.

'Well, our remit is to attract a whole audience,' Rosita Wolfe tells me a little later over the blasting Mozart. Rosita looks after marketing at the hall. 'The resident orchestra, the NSOI, plays here each Saturday evening, as you know; and the celebrities come – the Vienna Phil, the Berlin Symphony and so on. But we must offer other music too, not least to subsidise our classical programme. We have to subsidise or else get sponsorship, or else people could not afford

6

Classical, Contemporary And Jazz Music

to come. And we only have 1,200 seats or so, so we simply have a ceiling on the crowds we attract.

'But it isn't about having to offer other music here: it's our role to do so.' She mentions Ceol, the festival of trad music taking place around St Patrick's Day in March, for example, 'which we would like to develop along the lines of Celtic Connections in Scotland. We want new audiences to come in all the time, so that if we have a big trad night, we can attract audiences to classical music too. That crossover element is really important. French Québecois music, The Dubliners...we have room for them all here.'

'And so,' I say, 'is it difficult to change the perception that this venue isn't simply for classical music?'

'It is changing,' she answers slowly, 'but changing slowly: there is more variety here now and people are beginning to realise this. To put my marketing hat on, we want to be the centre of excellence for all music in Ireland, and that really does mean all music. Dublin and Ireland are changing too, and so our programme is affected by this. The Concert Hall has always seemed to be above some people, that's the sense anyway, and we're really trying to change that now. We have outreach going on all the time, programmes involving rap and so on, all to break down the perception that we're somehow above people. This year, we're concentrating on building audiences by getting people into the hall that have never been here before.'

'And what about the state of classical music in the city? In general?'

'We have the two RTE orchestras; and there are some other groups too, but in truth, we have limited opportunities for young musicians in Ireland. Having the Helix is great: it means we have another venue and this increases visibility generally.'

The Helix is a purpose-built complex of three auditoriums,

> **The Helix**
> Dublin City University
> Collins Avenue, Glasnevin
> Dublin 9 (700 7000)
> Three excellent venues in one at this brand-new concert venue in the city's northern suburbs.

located in the northern suburbs of the city. It is an impressive building and brand-new; and it is the sort of place I keep meaning to go to but scarcely ever do because it feels too far away. I feel a prickle of shame at the thought.

'But frankly,' and Rosita seems once more to take her marketing hat off momentarily, 'there's always a difficulty getting audiences to come. Dublin hasn't the appetite for classical music that other cities have. If you compare it to Vienna, for example, it's like a different world. And soloists and composers: so many of them have to go away just to get recognition. So part of our task is to build in a programme that supports young artists. Some of them are so well known outside of Ireland; and hardly known here at all! I don't know why that is, though I suppose part of it comes down to marketing, to people being afraid to market themselves. Some are happy to market themselves and do it well, but others much less so.

'And the media – they are less than willing to publicise music. The *Irish Times* publicises classical music, but the other papers hardly look at it. Maybe Ireland perceives itself as so literary-based that it is reluctant to look at classical music in the same way.'

I bring up the question of the hall's shortcomings.

'In terms of acoustics, the hall is pretty good – excellent, I think. But it isn't a purpose-built hall and we need a bigger venue for sure. We can't use the John Field Room if the main hall is in use, as you know.'

I nod.

'And the question of the new recital hall is in limbo too. And we are waiting to see if relocation is a live issue. So it's all up in the air. But we badly need a bigger hall and we need a recital hall. We want to be an outstanding cultural asset and to draw people in...it's as simple as that.'

THAT SAME weekend, I go along with my friend Ann-Marie to a piano recital at the Concert Hall. This is the kind of occasion the institution does well: the crowd seem well-heeled and comfortable and

6

Classical, Contemporary And Jazz Music

the atmosphere is pleasantly excited. People are anticipating a good night out. The performer tonight is the Macedonian pianist – the 'prodigy', as he has been described – Simon Trpceski and he is playing Rachmaninov's Sonata No. 2 and Prokofiev's Sonata No. 6. The performance is indeed prodigious and the evening brilliant. At the end, Trpceski contributes a crossover of his own. For his final encore, he gives a short speech: he will play, for the first time in Ireland, a traditional Macedonian folk tune which has been scored and arranged for piano by Zivojin Glisic: it is called Preludium and Pajdushka. I know nothing of Macedonian folk music, but Trpceski's performance contains a note of wildness and has as much impact on me as Rachmaninov did earlier. I think: crossover again.

The Contemporary Music Scene

THROUGHOUT this project, the notion of crossover, of cross-fertilisation, has been introduced by virtually everyone with whom I have spoken. It is crossover and cross-fertilisation of ideas and influences, they say, that gives Dublin's music scene its unique character and energy. And I have seen for myself how the traditional genres of music can never be viewed in isolation, because their practitioners no longer see themselves in this way. I notice it all over again as I begin looking at the contemporary music scene in the city – the music of which I have least knowledge.

In Queen of Tarts a few days later, on a cold, frosty afternoon, I order a chicken sandwich and look again at the information I have downloaded from the website of the **Contemporary Music Centre (CMC)**. 'Lost In Bar 20', it says. 'Just as in the 19th century composers, writers and artists would gather informally to discuss one another's work and explore the ideas of the day, this initiative aims to offer a platform to experiment with new work, listen to some of those rare second performances of recent compositions and generally discuss and debate issues in contemporary music.'

I feel a little dubious: salons conjure up for me not the 19th century but the 18th, when similarly themed salons would be presided over by

Contemporary Music Centre (CMC)
19 Fishamble Street Dublin 8 (673 1922) Excellent resource for anyone interested in Dublin's new music scene: the CMC library and archive are open to all and visitors are welcome

leisured ladies who provided the space, the cash and the patronage to artists. Maybe the title 'salon' wasn't such a good idea after all; and I remember an exchange with Ann-Marie a few nights previous.

'It reminds me of *Gosford Park*,' I said in the interval of the Trpceski recital. We were hanging over the banisters of the stairs at the National Concert Hall, looking at the pair of vast Waterford chandeliers which hung over the John Field Room. Crowds were queuing for coffee below.

'*Gosford Park*?' she said. 'Does it?'

'A bit: the whole thing of people gathered in the salon listening to Ivor Novello; while the servants sat on the stairs outside the door listening too – but they weren't allowed in. Of course, I'm sure it won't be like that at all. But still, maybe the title's a little bit – off.'

I could tell she thought so too, although at the time she merely told me to 'wait and see'. And I did, unusually for me, decide to reserve judgement.

I finish my sandwich and make my way down through Temple Bar to the CMC's headquarters in a narrow, high townhouse at Fishamble Street. *Messiah* was first sung right here, I think – as I always think when I walk down Fishamble Street. Purplish clouds are hanging in the sky and it feels like snow.

The building has been elegantly restored and is beautiful: the very door handles, tightly coiled and gold, are bespoke. Upstairs, the library is cool and white and already quite full of people and before too long it is packed. The organisers look a little taken aback at the turnout. The audience is something of a mixed bag and impossible to categorise, which is always a good sign: the long-haired and the sprucely besuited gather side-by-side and the

Dublin's own Messiah: Memorial to Handel, Fishamble Street

atmosphere is relaxed. People settle themselves on the ground, as they assuredly would not have done in the 18th century, and the salon begins.

I have said that I did not know what to expect, but this is not quite the case. My mind was anticipating electronics, lots of amplification, lots of squeaks and beeps, and so I am not so taken aback when the first piece turns out to be just like this. Darragh Morgan is the violinist and as he plays, electronic sound jumps across and below his notes and I'm conscious more than ever of my ignorance. I begin to realise how useful such a gathering is – even if I still have misgivings about the name. Audiences need – and certainly this individual audience needs – such music to be contextualised, even explained a little. So that when Frank Lyons explains his *Dazed by the Haze* composition, the music and the context all moves into focus in a way it could never have done before.

'It comes from Hendrix,' Frank tells us. 'I pulled notes from "Purple Haze".'

The audiences ask questions: Did he write the electronics and violin together? He did, he said, but there is a definite improvisational quality to the whole piece: Darragh was experimenting as he went along, while Frank himself fiddled with his

Classical, Contemporary And Jazz Music

6

laptop out of sight around the corner, changing the electronics as he went along. The mention of pulling notes from "Purple Haze" reminds me delightfully of Professor Dumbledore pulling thoughts from his head and sliding them into his Pensieve – and so I feel distracted by the thought and hardly hear the rest of the discussion.

Similarly, when Bill Campbell's *Prelude* and *Flight Home* is performed, the piece has a similar improvised quality. This is the first time he has heard the piece, Bill tells us, and he and Darragh discuss changes that might be made and future plans. Might it be expanded into a concerto? A little later, Fergus Johnson's *Extended* is performed: it has been inspired by Kandinsky's paintings and was originally an electric guitar solo. The audience begins to relax and respond with more confidence. When Simon Mawhinney's *Barcode III* finishes the salon, a member of the audience volunteers that it was 'like being able to hear colours'; both Simon and Darragh look pleased.

'To me, it's like little silver stars popping about,' Simon says. I feel the weight of my conditioning once more: this is not at all the sort of comment I expect to hear from a composer and it is both charming and disarming.

'WHEN I began working here,' says Karen Hennessey, 'I hardly knew what contemporary music was.'

We're sitting in the kitchen of the CMC a few days later. Karen organised the salon and has worked with the CMC for several years.

'And it is a confusing term: people ring up to talk to us about their latest rock album and so on. "Contemporary new music – isn't that what you do?" What it is really is this: it's what composers are composing today. The 1950s is generally used as the point at which similar music centres have begun their collections, but we have gone a little further back. Until now, there was nowhere for this earlier music to be archived in Ireland, but thankfully the National Library is now taking this slightly earlier material, so that from now on, our archive will hold a collection dating from the 1950s too.

6

Classical, Contemporary And Jazz Music

'Much of it today is not necessarily written material – we have a good deal of electronic also. That's where today we're getting crossover: in the universities, students are studying music but also producing it electronically; people are producing it in their bedrooms too.' She pauses and then says: 'And they are just as much composers as anyone else. That's the important thing.'

'Even though they might not conceive of themselves in that sense,' I say.

'Even if. It's still the case that they are composing original material.'

The CMC has existed since the 1980s. At the beginning it was housed in Georgian premises on Baggot Street and it moved to Temple Bar in 2001.

'We have great facilities now, a great library, and more space. We feel much more established ourselves and we jointly own the building with Temple Bar Properties, which is very important to us, since most of the arts organisations in Temple Bar lease their premises. Our role develops all the time, but it is primarily to document and support the work of Irish composers; that's really what we exist to do. We have an archive and a library, and a sound archive and a score archive with 3,000 scores and 5,000 recordings – and we're a public building. All sorts of people use the building: musicologists, students, artists and academics. But anyone can come and study or listen, or simply acquaint themselves with what's going on. And everything is online.

'We actively promote the work of composers: this has really developed over the last six years. I feel that it's a hard area. I worked in the arts for some years, but knew very little about contemporary music. And honestly, contemporary music has found it difficult up to now to connect with other art forms. We're building this up with open days, by connecting with other Temple Bar institutions and with city festivals too like Bloomsday.' Karen shrugs. 'But yes, it is difficult.'

I'm struck by this sense that the art form has no accepted name. 'Do you think that the label "contemporary music" is a good one?'

'Well,' she replies slowly, 'it's a funny one. In my opinion, the most exciting thing about any art form is what's new, and contemporary composers really are pushing boundaries and ploughing new ground all the time. So by rights, this music should be attractive and exciting to audiences. But I think perhaps it's an issue to do specifically with music. After all, the aural sense is extremely intimate – when you're in a concert, for example – and perhaps audiences find that very difficult and sometimes back off and return to what is familiar. The actual sounds in canonical classical music or rock music – people know these; they hear them on the radio all the time, in ads and on the television. But contemporary music is wholly new and people find this disconcerting. It's like learning a new language: you're in that country and suddenly, the language comes into focus, falls into place. Contemporary music is a bit like that: once you come to terms with the sounds and allow them to become familiar, then the language suddenly comes into focus and it becomes familiar. For example, I said I didn't know much about contemporary music when I arrived, but now, I am accustomed to contemporary music, so now I can look for what is unique and distinguishing about a certain composition.'

She stops for a moment and thinks. Then she says more confidently, 'But yes, I really do think it's a music thing: people at a Bowie concert want the greatest hits, they want what they know. But when they go to the theatre, they want the play to be entirely new. So that's a divergence of opinions that I find very interesting.'

I tell her my impressions of the salon. When they mentioned Jimi Hendrix, I say, I really sat up. The idea of all these different threads or influences was very stimulating, and very challenging. It made me sit up and pay attention – literally – and see what I could hear in it, and what ideas and links it created in my head.

'Well, you know,' she replies, 'contemporary composers really know their stuff: they aren't shutting anything off. They are in fact wide open to everything – entirely open – like the Jimi Hendrix thing.'

6

Classical, Contemporary And Jazz Music

We talk on for a while, speculating about the challenges.

'Perhaps it's a presentational thing too. Contemporary music is sometimes presented as part of a standard classical evening. They do it at the Concert Hall and also at the chamber music festival at Bantry House in Cork. It works really well, you know, and is usually accompanied by a talk.'

Context again.

'That's one way, but there are other ways of opening the audience to something new, of reaching them in other ways, of getting to people who go to galleries and other concerts, but who seldom go to contemporary music.

'The danger is that you think you have to incorporate visuals and funkiness in order to keep it trendy. So often, you really don't have to do anything with the music. All that funkiness sometimes isn't necessary. And there are other ways: the media could help too by simply being more interested; composers could market themselves better too – that's something we want to work on as well. People know about artists even if they hate the material. Just think about Damien Hirst.'

I think about Damien Hirst and my mind performs another one of its disconcerting leaps: from Hirst to Charles Saatchi's art collection and on to one of Nigella's recipes.

'But the composers seldom have that profile,' Karen goes on, oblivious to Nigella. 'In Aosdána, the Irish academy of artists, for example, there are far fewer composers than there are visual artists and writers.'

'Dead composers are very sexy,' I say. 'I mean, it isn't an essential problem with composers per se. Everyone knows about Beethoven and Bach.'

'Well,' she says and laughs, 'maybe live ones aren't. But then no – some live ones are too.'

I say vaguely, 'Maybe it's a question of definition.'

'How do you mean?'

'Well, maybe people don't like having to deal with an art form that can refer to Kandinsky one moment and Hendrix the next, and opera and animation the next. Maybe they want everything classified more neatly and less challengingly.'

'I just don't think it's that wide,' she replies slowly. 'Once you get a handle on it all, I don't think it's all that difficult. Of course, it can never be background music – never ever. It always has to be placed in context, and you always have to give it a chance.

'And of course we're bombarded by music too, and that's a problem. You have music all day long – at the supermarket, at the gym, walking down the street – and so sometimes it's difficult to decide to go and spend time and money listening to even more music; especially when there are so many other music forms as competition. Because of that, I think there is a case to be made for making it all free, always. It's a question of getting people to stick with it, to invest in it.'

A FEW days later, I went back to the Contemporary Music Centre to attend a seminar, which had also been organised by Karen. The point of the seminar is to look for ways in which contemporary music – for want of a better word – can be publicised more effectively and opened up to a wider and more receptive audience. If I felt stimulated and challenged by my talk with Karen, I emerged from the seminar feeling mildly depressed. One of the panel, a noted Irish composer, posited the idea that contemporary music neither catered to the Irish national self-image nor made money, and so was always destined to struggle. In comparison to the United Kingdom, he said, contemporary music was not afforded a place in national life; it was represented as having no firm place in the national story, when the truth was that this place was simply ignored. The media almost invariably neither previewed nor reviewed performances of major new compositions. 'The convergence of Boston and Berlin is destroying all art music,' he concluded. 'Long live the Revolution!'

The second panelist, introduced as an 'avid concert-goer', echoed Karen's worry that audiences could not be brought to accept the unfamiliar, and commented that sandwiching a new composition

6

Classical, Contemporary And Jazz Music

between two pieces by, for example, Brahms – as was often the practice at the Concert Hall – was not the best way of introducing new music to an audience. 'The bourgeoisie isn't capable of being shocked,' she said. 'It simply stays away.'

The third panellist, a prominent journalist, noted that the anti-intellectualism which is part of the fabric of Irish life was not conducive to the spread and establishment of classical or contemporary music. The media, he agreed, tended to back away from new music and this became a pattern in itself, one that was difficult to break. In all, it was a stimulating discussion, albeit less than optimistic; the weather played its apocalyptic part by repeatedly throwing hailstones on the windows through the whole course of the morning. I left, much enlightened and oddly, not pessimistic at all. I was conscious of a ferment of ideas bubbling away in the ether and simply seeking a wider and more receptive audience.

I immersed myself in contemporary music in the days that followed, although I felt continually hamstrung by the problems of what to call it. Contemporary music or art music or plain, bald 'new music': none seemed to be entirely satisfactory and nobody I spoke to seemed any clearer than I was. In the end, I decided to stop obsessing on it and try to look at the bigger picture.

The Crash Ensemble

'I WAS surprised by the sense of worry or anxiety that permeated the meeting.'

Once more, I'm in the Library Bar of the Central Hotel. This time, I'm having coffee with Donnacha Dennehy. He is one of the leading lights of the Crash Ensemble and it in turn has a high profile in the field of contemporary music. He is young and relaxed and articulate; he laughs a lot.

'People seemed anxious about the state of contemporary music in Dublin,' I continue, 'and anxious about getting people interested in it.'

'Well, the thing about Crash,' he replies, 'is that we have had a fair amount of interest in our music. There is some existing interest in the avant-garde in Ireland because of Joyce and so on, though of course he got a rough deal at the time; we have been able to draw on that pretty successfully. Put simply, people are more receptive to our ideas than you might imagine.'

It's a fairly upbeat initial assessment and I feel instantly cheered.

'That said...' and my heart sinks again. He laughs. 'No, that said,

Collision of Styles: The Crash Ensemble and the Library Bar

music always has a tough struggle, because of the massive success of U2, which has dwarfed the work of other people. There is much more interest today in rock and pop and techno, and there is always going to be a struggle to get people interested in contemporary music. So what we try to do is be innovative in our approach: we use multimedia, we bring people in from the theatre, video, amplification – and then the experimental rock crowd do come. So our concerts do well: sometimes we even have to turn people away, though of course the crowds are not on the scale of a rock band. But we're not doing too badly. One good thing is that the audiences at our concerts tend to be very disparate. Instead of a situation in which you see the same people coming along each time, we have a situation in which I never know who any of them are! This is bound to be a good thing. People from a jazz background, from a laptop background, all kinds.'

Then he shrugs.

'You know, we have come in for some flack for being popular, but I try and avoid the debates. I try not to get sucked in and I just concentrate on doing my own thing. Too much complaint just brings up a culture of complaint and that's very unattractive.'

I'm interested in this: it seems a very self-conscious and explicit sloughing off the weight of complaint, of begrudgery that is such a famed part of the national psyche. This idea of begrudgery is maybe a little clichéd too, but it exists, for sure.

6

Classical, Contemporary And Jazz Music

'What we like to do,' Donnacha continues, 'is have a variety of music: and we put beat-oriented pieces in the middle of other music. We keep it mixed up and that attracts people: people see it live and see the way it connects and they come away interested.'

'And where did your interest come from?'

'Well, I didn't come from a musical background,' he says. 'My father was a writer, so there was creativity there: he wrote radio dramas; and from the earliest age, I liked the idea of going to a room and writing. It came naturally, if you like. Then I went to the Academy of Music and I busked on Grafton Street. But I was always interested in experimental music – I was a big Bowie fan, and I loved Stockhausen – he came to Dublin when I was 12 and that was fascinating. And I also loved Bach, so I had very catholic tastes. All these influences have followed me into The Crash Ensemble.

'So I started writing at a very early age and studied flute. Then I went to study in Illinois and it was there that I really started getting into electronic music. They had these great big pieces of gear that would fill up an entire room and that would sometimes catch fire.' He laughs again 'And that was my first intensive experience of electronic music. I got into using computers and samplers: mixed media and stuff; it was great. After that, I lived in Holland for a while and in Paris. Then I wanted to come back here and set up a group that would experiment a bit and bring experimental music out of the ghetto.'

'Had these forms not been experimented with?'

'Well, there was something of a void in the market, really. It was a great time to set up a group. There was Concorde (the contemporary music ensemble) who do a great job, but their music was more or less acoustic – lunchtime concerts and so on – while we were coming out of the revolution made by minimalism; a lot of elements of pulse which was a big no-no in contemporary music for years.'

This is something I know nothing about. 'Really?' I say, feeling out of my depth once more.

'Yes, well, Adorno had – you know Adorno?'

I bridle at this: of course I know Adorno. I say: 'Yes.'

'Well, he had a massive impact on thinking in the avant-garde; the beep was tantamount to fascism. This kind of regularity, you know, in the post-war era was definitely frowned upon. Because the Nazis used music towards dangerously ideological ends: because the beat, the beep was associated with regularity and marching and so on – because of all this, there was a fear of it after the war too. But in the '60s in America, there was a real rebellion against that kind of thinking.'

I say again, 'Really?' Maybe I didn't know that much about Adorno after all.

'Yeah, but I really think there is a place for so many influences: there is a place for the pulse and the classic modernist position too. We've done some of them in the Crash. There's also a place for most adventurous, pulse-based music though, and electronics and animation too, that's what we tried to experiment with.

'We have got slated by the classical establishment, of course,' he says a little wearily, 'absolutely brutalised. Some of our work has gone down disastrously.'

I think: I can imagine the reaction. And I remember a conversation with a contact just a few days before. 'People like Donnacha Dennehy and Jürgen Simpson,' my friend had said, 'are two of the most interesting composers on the scene today. In some aspects, the traditional composers are a sort of dying breed. They can't survive on the commissions they receive and RTE can't commission work all the time, and so they get bitter. But many of the younger composers realise they must engage much more broadly and so they are more flexible in their attitudes.' Another contact said, 'The music schools churn out classically trained musicians who then can't get a job, while ignoring forms of non-classical music which is growing in popularity. The system makes no sense at all.'

I think about this as I listen to Donnacha describe being 'slated' by the classical establishment.

'So in that context, it's great when those concerts are sold out. It shouldn't really bother you, of course, but we put a lot of work into our pieces and it's good when we get a buzz back.'

I brandish the quotation from him gleaned from the CMC website and read it out:

'There is a whiff of high-class vandalism about my recent work. Is that snobbish? Well, it is not mere destruction! I am not interested in oh-so-dull arc forms or the "chill-out" static approach. Processes which undermine the integrity of my material provide the thrill factor

Crash Ensemble: A Short History

Crash Ensemble was founded in 1997 by Donnacha Dennehy, alongside composer Andrew Sinnott and clarinettist Michael Seaver. In the years since, Crash has established a reputation as one of Ireland's most energetic and innovative contemporary ensembles and has garnered glowing reviews in the process.

Crash has a foot in many camps. It blends together art forms that would seem to have nothing in common – electronics, animation, dance, video – and brings together composers, video artists and lighting specialists, in the process creating music and an experience that are altogether new. And in the process too, the ensemble attracts an audience as eclectic as is the music itself.

Crash has regularly performed work by important 20th-century composers including Reich and Stockhausen and has also commissioned a good deal of new work by young Irish composers like Siobhán Cleary. It founded the Contemporary Music Festival, which takes place each December in Dublin; and is also planning the creation of its own record label.

Members

Donnacha Dennehy	Michael Seaver
Fergus Shiel	John Godfrey
Malachy Robinson	David Adams
Susan Doyle	Richard O'Donnell
Ruth Hickey	John Godfrey
Natasha Lohan	James Eadie
Kevin Hanafin	Brona Cahill
Roddy O'Keefe	Ben Rogerson
Richard Sweeney	Kate Ellis

Classical, Contemporary And Jazz Music

in composing. My preoccupation with ideas of "urban" music remains.'

He laughs. 'Yes, I said that, but you know, it's true. In the music, the material is ripped apart; we single-mindedly go at it – which some people hate. I'm influenced by so many quarters though: electronic, ethnic music, the sean nos in Ireland, and by south Indian music. I

Some notable Crash performances:

Van Gogh Video Opera by Michael Gordon – 'We performed the world premiere of the new version of this in December 2003 (for three singers, amplified ensemble and video) – that went really well. We did a version with a local VJ called Tim Redfern. As for Michael Gordon himself, he is one of New York's Bang On A Can collective. We've done a lot of music by them over the years, as we share a similar kind of open-minded approach. They are very interested in the dialogue between experimental rock and adventurous new music.'

Junk Box Fraud by Donnacha Dennehy – 'This was one of the very first pieces we did, way back in 1997, and it was a defining piece for the Crash. This kind of defined the interdisciplinary nature of the group in that it not only involved a live amplified group but also video and multimedia, electronics, and a theatrical element. The live ensemble for this is made up of two female vocalists (one with dyed blue hair, the other dyed red), two pianos, clarinet, and trombone. The sounds of the vocalists blend with the electronics while their images, particularly the primary colours of their hair, interact with the technicolor computer-generated video! The piece progresses at a furious, thumping pace.'

Recent pieces – 'These include **I Like Things a Lot** by Andrew Hamilton and **Aria 51** by John Godfrey (who also plays piano in the group). "Aria 51" is for live piano and loads of boomboxes throughout the auditorium playing detuned versions of the live piano part. The European experimental music that we do would I suppose be represented by such composers as Michael Maierhof (of Hamburg), Gerhard Stabler (of Essen) and the Irish composer Jennifer Walshe. To give you an example, a piece by Maierhof which we performed last year involved flute, electric guitar and percussion distributed throughout the hall. The electric guitar was not played in the standard way but was used as a kind of prepared electronic instrument (with the amp up high). An amazing sound was produced by moving a small electric fan close to the sounding board. Maierhof's pieces often seem like intense sound sculptures punctuated with silences that highlight the intensity of the blocks of sound.'

6

Classical, Contemporary And Jazz Music

could rip apart the sean nos so that you can hardly recognise them: I like to take the rhythm and present it in a different way.'

'And I suppose that's why some people resent it,' I say feelingly. 'Some people can't stand the idea of sean nos being ripped apart,' and he nods.

'Yes. There is a sense in me that I dislike the status quo: that it "should be done in such and such a way". I instinctively don't bend to that.'

'So what's the future for the Crash?'

He sits up, talks enthusiastically. 'Well, we're setting up a label. It has bothered us for a long time that there isn't an appropriate label for our kind of music in Ireland. We want to be a label as well as a group. You know, so much material has fallen through the cracks and we want to catch it as it falls from now on. I think the establishment has ignored the CD for too long: there is a persistent idea that the score is the work of art and the CD isn't important; and we really want to change that. After all, there's no point trying to continue a tradition that means very little to us. Of course, the score is important but it isn't the be-all and end-all.'

'What will the label be called?'

'Hmmm...we dunno yet. We might call the Label "Crash" or "Semi-detached" or "Detour" – we haven't decided.

'We also want to tour more: we're off to Estonia soon as part of the Irish Presidency of the EU; and we hope to go to Poland and to The Netherlands too. And we want to make more connections with other groups overseas and on the fringes of experimental rock. The whole cross-fertilisation thing: you know, it's so important to the vitality of the music scene in Dublin. It's that aspect that is so great about the Dublin scene now; and it's interesting that the whole cross-pollination thing here is much more lively, more energetic than in other countries.

'I think it's partly because the scene here hasn't been so very policed: people have ignored it, have just let it get on with things. We're all a little suspicious of authority and of the classical establishment and all a little more into iconoclasm; we just have more opportunity to dip into other areas and gain from other influences. Of course, the contemporary scene in Holland, say, is much better resourced; but that makes it more policed too. Here and in New York, you have more free space: different things happen.'

I say: 'A bit like Temple Bar in the early days? It was ignored and all sorts of life throve there.'

Donnacha grimaces. 'Oh God. Well, it's not like that now – more like a 24-hour superpub.'

'So – just listening to your language: do you fear the Crash becoming established and changing for the worse?'

He nods vigorously. 'Oh sure – oh, we all fear that. So we know we have to keep on our toes. You always know after each concert how plugged in you were; and resolve to do better. We've worked a lot with new, younger composers: Judith Ring and Jürgen Simpson, for example; we've kept the influences moving all the time and we need to keep doing that.

'And we need more concerts, more ensembles in Dublin – and even a good deal more interactions going on too. But the scene needs more exposure, and more funding too – and we just need more critics. The old way of looking at music needs to be changed: the boundaries have been changed and we need critics who can respond properly to that. The old way of criticising doesn't really work for us.'

My mind flies back to the seminar. Do observers, journalists, critics all need to respond to the scene more imaginatively, I wonder? He nods.

'Oh yes.'

Going Native

LYCANTH is a choral piece, Jürgen Simpson tells me a few days later and is being sung by the National Chamber Choir in a few days' time.

'You know about the Living Music Festival, don't you?' he asks me. I nod.

RTE is sponsoring the second Living Music Festival, to be held at the Helix this weekend. The weekend theme is French contemporary

6

Classical, Contemporary And Jazz Music

Jürgen Simpson's Favourite Contemporary Music

I'm actually writing this in Dublin's National Concert Hall where we are rehearsing my all-time favourite piece: Stockhausen's electro-acoustic masterpiece *Kontakte*. Absolute magic and arguably the most important electronic work ever written. Like this? Then listen to Helmut Lachenmann, who mangles the sound of an orchestra and turns it into a growling, purring, roaring monster (try *Schwankungen am Rand*).

For anyone into the Aphex Twins, excellent *Selected Ambient Works Vol 2*, check out the very early electronic experiments of American composer Otto Luening (like *Low Speed* from 1952) and spot the difference!

If you fancy a musical nervous breakdown then I can't recommend Canadian composer Paul Dolden's *The Walls of Jericho* enough; there are up to 300 notes a second playing here! From the same part of the world but on a completely different trajectory is Do Make Say Think's album *Winter Hymn, Country Hymn, Secret Hymn* which along with Norwegian band Supersilent 1-3 is some of the best experimental rock/jazz I've heard.

Here in Dublin there is a constant brewing of eclectic experimental activity. Some of my favourites include the side-splittingly hilarious **The Warlords of Pez**, and the excellent and slightly more serious **Trouble Penetrator**. Some of the best experimental performers here include laptop wizz Keith O'Brien (aka **Amoebazoid**) and free jazz pianist **Paul Smyth**, both of whom must be experienced live. If you like slightly more beats based electronic music then check out **Spectac**'s excellent debut *Rabbid* on Dublin's Front End Synthetic label or **Ambulance**'s *The Curse of Vale do lobo* on Planet Mu.

Enjoy!

music and is supported by the French Embassy in Dublin – but the Irish scene will get a fair crack of the whip too. The Crash Ensemble will be performing and several new young Irish composers, including Jürgen, will be premiering pieces specially commissioned by RTE.

'It's set around God's banishment of Nebuchadnezzar,' he tells me. 'You know about Nebuchadnezzar?'

Classical, Contemporary And Jazz Music

6

'He went mad and ate grass, did he?'

'And was transformed into a werewolf, yes. That's what lycanthropy is: the power to transform oneself into a wolf; or a form of madness in which you think you can make that transformation.'

I remember a comment I read in a history book a few weeks before.

'In medieval times, when English colonists in Ireland went native and adopted Irish "habits", they were compared to Nebuchadnezzar,' I say.

'Really? How?'

'I have it in my bag,' I say. I pluck a photocopy out of a file. 'It's from the Tudor period, about the oldest Hiberno-Norman colonists who went native.' I read the passage aloud.

> These were the Irish customs which the English colonists did embrace and use after they had rejected the civil and honourable laws and customs of England, whereby they became degenerate and metamorphosed like Nebuchadnezzar who, although he had the face of a man, had the heart of a beast…for, as they did not only forget the English language and scorn the use thereof, but grew to be ashamed of the very English names, though they were noble and of great antiquity and took Irish surnames…

We laugh; the colonial language and imagery is startling.

As I speak to Jürgen, I have the sense of a furious creativity working away, making connections and forming ideas. And a furious energy too: he is accordionist with The Jimmy Cake, lecturer, and composer, all at the same time.

'I grew up in a very music-oriented background,' he says. 'My father was a piano tuner for U2, Chris de Burgh and Phil Lynott. My big claim to fame was that I was shown around Windmill Lane on Phil Lynott's back! Then I moved to southern Germany and played jazz. When I was 17 I moved to Galway and learned the accordion. I played in a trad band, and I also had the whole classical repertoire in my head – Bach to Chopin – too and this was very helpful, very healthy.

'More recently, I moved to County Clare with a friend of mine

6

Classical, Contemporary And Jazz Music

215

and we set up a studio and got very interested in ambient techno – very influenced by the British scene. But I became more and more influenced by Cage and Stockhausen, so I left that whole area behind and I did the music technology course at Trinity.'

'The one that Donnacha Dennehy lectures on?'

Jürgen nods. 'That's the one. Donnacha taught me. I finished my Masters by writing my first opera, *Neshika*, which is Hebrew for "the kiss". So I got very interested in the electronic, contemporary music world. *Neshika* was completely electronic: it was based on the idea of Judas Iscariot from two different angles: one moving backwards in time and the other forwards through time, and the two timelines converging at the moment of the betrayal, the kiss. My idea was that the betrayal was necessary, as proposed by biblical history. So where did Judas fit into that? He hardly had a choice, after all.

'My first big collaboration was with Kevin Volens; and then I did some work with Raymond Deane. From there, I worked on more classical music and then I worked on my second opera *Thwaite*.'

I know about *Thwaite*. It was awarded top prize by the Genesis Foundation and was performed by the Almeida Opera in London and also by Opera Theatre Company in Dublin.

'That was a big deal,' I say.

'Well, it got a terrific reception,' he replies with refreshing clarity. 'It was an extension of the *Waiting for Godot* idea, only in *Thwaite*, people are waiting for each other. Everyone is claiming to be the Messiah and in the end everyone kills each other: nobody is the Messiah, of course, so nobody is resurrected. At the end,' he says comfortably, 'there are just dead bodies everywhere.'

I wish I had seen it. I ask him to talk about the sense of energy I have so strongly perceived in Dublin.

'Well, what binds it together is the various hubs of energy in the music scene in Dublin – and for me, the music course at Trinity binds it all together. Donnacha Dennehy, Roger Doyle, Fergus Johnson and others: all active in many scenes and aware of many traditions; all coming together and opening up all sorts of ideas to each other; opening up to all different types of media.'

'I suppose,' I say suddenly, 'like this kind of energy is always latent – it simply needs to be harnessed.'

'Well, exactly, and there is a real community of Dublin, a very strong community that facilitates this kind of approach. For example, we had a concert in Vicar Street on Monday night which exemplified this attitude: Turn was there and The Jimmy Cake and others – and all collaborating with each other. That's just one example of collaboration. The Jimmy Cake, of course, is collaboration on a wider scale: nine friends getting together and forming a band. But it's all part of the energy of the Dublin scene. Artists respect each other more and it works. The Jimmy Cake was originally a college band, percussion-oriented and students, with female singers. It got more interested in experimental stuff, and got a little cult-ish. It stopped for a while and then it formed again for a single concert, in a slightly different form. There were seven of us in the line-up at that point. Then we recorded an album called *Brains*, which was well received; and it all went from there. I think it's a little bit like the Icelandic scene: there is music being written that hasn't really been written before.

'Because the lineup in The Jimmy Cake is so big, there's no room for ego: it's all very optimistic and unegotistic. We're loud but pretty delicate: two guitars, bass, drums, trumpet, saxophone, piano, accordion, and clarinet. The sound is very – traditional, I suppose, but also very contemporary; and we bring lots of live energy to the stage and to our ensemble playing. It's a little like traditional Irish playing methods: everyone plays homophonic lines and then moves away from them. It's great fun.' Jürgen pauses and then adds enthusiastically, 'And we're going on a tour of eastern Europe in the spring.'

I think: God, everyone is going to Eastern Europe in the spring. But no, the Irish presidency of the EU has opened up all kinds of opportunities to Irish musicians, and more events are happening in Dublin as a result of it too. The BBC and RTE, for example, has announced plans for a simultaneous live concert in Belfast and Dublin on 1 May, to coincide with the official entry of ten new member states to the EU. The concerts are part of its Music Live festival.

'The only problem is logistics,' Jürgen says. 'We're such a big band, you know? And it's so difficult in practical economic terms.' Then he echoes Donnacha's comments about the kind of audiences The Jimmy Cake receives. 'We have a very varied audience: we expect young people in the crowds, but their parents come too. They presumably heard us in their children's music collections and came along to see what's going on.'

I talk to him too about the seminar of a few days previous, which has impressed itself on my mind. I imagine he is optimistic about the future of new music in Dublin, I ask – but how will it develop?

'Well, the scene has already developed. I mean, five years ago, contemporary music seemed very bounded; but we began to talk about it and see how we could broaden it. People seemed happy to stay inside their boundaries: people who were involved in the highbrow, which developed from the western classical field, were unaware of the kind of music that I was interested in – and so on. So we tried to get people interested in the in-between, in the music that fell into the gaps.

'But now, things have changed. A lot of people are working in those gaps – the Crash Ensemble, of course – but others too. People are becoming aware and more people are working in the scene. The thing is, if you don't expect there to be boundaries, the boundaries disappear! You have to show a little imagination too: advertise the concerts on techno and electronica websites as well as on conventional media, and people come. They really will come. It means that people, who ordinarily wouldn't, came to see my opera for example, because they know about my work with The Jimmy Cake. My opera deliberately had an electronic section in Act Three, and that brought people in. It's really not difficult.

'My own work has been well received in England, but hasn't been performed in Europe yet. England has been the biggest place for me and Irish people have reacted to that acknowledgement; it was an opera and so people reacted well to that. British people responded so well, but in Ireland, we still feel that other people need to acknowledge work before we feel confident to do so. We have a lack of confidence in our own taste, especially in the classical world. There is a sense that some of the Concert Hall audiences are very cautious – they squint at the music, if I can put it that way. I have huge problems with that, and that is why the whole performance aspect of my career is so important to me.' He pauses.

I say: 'Thank God for The Jimmy Cake?' and he laughs.

I HAVE two concerts booked for the Living Music Festival. When I enter the atrium of the Helix the following Friday afternoon, there are already a good many people milling around. I am ridiculously early and I know now why I sometimes avoid coming to the Helix. The transport chaos in Dublin is now of the order that one has to set aside hours to get anywhere; and so I caught my bus at Merrion Square at 3pm for a 5pm show. Now it is just after 4pm, so the traffic was pretty bad but not disastrous, and I have an hour to spare. I have a cup of coffee, read the programme, watch the people loitering around and take in the high surroundings of the Helix.

It is an impressive venue. The main Mahony Hall seats some 1,200 people and the two other halls, The Theatre and The Space, cater for smaller numbers. The programme is eclectic and colourful, from full orchestra through to cabaret nights and ABBA tribute concerts. Camille O'Sullivan is performing soon, I notice; Mark Rylance of the Globe Theatre in London is giving a full-day theatre masterclass; there are all manner of things going on.

The programme might be sharp, but the main atrium is rather less impressive. Long sheets of perforated metal are bolted together, Meccano-style, to form the staircases to the upper floors; they jar with the ill-fitted red carpet on the floor. But as I sit and observe, I feel it is disagreeable even thinking about the weaknesses of the building today: such is the buzz in the air that it seems to be going against the grain. And besides, the building is new and deserves some settling time. So I look again at the programme.

'That this festival is happening for a second time is a miracle,' notes the introduction. 'Long may the miracle continue!'

6

Classical, Contemporary And Jazz Music

The comment also jars. I realise that I'm not accustomed today to hearing even the slightest note of defensiveness from Dublin's music scene, and so hearing it repeatedly emanating from contemporary music is a little perplexing.

Lycanth is performed in the main Mahony Hall, which, in contrast to the atrium, is decked coolly in pale wood; it is respectably full for a Friday afternoon.

'It's a lovely venue, isn't it?' I hear my neighbours say approvingly. 'Much nicer than the Concert Hall.'

The National Chamber Choir – 16-strong – is an impressive outfit with a sense of real panache and they acquit themselves admirably; they are accompanied for several pieces by a guest ensemble. The music in the programme – all French and Québecois, with the exception of *Lycanth* – seems difficult and technically stretching. *Lycanth* itself is disturbing: the electronic background shudders and vibrates deeply and hums in my fingertips. Later, on the bus home, I happen to overhear choir members talking behind me and I eavesdrop shamelessly. They did find today's music difficult, they say; contemporary music is very challenging; the rehearsals stretched for weeks. Was it worth it? They mull it over as the bus rumbles into town. Yes, they finally agree; yes, it was worth it.

Sundays at Noon

ONE OF the longest running features of the music world in Dublin has been the Sundays at Noon concerts in the **Hugh Lane Gallery** on Parnell Square. The gallery is one of Dublin's cultural gems. Its fine Georgian home is Charlemont House, which overlooks the Garden of Remembrance and the grounds of the Rotunda Hospital and Gate Theatre. This area of town is still fairly frayed around the edges, but the Hugh Lane sits on a long terrace that also houses the Dublin Writers' Museum and the Irish Writers' Centre. Dublin city centre is flat, flat, flat, but this district lies on a rise and offers a sense of space and height. And Charlemont House itself was one of

Hugh Lane Municipal Gallery of Modern Art
Parnell Square, Dublin 1
(874 1903)
This excellent gallery is housed in the beautiful Charlemont House and features a concert each Sunday at noon.

the finest townhouses in the city when it was first built, and it remains a splendid example of its kind.

The Municipal Gallery was founded in 1908 in order to provide the city with a gallery of modern art; it moved into Charlemont House in 1933. Hugh Lane was the prime mover behind the campaign to get the gallery off the ground: he donated much of his own collection and put forward the cash necessary to acquire even more. But the authorities dragged their heels over providing a permanent home for the collection and finally, Lane willed much of his collection to the National Gallery in London instead. He died on the *Lusitania* in 1915 without ever fully clarifying his will and so the scene was set for a bitter battle of wills between London and Dublin which was only resolved in the 1950s. Today, many of these important pieces are rotated between the two institutions.

The cool and harmonious interior of the Hugh Lane is a treasure in itself but it also offers all sorts of artistic riches, including work by Manet, Degas and Renoir. The Sundays at Noon series began in 1976 and now takes place in the long ground-floor saloon, which is lit from above by a domed skylight. It is a beautiful space and almost full when I arrive on a Sunday morning in early February.

The series has probably maintained itself for so long because it has been wise enough never to tamper or fiddle with its essential ingredients: its timing, its slot, and its basic format. Ever since it

6

Classical, Contemporary And Jazz Music

began, it has been in the Hugh Lane at noon on Sundays – and so people build it into their weekend plans and it becomes an accepted feature of weekend life in the city. The series began with a programme featuring Bach's complete sonatas for violin. But in the years since, it has evolved as the city's music scene has evolved, and includes a wide variety of music in its programme. This spring, the National Chamber Choir is preceded by a season of guitar music; Mozart was played in January; Concorde is scheduled to perform in March. And today, a jazz trio called Evidence, with Ronan Guilfoyle on bass, is all set up and ready to go.

Ronan is one Ireland's foremost jazz composers and performers. He was also instrumental in setting up the full-time jazz course at New Park School in the southern suburbs of the city – the first established jazz course in Ireland. He still teaches at New Park today. Gavin O'Sullivan, who runs the Sundays at Noon series, had told me a few days before, 'Ronan has no hang-ups. He's a working musician, and a composer too, so he's much more practical about all this. He's a member of Aosdána and he has a tremendous breadth of knowledge. He certainly isn't above performing with his students.'

I look at the two younger members of the trio: Sean Carpio on drums and Greg Felton on piano. They are both very young – maybe early 20s? Then I glance back at the entrance: the large room is full now and I see Gavin having to turn people away apologetically. Today, Evidence is playing Thelonious Monk. 'Evidence,' the programme says, 'named after one of Monk's great compositions, is dedicated to playing the music of Monk and exploring both the lesser-known pieces and exploring new angles in the better-known ones.' Sounds great. I sit back and take in the great room, the vaulted ceiling. The piano sits in the centre of the floor, with seats laid out in front and in the wings; sunshine slants through the stained glass skylight. The audience is enormously mixed: young jazz heads mix with scarf-enveloped seniors and a sprinkling of fortunate tourists.

Before me, behind me, on either side, hang some of the gallery's great treasures. I can see Renoir's *Les Parapluies* straight ahead, Monet's *Waterloo Bridge* and Manet's *Eva Gonzalez*; behind me sits

Degas' sculpture of *Thoroughbred Horse Walking*. Beside it is a glowing still-life: Fantin-Latour's *Blush Roses*. The music begins.

Ronan Guilfoyle is effortlessly cool. He looks as though he is half-dead with a heavy cold, but he smiles his way through the performance, gliding effortlessly across each complex piece and playing them smoothly, lustrously, like butter or toffee. Sean and Greg smile too as they play: all three give the impression of enjoying themselves on a profound level. In *Les Parapluies*, the lady with the basket seems taken aback: I fancy that her expression changes to shock that such a thing is going on, but the child beside her seems delighted.

'I'M A self-taught musician,' Ronan told me later. 'I heard both classical and jazz at home when I was a child. My father was into both in a big way: he was specifically interested in classical from about 1880 and jazz from 1945. Music was always on: we used to have speakers in all the downstairs rooms in the house, with classical on the radio and jazz on his records. So we were raised with Bartók, Prokofiev, Stravinsky, Sibelius, and Ravel and then Miles Davis, Charlie Parker, and Earl Garner. It meant that both languages were entirely familiar to me; and it meant that this music was never difficult or dark; it was normal and natural.

'I got into rock music for a while by looking for it, because in those days you didn't just come across it, and there wasn't the same pressure to like it. We used to go on holidays to Skerries and I got into the music they played on the jukebox; I started buying Slade singles – terrible stuff – and then moved onto Black Sabbath for about a month; and then onto King Crimson. Of course,' and he raised his eyes wryly, 'what I was really doing in hindsight was always looking for complex music, because of course my ear was accustomed to it. Then I heard Cream and thought I would like to learn bass. I bought a bass when I was 18 and taught myself to play – by which stage I wasn't into Cream anymore. What I was really doing, of course, was coming slowly back to jazz.'

6

Classical, Contemporary And Jazz Music

He talked about his seminal influences. The Mahavishnu Orchestra, he said, was up there at the top of the list.

'*Birds Of Fire* in 1973 changed my life. It was truly complex music, combining the virtuoso style of jazz with the energy of electric rock music; it was a real masterpiece. And that set me on the path back towards jazz. It was all very adolescent, of course. I was easily influenced.'

And as for being self-taught – well, it wasn't exactly a choice.

'It wasn't that I didn't want to be taught the bass,' he said and paused. 'It was that there was really nobody to teach me, so I had to

Great Days of Jazz

The jazz scene in Dublin has expanded enormously in the last few years and today, while dedicated jazz spaces are still few and far between, there are high-quality jazz nights to be had at venues across the city centre. JJ Smyth's leads the way, with **Isotope (map: 3)** resident on Thursday nights and **Pendulum (map: 3)** on Sundays – both attracting the very best players and most discerning audiences. Isotope concentrates on classic jazz, Pendulum showcases new talent on the Dublin scene. On a Friday night, the relatively new jazz night at the **Wellington (map: 6)** leads the way; and Conway's pub – otherwise small and quiet – features Thursday jazz nights in its upstairs **Boom Boom Room (map: 22)**. The International hosts jazz nights on Tuesdays (**The Dirty Jazz Club – map: 13**).

The city also caters for the Sunday jazz brunch crowd, with a positive host of competitors kicking off the action at noon or thereabouts. The best of this particular bunch? – **Zanzibar (73)**, **Café En Seine (75)**, **Ron Black's (76)** and the **Globe (74)**. These sessions are probably not for the serious of heart, but hell – the food is good.

Pendulum at JJ Smyth's, 12 Aungier St, Dublin 2 (475 2565); 8pm, 5 euro
Dirty Jazz Club at The International, 23 Wicklow St, Dublin 2 (677 9250); 9pm, 5 euro
Isotope at JJ Smyth's, 12 Aungier St, Dublin 2 (475 2565); 9.30pm, 7 euro
Wellington, 1A, Upper Baggot Street, Dublin 4 (660 7344) 9pm, 7 euro
Boom Boom Room at Conway's, 70 Parnell Street, Dublin 1 (873 2687) 8.30pm, 3 euro

Classical, Contemporary And Jazz Music

teach myself. I taught myself to read by buying Bach piano music. I gravitated into the Dublin jazz scene; and of course I'm still learning now.'

I asked him about the jazz scene in the city back in the '70s compared to the present day.

'It was very small back then, but there were great players. I played in the Tommy Halferty Trio which taught me so much; it was a great education. I learned jazz in much the same way people in America had learned 20 years ago, before jazz education came along – by simply learning on the job. There were great players, but it was a small scene.'

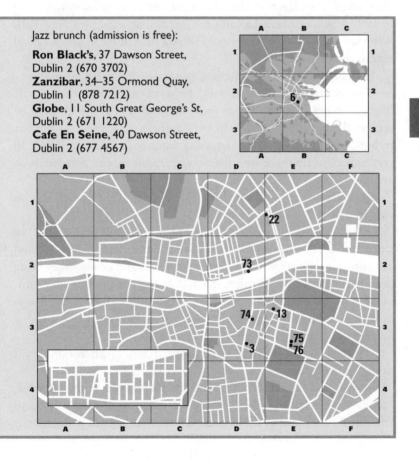

Jazz brunch (admission is free):

Ron Black's, 37 Dawson Street,
Dublin 2 (670 3702)
Zanzibar, 34–35 Ormond Quay,
Dublin 1 (878 7212)
Globe, 11 South Great George's St,
Dublin 2 (671 1220)
Cafe En Seine, 40 Dawson Street,
Dublin 2 (677 4567)

6

Classical, Contemporary And Jazz Music

'So you must have been conscious of the need for education?'

Well, I'm an evangelist when it comes to teaching this music. I firmly believe in its worth – and besides, I enjoy teaching. What happened was that I went to New Park in 1984 to take lessons in counterpoint. I did no formal training though, and sat no exams. The administrator of the school, Simon Taylor, was a classical guitarist and he asked Tommy Halferty and me to play one day. The concert was a great success: everyone loved the spontaneity of the music: it seemed miraculous to them, although of course we had played together for so long that it was second nature to us. Then, after that, they asked us to teach at the school and then a course evolved until in 1997 when we opened a full-time jazz course. And now New Park is the only school in the country to offer a full course in non-classical education.'

He added: 'Which is a disgrace, of course, but there we are.'

'We see the benefits of it now,' he went on. 'The earlier people begin learning jazz, the better they are. The results are clear to be seen in the new young bands in Dublin these days: their skills, their technical skills are so finely honed. I want to see new, young Irish jazz musicians up there with their counterparts in, say, Sweden, who are at a level aged 13 that today we reach aged 18.'

I knew that the jazz scene has expanded in recent years – serious jazz too.

'Absolutely. Well, we have 70 people on the full-time course, so since 1997, 120 people in Dublin have gone through the course and are now out in the city. They come to concerts and venues; they bring their friends – we have critical mass. And there is more money now, more support – and great musicians visit Dublin too. When I was growing up, big musicians hardly ever came, but now there is also a lot more of that.'

'There is jazz all over the city now on a Sunday afternoon too,' I said. 'You can hear it inside bars all over the place.'

Ronan said hesitantly: 'Yes, and the players are probably great, but they are terrible venues – truly terrible. People aren't going to specifically hear jazz at those venues, after all; they are going for the

Classical, Contemporary And Jazz Music

ambience, for the brunch and coffee, and to chat to friends. The best nights are the dedicated jazz nights: Sundays in JJ Smiths, Friday in the Wellington, Sunday in the Boom Boom Room on Parnell Square, and Thursdays in JJ Smyths. And all the visiting musicians too – so there are great things happening; the audience is there and the promoters have the money to put on concerts. The Arts Council is conscious of the need and demand now and are willing to fund the scene too.

'In the past, you know, jazz musicians weren't organised and politicised. Today though, they are more aware of the system and how to use it. And I'm certain that there will be jazz taught in the universities within five years. So it's all change, and we're catching up with other countries too.

'You know, America is dead for jazz.' He shook his head wonderingly. 'The society from which it sprung wouldn't know the difference between Duke Ellington and the Duke of York. It's all hip hop and rap. Classical, meanwhile, is kept afloat by donations from the liberal elite, and jazz can't compete with that. So the music is great, but there is no money to keep it going; and there is only a scene in a handful of the big cities: Philadelphia, New York, Boston, and Chicago. Jazz is the greatest gift America has given the world and it's not supported at all in America itself. In fact, jazz musicians in America are desperate to get to Europe, because it's subsidised over here. Even Ireland, although it's still on the lowest rung of the subsidy ladder compared to other EU states, is still far better off than the United States. The musicians earn no money.'

He told me a few mournful jokes: How do you earn two million dollars from a jazz concert? Invest six million. What's the difference between jazz and a pizza? A pizza will feed a family of four.

'Anyway...'

'Anyway...what are you working on, composition-wise?'

He laughed. 'I'm snowed under at the minute, because I'm working on five pieces. I have a piece in progress for the Manhattan School of Music Jazz Philharmonic: that's their combined symphony and jazz orchestra – 120 musicians in total. I

6

Classical, Contemporary And Jazz Music

have completed one movement of a three-movement piece; and the rest is due to be performed in September. I'm writing a piece for the 25th anniversary of the Cork Jazz Festival; the Mermaid Arts Centre in Bray has commissioned a piece; and I'm also writing a piece influenced by the music scene in Cairo. Do you know the novels by Naguib Mahfouz?'

'I do.' We talked for a while about Cairo, about the Levant; kicked a few book titles around.

'Anyway, I always loved those novels, so I went and did some work on them, some reading. I'm going to Cairo in April to look at the music scene there and write a piece based on my experience. It's going to be performed later in the year at the Chester Beatty Library. And finally, I'm writing a piece for an English woodwind outfit. So it's all a bit of a whirl.'

So it all broke down in the end – as I knew it would. It went spinning from the National Concert Hall's 'Tribute to Brendan Kennelly' all the way through to the banks of the Nile at Cairo. And that's life in Dublin: that's the reality of the music scene in this city. Long may it continue.

Conclusion

The Tipping Point

'CANNES. Berlin. Sundance. Now it's our turn.'

The large advertisement by the bus stop is for the Dublin International Film Festival, then just getting underway. I walk towards it, then stop and look again. The poster jars with me somehow – it jars in its defensive tone, its need to be defined according to the greats of the film festival calendar. Why does the Dublin jamboree compare itself to Cannes, Berlin, and Sundance? Why does it feel the need?

I think about the poster over the next few days and realise the reason why it has had such an impression on me. I have been comparing it mentally with Dublin's music scene, which seems to simply get on with the job, which seems scarcely to compare itself to anything. Frankly, this has startled me; it seems not to square with the preconceptions I brought with me. Until 15 years ago, even until 10 years ago, the music scene seemed to operate in the time-honoured way – by continually glancing over its shoulder to see what other people thought of it. Not any more – or at least not so much. Of course, there is still a hunger to break markets abroad in Europe, Australia and Canada and most of all, in the United States. But the anxious need to please, to react against, to imitate, this seems entirely gone.

I remember this poster a few days later.

'It's true. People are not keeping to their own cliques: they're meeting up and mixing it up.'

I'm sitting in the bar at the Village. It's long and sleek and tastefully lit: above me is a glazed roof and beside me is John Hennessy, who managed the venue and Whelan's next door.

'He works all night,' I had been told. 'Try calling him after 4pm.' I did finally track him down and I did finally meet him and now we're both drinking coffee. John has worked in Whelan's for five years: he started off as a barman and then became the booker for the venue. The Village opened a year ago.

It's a larger venue which is more modern, more elegant; and John tells me that the music here is more progressive than is Whelan's which is considerably more indie- and guitar-based.

'And people don't like Whelan's to be messed with: they feel it already has cohesion and integrity. Whereas the Village is still finding its space; it has the room to manoeuvre and evolve and be freer with its plans. The Village is into soul, hip hop, funk, and trad sometimes, but not commercial music. It's finding its place. And,' he says to me explicitly, 'we're not simply interested in naked commercialism; we want other good things.'

Many people were involved in putting together the Village. John's partner Derek Nally works with him on the creative side, but John tells me he was given a free hand early on in the relationship when it came to booking. Together, the venues offer something that never existed up to this point.

I say, 'Do you mean that Dublin needed a larger venue to pull everything together?'

I have heard this before, of course: the city doesn't have enough venues and it also doesn't have enough of the right kind of venue.

'I think so. People get frustrated, you know, and bored with tiny venues after a while. But the Village isn't vast either: there's room for about 800, so it's just a right size. It just plugged a gap, because we needed a space to fill between Whelan's: 450, and the Olympia: 1,200.'

He sips his coffee and says, 'This is why it's so important. Take an outfit like The Redneck Manifesto: they needed to move from Whelan's into a larger venue before going to the Olympia. That's why the Village is so important: otherwise acts like The Rednecks would fall through the gaps. Now The Rednecks and others like them can leap into an even bigger venue again.' John leans forward. 'And they're an incredibly exciting band: there is so much going on there.'

So much has been going on in Dublin's musical education over the last few years. People are coming up to speed – the scene is coming up to speed – and I see that a venue like the Village has come into being, directly from this education.

'Everyone was suddenly saying: "Someone needs to do something!" and we did it. This in turn will influence other changes, and other developments. Everything will spin on a little faster.'

He turns and looks out at Wexford Street – once a little grimy and now a little more polished up without being too glitzy, or too fake. The chains of coffee houses, the butcher shops, the Swedish furniture shops and greengrocers – they all exist side by side now.

'Camden Street–Wexford Street is becoming a really interesting strip – not in some über-trendy way, but there are good venues, good bars, friendly venues, and no agendas. It's all still finding its way, but this is a good part of town and is still evolving – like the Village itself, if you like.'

One of the staff appears, lugging a large blackboard. The evening menu is now on stream: I could have seabass if I wanted, or lamb or a number of vegetarian options.

'The quality is there now,' John says. 'Dublin was ignored for so long because there wasn't so much going on. The '80s damaged the city: anyone and everyone was being signed up to record labels when they really shouldn't have been. Now, thank God, it's different. Now, it's all about slowly, steadily and confidently building up: there is such a wealth of music too, such a variety of music, and such a collision of styles. Because there are not so many cliques, the creative energy has exploded and all the stagnation is gone. The ten-piece instrumentals like The Jimmy Cake, the singer-songwriters like Damien Rice, David Kitt – all meeting up, all around in the same scene, and all doing their own thing. And so it has just rolled.

'And people have got over themselves: there is none of this rubbish about people noticing us.'

I suddenly think again about the poster for the Dublin Film Festival. 'Berlin, Cannes...'

'And that in turn provides more energy,' John continues. 'I suppose you could call it the tipping point. Of course, we want people to do well abroad – don't get me wrong. The Thrills selling out Brixton Academy is great, Snow Patrol in the British Top Five singles, Damien Rice playing a stadium tour to 5,000 a night in America and on the Letterman show. All that is brilliant; all that is really great. And it leads to more exposure for smaller bands too.'

'I suppose it simply taps into a wider context,' I say. 'A more confident country. The zeitgeist and all that.'

John nods. 'Yeah – I think so. There are remarkable things too. There is less of that corrosive cynicism that we used to have everywhere. Journalists, promoters – they really believe in the bands now and so that cynicism is dispelled. It's just a habit of mind, after all it's not something natural or essential in Ireland; and it can be dispelled. People believe in it all, really wholeheartedly. And the best thing is that the scene here isn't looking for that kind of affirmation, as it might have done in the past. It's just getting on with it. People are playing around with their own original work: they aren't picking up work from abroad, as they might have once done.'

'Well,' I say. 'You don't do your best work when you're glancing over your shoulder.'

John nods again.

'Exactly. And today in Dublin, if you're bored – well, you're only bored because you're boring.'

Appendix

Getting Here and Away...By Air

Dublin Airport is located about 10 kilometres north of the city and offers direct flights to the UK, Europe and North America. The Irish airports authority is **Aer Rianta** (814 1111). The airport is linked to the city centre by **coach** only – there are **no train** connections to the city. **Airlink** coaches, run by Dublin Bus, offers connections to the city centre and main train stations (844 4265); the private **Aircoach** runs to the city centre and main south city hotels (844 7118). Both services depart from just outside the main terminal building. **Cabs** should cost approximately 10–15 euro for a fare to the city centre; don't feel you need to tip.

Getting Here and Away...By Sea

Irish Ferries sails from Dublin Port to Holyhead (661 0715); and **Stena** from Dun Laoghaire to Holyhead (204 7777).

Getting Around

The bad news first: public transport is hellish in Dublin. Traffic congestion is so bad that it's very difficult to get anywhere fast. There is no Metro service in Dublin, so you usually need to rely on **Dublin Bus** (872 0000). The exception to this is the **DART** train (836 3333), which hugs the coast of Dublin Bay from **Howth** and **Malahide** in the north, through the **city centre** and **Dun Laoghaire**, to **Greystones** in the south. It's generally very pleasant – except at rush hour – and it offers great views of the bay. DART trains stop in the city centre at **Connolly**, **Tara Street** and **Pearse** stations.

The good news is that Dublin city centre is very compact and eminently walkable. In fact, it's the classic walker's city and you probably won't need to take a bus anywhere! And avoid **driving** in the city centre: it really isn't worth the hassle.

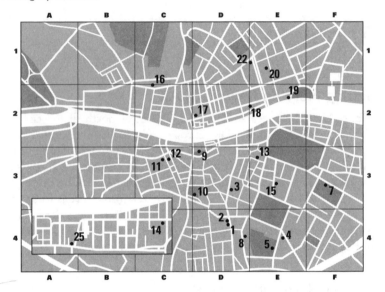

The Music Venues

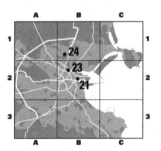

South of the River

Whelan's (1) 25 Wexford Street, Dublin 2 (478 0766) – Long-established and treasured live music venue on the Camden Street-Wexford Street strip.

The Village (2) 26 Wexford Street, Dublin 2 (475 8555) – Next-door to Whelan's, larger and more slick, the Village offers live music nightly, as wellas food and good coffee all day.

JJ Smyths (3) 12 Aungier Street, Dublin 8 (475 2565) – The city's best jazz and blues venue: music is on offer nightly, with Thursday and Sunday the main jazz nights.

Sugar Club (4) 8 Lower Leeson Street, Dublin 2 (878 7188) – A mixed bag of music here – but the main draw is the stylish venue itself, with its plush cinema-style seating.

National Concert Hall (5) Earlsfort Terrace, Dublin 2 (475 1572) – The main city-centre classical music venue, offering a large auditorium and smaller recital space. A mixed bag of musical tastes, though classical continues to dominate.

The Wellington (6) IA Upper Baggot Street, Dublin 4 – Lots of live music on offer here, but the main draw is the quality jazz on Friday nights.

O'Donoghue's (7) 15 Merrion Row, Dublin 2 (677 8312) – Small and always crowded, this famous old pub offers good Guinness, an impressive collection of photographs on the walls and lots of live music too.

The Harcourt Hotel (8) 60–61 Harcourt Street, Dublin 2 (478 3667) – You can listen to music here most nights of the week – and into the early hours too. Musicians tend to gravitate here when sessions are finishing elsewhere: just turn up and you can usually rely on an impromptu session.

Christchurch Cathedral (9) Christchurch Place, Dublin 8 (677 8099) – The Christchurch bells ring each Sunday morning from 10am; the Cathedral Choir sings each Sunday at 11am service.

St Patrick's Cathedral (10) Patrick's Close, Dublin 8 (475 4817) – Try choral matins here, each Sunday at 11:15am; and don't forget to look at Swift's memorial.

Vicar Street (11) 99 Vicar Street, off Thomas Street, Dublin 8 (454 6656) – Newish but already established as one of the city's best live music venues.

Mother Redcap's (12) 40–48 Back Lane, Christchurch, Dublin 8 (453 8306) – A great rambling barn of a place and a famous venue in the city. It offers trad music throughout the week, with jazz and blues on Fridays and Saturdays.

The International (13) 23 Wicklow Street, Dublin 2 (677 9250) – Old and atmospheric city-centre boozer, with music and comedy nights on offer on the upper floor.

The Oliver St John Gogarty (14) 58–59 Fleet Street, Temple Bar, Dublin 2 (671 1822) – Unashamedly commercial, but featuring trad music each night and all day on Saturdays.

St Ann's Church (15), 18 Dawson Street (676 7727) – Elegant St Anne's holds regular lunchtime recitals for fans of choral music.

Olympia (25) 72 Dame Street, Dublin 2 (679 3323) – The Olympia is one of Dublin's most successful venues and plays host to the city centre's concerts, as well as regular theatre. venue in the city's northern suburb.

North of the River

The Cobblestone (16) 77 North King Street, Smithfield, Dublin 7 (872 1799) – This pub's future was uncertain at time of writing – but ring and check, because the Cobblestone offers Dublin's best trad music.

Hughes (17) 19 Chancery Street, off Church Street, Dublin 7 (872 6540). One of the city's oldest trad venues, with music sessions nightly.

Spirit (18) 57 Middle Abbey Street, Dublin 1 (877 9999) – New venue on the site of the former Irish Music Hall of Fame, featuring main auditorium, bars and chill-out rooms.

Liberty Hall (19) Eden Quay Dublin 1 (872 1122) – Liberty Hall is the tallest and quite possibly ugliest building in Dublin, but don't allow this to distract you … the newly revamped venue here offers a good and varied diet of music.

St Mary's Pro-Cathedral (20) Cathedral Street, Dublin 1 (874 5441)
– The city's principal Catholic Church. The Palestrina Choir sings each
Sunday at 11am.

The Point Depot (21) East Link Bridge, North Wall Quay, Dublin (636
6777) – The city's biggest music venue: vast and barn-like, it is used mainly
for big-name concerts and other spectaculars.

The Boom Boom Room (22) Conway's, 70 Parnell Street, Dublin 1
(873 2687) – The upper room of the otherwise quiet Conway's pub
features live music nightly, including jazz on Sunday nights.

St Francis Xavier Church (23) Gardiner Street, Dublin 1 (836 3411)
– The Dublin Gospel Choir sings each Sunday evening at 7:30pm.

Helix (24) Dublin City University, Collins Avenue, Glasnevin, Dublin 9
(700 7000) – Three excellent venues in one at this brand-new concert
venue in the city's northern suburbs.

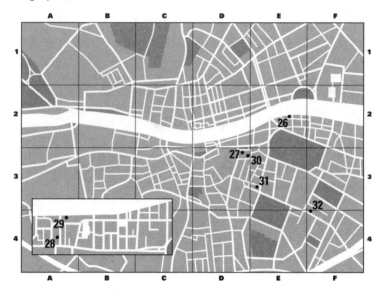

The Pubs and Bars

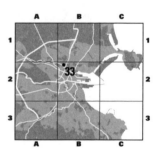

South of the River

Mulligan's (26) 8 Poolbeg Street, Dublin 2 (677 5582) – Dublin's most famous boozer, reputed to offer the best 'pint of plain' in town.

The Stag's Head (27) 1 Dame Court, off Dame Street, Dublin 2 (679 3701) – Polished wooden bar, gleaming mirrors and good pub grub in this old, old bar. A treasure.

The Front Lounge (28) 33–34, Parliament Street, Temple Bar, Dublin 2 (670 4112) – Beloved of the trendy and the gay and one of the few excellent watering holes in Temple Bar.

The Octagon (29) Clarence Hotel, 6–8 Wellington Quay, Temple Bar, Dublin 2 (670 9000) – Famously owned by U2 and hyper-trendy, this still manages to be pleasant and discreet. Lovely in the afternoon for a quiet drink and a bowl of designer crisps.

The Library Bar (30) Central Hotel, 1-5 Exchequer Street, Dublin 2 (679 7302) – Upstairs in the Central Hotel you'll discover the Library Bar, got up in the manner of an old gentlemens' club, with thick carpets, winged-backed leather armchairs and leather-bound volumes on the walls to boot.

Bruxelles (31) 7–8 Harry Street, Grafton Street, Dublin 2 (677 5362) – Loud, raucous and good fun, with a penchant for very, very loud rock music.

Doheny and Nesbitt (32) 5 Lower Baggot Street, Dublin 2 (676 2945) – The best of the bunch in Dublin's Georgian heartland: old-fashioned and atmospheric with lots of mirrors and wood.

North of the River

The lion's share of good drinking places is south of the river – but try both Hughes and the Cobblestone (see Music Venues) or…

Kavanagh's (The Gravediggers) (33) 1 Prospect Square, Glasnevin, Dublin 9 – The Gravediggers takes its name from the proximity of Glasnevin cemetery, resting place of many of Ireland's national heroes. It's an old-fashioned mellow sort of place, with buckets of atmosphere.

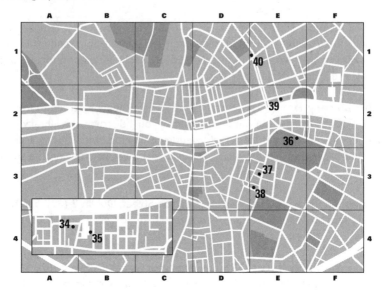

Dublin On Stage

South of the River

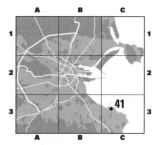

Project Arts Centre (34) 39, East Essex Street, Temple Bar, Dublin 2 (679 6622) – The largest cultural resource in Temple Bar, newly rebuilt in 2000 and offering two theatre spaces for innovative and cutting-edge art.

The Ark Children's Cultural Centre (35) 11A Eustace Street, Temple Bar, Dublin 2 (670 7788) – Wonderful building and cultural resource, offering regular shows and entertainment throughout the year.

Samuel Beckett Centre (36) Trinity College, Dublin 2 (608 2266) The Beckett offers student shows, as well as high-quality fringe theatre.

Bewley's Café Theatre (37) 78 Grafton Street, Dublin 2 (635 5470) – This small, charming venue offers a good diet of excellent lunchtime and evening shows.

Gaiety Theatre (38) 8 South King Street, Dublin 2 (677 1717) – The Gaiety is famous for its Christmas panto, a fixture on the Dublin entertainment calendar. But it's home to a good deal more besides – everything from popular theatre and comedy to concerts and opera is staged here and the crimson and gold interior is pure Victorian.

Pavilion Theatre (41) Marine Road, Dun Laoghaire, Co Dublin (231 2929) – Overlooking the harbour at Dun Laoghaire: come for a walk by the sea and then take in a show. The theatre is next door to the DART station.

North of the River

Abbey Theatre (39) 26 Lower Abbey Street, Dublin 1 (878 7222) The most famous of the Dublin stages, still offering a combination of Irish and European classics and new writing on its two stages.

Gate Theatre (40) 1 Cavendish Row, Parnell Square, Dublin 1 (874 4045) – Dublin's most elegant theatre features an intimate and democratic auditorium; a cosmopolitan range of European and American drama is supplemented by occasional new Irish writing.

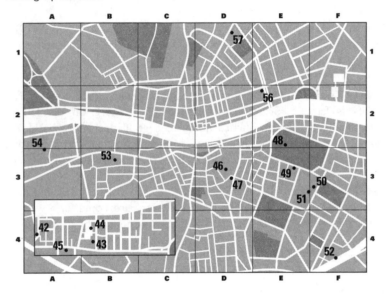

Shops and Attractions

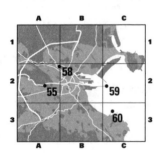

South of the River

Contemporary Music Centre (42) 19 Fishamble Street, Temple Bar, Dublin 8 (673 1922) – Excellent resource for anyone interested in Dublin's new music scene: the CMC library and archive are open to all and visitors are welcome.

Irish Film Institute (43) 6 Eustace Street, Temple Bar, Dublin 2 (679 3477) – Two art-house cinemas, plus bar, restaurant and bookshop – all grouped around a glazed atrium.

Meeting House Square (44) Temple Bar, Dublin 2 – This is one of Dublin's most agreeable public spaces, offering a Saturday food market and summer entertainment and open-air movies.

City Hall (45) Dame Street, Dublin 2 (672 2204) – Gloriously restored reminder of Dublin's eighteenth-century architectural heyday.

Chester Beatty Library (46) Clock Tower Building, Dublin Castle, Dublin 2 (407 0750) – This is perhaps Dublin's most impressive and fascinating museum, offering a splendid collection of Islamic and Oriental art in splendid new surroundings.

Road Records (47) 16B Fade Street, Dublin 2 (671 7340) – The best independent music store in town.

Trinity College (48) College Green, Dublin 2 (677 2941) – The biggest tourist destination in Dublin, but still worth a look: beautiful Georgian architecture, harmonious quadrangles and that famous Book of Kells...

Celtic Note (49) 12, Nassau Street, Dublin 2 (670 4157) Despite the forbiddingly commercial windows and situation on the Nassau Street tourist strip, Celtic Note stocks a good stash of Irish music.

National Gallery of Ireland (50) Merrion Square West, Dublin 2 (661 5133) – This has always been an impressive gallery, but the beautiful new Millennium Wing has drawn even more visitors.

Natural History Museum (51) Merrion Street Dublin 2 (677 7444) – Maintained as an example of the Victorian mania for collecting, preserving and archiving, this museum features a vast range of stuffed mammals and reptiles and insects pickled in brine. Perfect for the children, of course, and for any adult who enjoys the ghastly side of life.

Grand Canal and Patrick Kavanagh Memorial (52) – The canal snakes through the south city and is good for a walk and a look at the swans. Patrick Kavanagh reclines on his bench at Baggot Street Bridge.

Guinness Storehouse (53) St James's Gate, Dublin 8 (408 4800) – Unlike many visitor experiences, this one comes up with the goods: entertaining and informative exhibition spaces and the fabulous lofty Gravity Bar, offering 360° views of Dublin.

Irish Museum of Modern Art (54) Royal Museum, Military Road, Kilmainham, Dublin 8 (612 9900) – Excellent gallery in superlative surroundings; and don't forget to check out the formal gardens and bookshops too.

War Memorial Gardens (55) South Circular Road, Kilmainham, Dublin 8 – These austerely beautiful Lutyens-designed gardens include sunken rose gardens and long lawns running down to the Liffey.

South Wall (59) – You really need a car – point its nose in the direction of the Pigeonhouse power station and keep on driving. But when you get there, it's the best walk in town.

Dun Laoghaire Piers (60) Dun Laoghaire Seafront, Co. Dublin – Good for a bracing constitution; and when you're finished, check out any of the new bars and cafés nearby.

North of the River

General Post Office (56) O'Connell Street, Dublin 1 (705 7000) – This imposing building was the focal point of the 1916 Easter Rising and remains a potent symbol of Irish nationhood today.

Hugh Lane Municipal Gallery of Modern Art (57) Parnell Square, Dublin 1 (874 1903) – Excellent gallery, housed in beautiful Charlemont House and featuring a concert each Sunday at noon.

National Botanic Gardens (58) Finglas Road, Glasnevin, Dublin 9 (837 7596) – The Gardens have recently been thoroughly overhauled and now feature a new Visitors' Centre and inevitable café. The splendid glasshouses are worth a visit in themselves.

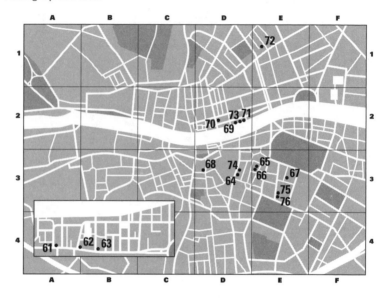

Cafes and Restaurants

South of the River

Queen of Tarts (61), 4 Cork Hill, Dame Street, Dublin 2 (670 7499) –
Tiny – but one of the best cafés and pastry shops in town, with everything
home-made on the premises.

The Mermaid Café (62) 69–70 Dame Street, Dublin 2 (670 8236) –
Pricey but excellent contemporary cuisine. Or, if you're feeling in the
mood for utilitarian chic, try the attached Gruel Café next door.

Monty's of Kathmandu (63) 28 Eustace Street, Temple Bar, Dublin 2
(670 4911) – You mightn't imagine Dublin was the place to come for good
Nepalese grub, but come here and think again. A gem.

Simon's Place (64) 22 George's Street Arcade, South Great George's Street, Dublin 2 (679 7821) – Great soups, sandwiches and cinnamon buns at this very trendy city-centre café.

La Corte (65) Top Floor, Powerscourt Townhouse Centre, South William Street, Dublin 2 (633 4477) – Good Italian coffee and lunches in this lofty café under the Powerscourt glazed roof.

Fresh (66) Top Floor, Powerscourt Townhouse Centre, South William Street, Dublin 2 (671 9669) – First-class vegetarian and vegan restaurant.

Dunne and Crescenzi (67) 14 and 16 South Frederick Street, Dublin 2 (677 3815) – Brilliant and authentically Italian café and wine shop, offering excellent lunches, snacks and coffee.

Leo Burdock's (68) 2, Werburgh Street, Dublin 8 (454 0306) – This is the best and most authentic 'chipper' in town: the regular queues are the proof of the pudding...

Globe (74) 11 South Great George's St, Dublin 2 (671 1220) – The Globe was one of the first wave of new and fashionable Dublin hostelries and it's wearing its age well: good for lunch and evening drinks as well as weekend music.

Cafe En Seine (75) 40 Dawson Street, Dublin 2 (677 4567) – This joint was recently expanded and is now larger than your average Olympic stadium. Well, we exaggerate. But it's beautiful – expensively kitted out in the manner of a Parisian watering hole and very popular.

Ron Black's (76) 37 Dawson Street, Dublin 2 (670 3702) – Expensive clothes, expensive drinks, expensive clients: Ron Black's is a relatively new addition to the pub scene in Dublin and the place to go if you are in the mood for über-chic surroundings.

North of the River

Café Cagliostro (69) Blooms Lane, 24 Ormond Quay (888 0860) – Brand-new, tiny and fabulous, Café Cagliostro is one of the main tenants in the new Bloom's Lane courtyard, just off the city quays. It offers excellent coffee and hot chocolate, as well as a chaste but excellent selection of Italian sandwiches and desserts. Also check out the *Enoteca della Langhe* wine bar across the courtyard for a glass of red and a game of chess.

Romano's (70) 12 Capel Street, Dublin 1 (872 6868) – Ignore the appalling décor and concentrate on the excellent pizza and pasta, all made with organic Italian flour.

Winding Stair Café (71) 40 Ormond Quay Lower (873 3292) – The most charming bookshop in the city is also a café on three floors, looking south across the river and the Ha'penny Bridge.

The Cobalt Café (72) 16 North Great George's Street, Dublin 1 (873 0313) – The food is uneven here, but the café itself is beautifully elegant, with regular exhibitions and concerts featuring too.

Zanzibar (73) 34–35 Ormond Quay, Dublin 1 (878 7212) – If you like your bars exuberantly themed, then look no further than Zanzibar, which is kitted out like an East African film set – full-size palm trees and all. Great fun and very popular.

Accommodation

South of the River

The Clarence Hotel 6-8, Wellington Quay, Temple Bar, Dublin 2 (407 0800) – We had to mention it – it's owned by U2 and is *very* stylish and *very* exclusive and right in the heart of the city.

The Shelbourne Hotel 27 St Stephen's Green, Dublin 2 (663 4500) – The Shelbourne is the grand old lady of Dublin hotels: lately acquired by Marriott, it still boasts an atmosphere of its own.

The Merrion Hotel Upper Merrion Street, Dublin 2 (603 0600) The Merrion Hotel is the ultimate in refined and understated elegance in the city and boasts splendid bedrooms and drawing rooms, as well as all the usual facilities.

The Central Hotel 1–5 Exchequer Street, Dublin 2 (679 7302) – Stitched into the very centre of the city, the Central boasts the Library Bar, complete with big fires and comfy armchairs – perfect for a late-night drink.

Jury's Inn Christchurch Christchurch Place, Dublin 8 (454 0000) – Jury's are a big chain in the city – there's another Inn at the **Custom House** on the city quays – and are a little lacking in character. But on the plus side, they offer comfortable standard rooms and good value rates.

The Mespil Hotel Mespil Road, Dublin 4 (667 1222) – Overlooking the Grand Canal and only a few minutes walk from town, the Mespil offers pleasant rooms, reasonable rates and a sense of space.

Harrington Hall 70 Harcourt Street, Dublin 2 (475 3497) – This impressive small townhouse offers Georgian elegance and a welcome note of personal service.

Avalon House 55 Aungier Street, Dublin 2 (475 0001) – This friendly hostel is not exactly posh, but it's clean, comfortable, pleasant – and just a moment's stroll from Grafton Street.

North of the River

The Morrison Hotel Ormond Quay, Dublin 1 (887 2400) – Stylish hotel on the city quays. Fashion guru John Rocha was the creative force behind the Morrison's chic interiors.

The Gresham Hotel 24 Upper O'Connell Street, Dublin 1 (874 6881) – The Gresham has long anchored O'Connell Street and a new makeover has restored its elegance once again.

Bibliography

Asbury, Herbert *Gangs Of New York*. New York: Knopf, 1928.

Bernelle, Agnes *The Fun Palace: An Autobiography*. Dublin: Lilliput, 1996.

Deane, Seamus (ed.) *The Field Day Anthology Of Irish Writing* (four vols). Derry and Cork: Field Day, 1991–2002.

Friel, Brian *Performances*. London: Faber, 2003.
Dancing At Lughnasa. London: Faber, 1990

Giraldus Cambrensis/Gerald of Wales *Expugnatio Hibernica (The Conquest of Ireland)*. Dublin: Royal Irish Academy, 1978.

McGuirk, Niall *Document: A Story Of Hope*. Dublin: Hope, 2002.

O'Casey, Sean *The Plough And The Stars* and *Juno And The Paycock*. London: Faber, 1988.

Swift, Jonathan *A Modest Proposal*. Harlow: Longman, 2001.

Topographica Hibernica (The History And Topography Of Ireland). Harmondsworth: Penguin, 1982.

Index